JEWISH APPROACHES TO SUICIDE, MARTYRDOM, AND EUTHANASIA

JEWISH APPROACHES TO SUICIDE, MARTYRDOM, AND EUTHANASIA

EDITED BY
KALMAN J. KAPLAN AND
MATTHEW B. SCHWARTZ

JASON ARONSON INC.
Northvale, New Jersey
Jerusalem

This book was set in 11 pt. Weiss by Alabama Book Composition of Deatsville, Alabama.

Material reprinted in "A Dialectic on Life and Death: Elie Wiesel, from the Tragic to the Midrashic Mode," by Joseph Lowin, is excerpted from *The Fifth Son*, Elie Wiesel (Summit, 1985). © Elie Wiesel, 1985. Reprinted by permission of author.

Copyright © 1998 by Kalman J. Kaplan and Matthew B. Schwartz.

10 9 8 7 6 5 4 3 2 1

All rights reserved. Printed in the United States of America. No part of this book may be used or reproduced in any manner whatsoever without written permission from Jason Aronson Inc. except in the case of brief quotations in reviews for inclusion in a magazine, newspaper, or broadcast.

Library of Congress Cataloging-in-Publication Data

Jewish approaches to suicide, martyrdom, and euthanasia / Kalman J. Kaplan, editor : Matthew B. Schwartz, associate editor.
    p.   cm.
    Includes bibliographical references and index.
    ISBN 0-7657-5967-5
    1. Suicide—Religious aspects—Judaism.   2. Martyrdom (Judaism)
    3. Euthanasia—Religious aspects—Judaism.   4. Judaism—Doctrines.
    I. Kaplan, Kalman J. II. Schwartz, Matthew B.
BM635.4.J38   1997
296.3'697—dc21   96-40897

Manufactured in the United States of America. Jason Aronson Inc. offers books and cassettes. For information and catalog write to Jason Aronson Inc., 230 Livingston Street, Northvale, New Jersey 07647.

Contents

Prologue ... vii

I SUICIDE IN JEWISH, GREEK, AND CHRISTIAN THOUGHT

1 Freedom, Creativity and Suicide in Greek and Biblical Thought: The Anomaly of Masada
Kalman J. Kaplan, Ph.D., and Matthew B. Schwartz, Ph.D. ... 5

2 Maimonides, and Freud, on Self-Destructiveness
David Bakan, Ph.D. ... 22

3 Fatalism and Suicide in Greek and Biblical Thought
Kalman J. Kaplan, Ph.D., and Constantino V. Riccardi, M.A. ... 27

4 The Fatalism of "Aher"
Matthew B. Schwartz, Ph.D. ... 35

5 The Death of Jesus and Anti-Semitism
Kalman J. Kaplan, Ph.D. ... 37

II SUICIDE AND EUTHANASIA IN JEWISH AND AMERICAN LAW

6 Suicide in Jewish Law
Fred Rosner, M.D., F.A.C.P. ... 61

7 Shneidman's Definition of Suicide and Jewish Law: A Brief Note
Kalman J. Kaplan, Ph.D. ... 78

8 Euthanasia as a Halakhic Option
Bryon Sherwin, Ph.D. ... 80

9 Kevorkianism—Judaic and Logotherapeutic Reactions
Reuven P. Bulka, Ph.D. ... 98

10 Dr. Kevorkian and the Rabbis, Detroit, 1996:
A Brief Historical Note
Matthew B. Schwartz, Ph.D. 114

11 Euthanasia and Physician-Assisted Suicide in America
Today: Whither Are We Going?
Joseph Richman, Ph.D. 116

III SUICIDE AND SUICIDE-PREVENTION IN BIBLICAL AND GRAECO-WESTERN NARRATIVES

12 Suicide, Sacrifice, and Self-Esteem in Biblical versus
Greek Stories of Creation
Kalman J. Kaplan, Ph.D. 133

13 A Dialectic on Life and Death: Elie Wiesel, from the
Tragic to the Midrashic Mode
Joseph Lowin, Ph.D. 143

14 The Blood of Thy Brother: Antigone Suicides,
Cain Doesn't
Matthew B. Schwartz, Ph.D., and Kalman J. Kaplan, Ph.D. 159

15 Job—A Biblical Message About Suicide
Israel Orbach, Ph.D. 168

16 Moses: "Kill Me I Pray"
Stanley S. Selinger, Ph.D. 176

17 Jonah versus Narcissus: A Biblical Approach to
Suicide Prevention
Kalman J. Kaplan, Ph.D. 186

Epilogue 197

Index 203

Prologue

We are all aware of the controversy in the United States concerning legalized abortion emerging from the Roe v. Wade decision of 1973. Pro-abortion forces have advocated "freedom of choice" while those in the anti-abortion camp have marched under the banner of "right to life." More recently the "right to die" debate has begun to rage across America, spurred on by the assisted suicides conducted by Dr. Jack Kevorkian in Michigan. Although Kevorkian has limited his practice to adults who presumably "want to die" (as elusive, transitory, and ambivalent as that urge typically is), many of the issues he raises are strikingly similar to those raised over 80 years ago (1915) by a Chicago physician by the name of Harry Haiselden. Dr. Haiselden campaigned to euthanize deformed infants and even made a movie, *The Black Stork*, to propogate his views. This movie played in theaters in America for a quarter of a century. The questions underlying both movements are simply: "Which lives are not worth living?" and "Who will make that decision?"

The right to euthanasia (a combination of two Greek words meaning "a good death") and assisted suicide have been advocated by the Hemlock Society. At the same time, the New York State Task Force on Life and Law (1994) unanimously recommended that New York laws prohibiting suicide and euthanasia should not be changed. Assisted suicide has been the subject of two recent rulings by the Second and Ninth District Court of Appeals and will now be heard by the United States Supreme Court.

This volume will attempt to explore the philosophical and religious underpinnings underlying the various positions on these contemporary issues. The position of the Hemlock Society must be seen in the context of the Stoic school of thought in ancient Greece and Rome. Life belonged to the individual and he could do with it what he wished. Suicide, in fact, was equated with freedom. Judaism and other biblical religions have strongly denounced this position, stressing the sacredness of life and the idea that life is entrusted to the individual by God. The individual here has no more right to kill himself (or even injure himself) than he does to take another's life. Freedom is equated with following God's commandments. A striking difference emerges between Jewish law and Anglo-American law in terms of people's responsibility for one-another. Anglo-American law has not typically assigned tort liability for nonfeasance (i.e., sins of omission) but only for misfeasance (i.e., sins of comission). Jewish law, in contrast, has typically assessed liability for nonfeasance as well. This difference can become critical with regard to suicide prevention. The providing of social support—for example, affordable home care—can often help alleviate the distress experienced by the family of a seriously ill patient and may lessen some of the pressure for assisted suicide and euthansia.

We try to explore these issues in depth in this volume. Specifically, we examine three aspects of Jewish civilization: (1) life, death, and suicide in ancient and traditional Jewish, Greek, and Christian thought, (2) suicide and euthanasia in Jewish law, and (3) suicide and suicide prevention in biblical versus Graeco-Western narratives.

The editors conclude this volume with a comparison of the mass suicides at Waco and Masada, in an attempt to understand what is unique about Jewish ideas about life and death, and about suicide and martyrdom and how these differ from superficially similar ideas in other religious cultures. Life, in Judaism, is preferable to death. The Jewish martyr, unlike some other martyrs, does not court death, but he will let himself be killed under certain prescribed circumstances. For the Jew, death may sometimes be unavoidable, but in itself it provides no theological gain.

I

Suicide in Jewish, Greek, and Christian Thought

The first paper, "Freedom, Creativity and Suicide in Greek and Biblical Thought: The Anomaly of Masada," by Kalman J. Kaplan and Matthew B. Schwartz, compares the place of suicide in biblical-rabbinic and Greek thought. Although freedom is linked to the study of Torah in Jewish thought, it is coupled with suicide in aspects of Greek thought, sometimes in the sense of freeing body from soul. Josephus' narratives of the mass (collective) suicides at Jotapata and Masada are discussed in this context. The second paper is by the most distinguished psychotheologian, David Bakan, and is entitled "Maimonides, and Freud, on Self-Destruction." Freud's conception of "repression" is compared with Maimonides' "interference with intellectual apprehension" in this regard. Bakan suggests that Maimonides' view considers the resultant vacuity in consciousness, which may play a role in the psychodynamics of suicide. A second factor in self-destructiveness for both Maimonides and Freud, according to Bakan, is the interiorization of the angry God imposed by the angry Moses.

The final three papers in this section deal with the issues of fatalism and freedom in Greek versus Hebrew thought. In the first paper, Kalman Kaplan and Vince Riccardi, an instructor in philosophy and religion, author, and the producer of an acclaimed video drama on suicide, collaborate to examine the link between Greek fatalism and self-destructiveness and how the biblical world overcame this closed view to proclaim the possibility of change and renewal. In the next paper, Matthew Schwartz analyzes the response of the Mishna to the fatalistic pessimism endemic to Greek and Roman stoicism. The tragic case of "Aher," Elisha ben Avuyah, the second-century rabbi who turned violently against his people, is discussed. Finally, Kalman Kaplan examines the insistence by Christian theologians on the voluntary aspects of the death of Jesus, and traces its origins in Greek tragedy. This paper examines the implications of this viewpoint on the emotions of believing Christians as the survivors of an "altruistic suicide" and, specifically, how this may have affected the sad historical phenomenon of outbreaks of historical anti-Semitism during the week of Easter.

1

Freedom, Creativity and Suicide in Greek and Biblical Thought

The Anomaly of Masada

KALMAN J. KAPLAN, PH.D.
MATTHEW B. SCHWARTZ, PH.D.

Freedom and creativity are seen very differently in Greek and Hebrew writings. In the Greek and Roman world, they come to be equated with the right to suicide. The Hebrews, in contrast, generally condemn suicide and see freedom and creativity in the context of living in obedience to God. The anomaly of the mass suicide at Masada is discussed in this context.

Freedom is a central and fundamental idea in the literature and thought of both the ancient Greeks and the Hebrews. But the way in which each culture understood and dealt with freedom was very different. To the Greeks freedom is a struggle against the control of others and an effort to establish some sense of control over one's own life. The highest form of control over one's self is the freedom to decide whether to continue to live or to die; i.e., to suicide. Suicide thus becomes a creative act and an intensely important issue in Greek thinking, a subject discussed at length by many of their best writers (e.g., Plato, Cicero, and Seneca), who never found satisfactory resolution.

The Hebrews, in contrast, see freedom as a central feature of their foundation stories; for example, the freeing of the Hebrews from the bondage of Egypt. However, the issue of control is resolved in a direct manner. Man's true freedom is in a moral sense. God gives him freedom to make decisions as to whether he will or will not follow God. If he acknowledges God's rule over the earth, then he has freedom from the urge to self-destruction. More, he can be creative in living—a partner, not a rival, of God in the ongoing work of Creation. Thus freedom can be achieved, but only in the acceptance of the realities of man's relationship with God. This sets the stage for a striking psychological contrast. For Greeks and Romans, suicide represents a very high form of creativity. For the Jews, life itself is the essence of creativity and suicide only destroys this opportunity.

THE GREEKS

Greek attitudes toward suicide can be placed in three camps: Pythagoras, Aristotle and the Epicureans were opposed to it, Plato and Socrates took a guarded middle position and the Cynics and Stoics accepted it. Let us give some examples:

Pythagoras

Athenaeus, a spokesman for the Pythagoreans in the third century, stated the Pythagorean and Orphic positions as follows:

> that the souls of all men were bound in the body, and in the life which is on earth, for the sake of punishment; and that God has issued an edict that if they do not remain there until he voluntarily releases them himself they shall fall into more numerous and more important calamities. On which account all men, being afraid of those threatenings of the gods, fear to depart from life by their own act, but only gladly welcome death when it comes in old age, trusting that the deliverance of their soul will take place with the full consent of those who have the power to sanction it. And this doctrine we ourselves believe. (Athenaeus, *The Deipnosophists*, 2:216)

Suicide is thus a rebellion for the Pythagoreans against an almost mathematical discipline set by the gods. Death comes when it should and then it can be welcomed. There are a set number of souls, according to Pythagoras, available to the world at any one time. Suiciding creates a gap through upsetting this mathematical equilibrium and thus must be rejected. Despite this philosophy, however, several accounts portray Pythagoras as letting himself be killed or actively committing suicide. In an account by Diogenes

Laertius, Pythagoras allows pursuers to catch and kill him rather than trample on a field of beans (8:45).

Socrates and Plato

Three general themes in the teaching of Socrates ease the road to suicide in the classical period. First, several references are made to the nature of the afterworld. Hades (if it exists at all) is not so frightening a place as it was to the Homeric hero. In the closing section of Plato's *Apology* (41a–42a) Socrates asks rhetorically:

> If on arrival in the other world, beyond the reach of our so-called justice, one will find there the true judges who are said to preside in those courts, Minos and Rhadamanthes and Aeacus and Triptolemus . . . to meet Orpheus and Musaeus, Hesiod and Homer . . . would that be an unrewarding journey? . . . What would one not give . . . to be able to question the leader of that great host against Troy, or Odysseus, or Sisyphus . . ."

At the conclusion of Plato's *Republic*, Socrates relates the myth of Er which describes the Good Man's rewards in the life after death:

> These . . . are the prizes and rewards and gifts which the just receives from gods and men while he is still alive, over and above those which justice herself brings him. Yet they are nothing in number and magnitude when compared to the things that await the just man and unjust man after death . . . (*The Republic* 10:3, 1. 614)

Secondly, the idealized harmony of man in the status of classical Greece gives way in Plato's thinking to a sense that the relationship between body and soul is conflictual and unfortunate. "The soul is a helpless prisoner chained hand and foot in the body, compelled to view reality not directly but only through its prison bars, and wallowing in utter ignorance," (*Phaedo*, 83a). The evil acts of the body pollute the soul and prevent it from achieving a complete and clean separation and returning to the world of Ideal Forms. Only the soul can perceive Ideal Truth but it cannot do so as long as it must perceive Reality by use of the five bodily senses. Thus, the real attainment of truth can come only in the higher world when souls can perceive directly without the interference of the body. This idealizing of a state of existence after life is not necessarily a direct call to suicide, but it does foster an atmosphere of thought in which earthly life is belittled and the philosopher is encouraged to believe that separation from earthly life is the only road to the ideal human existence.

The third point of departure facilitating suicide is exactly this—Socrates' general view that philosophy is "preparation for death". This view is expressed in different forms upon a number of occasions. While awaiting execution, Socrates maintains in an argument to Simmias and Cebes:

> Other people are likely not to be aware that those who pursue philosophy aright study nothing but dying and being dead. Now if this is true, it would be absurd to be eager for nothing but this all their lives, and then to be troubled when that came for which they had all along been eagerly practicing. (*Phaedo*, 64a)

In a subsequent passage, Socrates again emphasizes that philosophers desire death, though he leaves the reasons vague:

> And they would be speaking the truth Simmias, except in the matter of knowing very well. For they do not know in what way the real philosophers desire death, nor in what way they deserve death. (*Phaedo*, 64b)

Later in this dialogue, Socrates further explains the linkage between philosophy and death—death frees the soul!

> For, if pure knowledge is impossible while the body is with us, one of two things must follow, either it cannot be acquired at all or only when we are dead; for then the soul will be by itself apart from the body, but not before. (*Phaedo*, 66e)

Socrates goes on to argue that, "The true philosophers practice dying, and death is less terrible to them than to any other men," (*Phaedo* 68a). His argument continues along the line that unlike the ordinary man, only the philosopher understands that death is not a great evil. "You know, do you not that all other men count death among the great evils" (*Phaedo*, 68d).

Given the preference for death over life, it seems only a short step for Socrates to be asked "then why not suicide?" Indeed, Cebes has already asked this very question. "Tell me then, Socrates, what are the grounds for saying that suicide is not legitimate. I have heard it described as wrong . . . but I have never yet heard any definite explanation for it," (*Phaedo*, 62a). Socrates concedes Cebes' point, "It probably seems strange to you that it should not be right for those to whom death would be an advantage to benefit themselves, but that they should have to await the services of someone else" (*Phaedo*, 62b) but goes on to give Cebes the famous guard-post allegory as an argument against suicide. Life is a sorry business but we must not leave our guard-post unless we are relieved:

> The allegory which the mystics tell us—that we men are put in a sort of guard-post, from which one must not release one's self or run away—seems to me to be a high doctrine with difficult implications. "All the same, Cebes, I believe that this is true; that the gods are our keepers, and we men are one of their possessions . . . If one of your possessions were to destroy itself without intimation from you that you wanted it to die, wouldn't you be angry with it and punish it, if you had any means of doing so? . . . so if you look at it this way I suppose it is not unreasonable to say that we must not put an end to ourselves until God sends some compulsion like the one which we are facing now?" (*Phaedo*, 62b–c)

Aristotle

Aristotle seemed less obsessed with the idea of suicide than his mentor Plato, and the subject occupies only a few lines in his many extant writings. He argued that suicide for certain reasons is the act of a coward—suicide as an escape from "poverty or disappointed love or bodily or mental anguish is the deed of a coward. . . . The suicide braves death not for some noble object but to escape ill" (*Ethics*, 3.7). Aristotle added that suicide is an injustice against the state that the state may punish. Unlike Socrates' allegory in *The Phaedo*, Aristotle made no mention of man being the property of the gods, but only as obligated to the state:

> But the man who cuts his throat in a fit of temper is voluntarily doing an injury which the law does not allow. It follows that the suicide commits an injustice. But against whom? Is it not the State rather than himself? For he suffers of his own volition, and nobody suffers injustice voluntarily. It is for this reason that the State attaches a penalty, which takes the form of a stigma put on one who has

destroyed himself, on the ground that he is guilty of the offense against the State. (*Ethics*, 5.11)

Stoics

The Stoics seem to regard neither life nor death as very important. Yet they seem almost obsessed with the idea of suicide as a way of overcoming their fear of death. In a sense, the Stoic attempts to conquer death by choosing it on his own terms. At best the philosopher should commit suicide not to escape suffering, but to avoid restrictions in carrying out life. He should be as unaffected by suffering as by any other emotion.

A central problem prompting the assumption of the Stoic philosophy of life is a pervasive fear of a loss of control, ultimately of the final control over life itself. For the Stoic, cheerfulness is no more than a philosophical duty, and does not indicate an underlying optimism. The Stoic does not accept the idea of a caring and loving deity and he is also too much of a thinker to place much permanent value on so limited a prospect as human success. He knows that he must fulfill his moral and social duty, but he can never desire reward, recognition or love and can never even feel secure that his good acts will produce a good result.

Zeno, the Greek founder of Stoicism, defined the goal of life as living in agreement with nature (*Diogenes Laertius*, 7:87). If the agreement exists, life is good; if it does not exist, suicide becomes the wise choice (*Ibid*, 7:130). Thus Zeno was said to have suicided out of sheer irritation (perhaps with imperfection itself) when he wrenched his toe upon stumbling on his way home from school. He held his breath until he died (*Ibid*, 7:20). His successor Cleanthes fasted initially to cure a gumboil but ultimately "as he had advanced so far on his journey toward death, he would not retreat," and he starved himself to death (*Diogenes Laertius*, 7:176).

Cicero argues that suicide is no great evil. "When a man's circumstances contain a preponderance of things in accordance with nature, it is appropriate for him to remain alive; when he possesses or sees in prospect a majority of the contrary things, it is appropriate for the wise man to quit life, although he is happy, and also of the foolish man to remain in life although he is miserable," (*De Finibus* 3:60). "And very often it is appropriate for the wise man to abandon life at a moment when he is enjoying supreme happiness, if an opportunity offers for making a timely exit. For the Stoic view is that happiness, which means life in harmony with nature, is a matter of seizing the right moment. So that Wisdom her very self upon occasion bids the wise man to leave her," (*De Finibus* 3:61). To Cicero, appropriate means in accordance with nature, and self-love is in accordance with nature. Thus, suicide is a useful action for the wise man who wishes to remain in accord with nature.

In the *Tusculan Disputations*, Cicero depicts death as freeing man from chains. The gods in their benevolence prepare for man a haven and refuge after he departs from worldly life (1:18). Some philosophers, he notes, disagree with this and some Stoics even feel that the soul is not immortal. Indeed, earthly life is not wholly evil; however, the afterlife holds far more joy (1:84).

Cicero cites the previously mentioned examples of the deaths of Socrates and Cato to show that suicide is permissible but only when the gods themselves have given a valid reason. One must not break the prison bonds except in obedience to the magistrate. The soul should be dissociated from the body during life by means of philosophy and virtue, so that his life will most closely resemble and best prepare the soul for afterlife. It is highly desirable for one to quit the sorrows of this world to gain the joys of the next (1:71–75).

Suicide also was a major topic in the letters of Lucius Anneaus Seneca, the brilliant Roman writer and statesman. The younger Seneca's writings show a deep concern and awareness of death. One must continue to try, but not because there is any hope of success. Pacurius held his own wake every night believing that any one who can say "My life is lived," rises daily from his bed to a sense of something gained (*Ep* 12:8–10).

One may hope for good, but must always be prepared for the worst. People discover too late that they "stand in the shadow of death of exile and suffering," (*Ep* 24:12–15). Thinking man does well to feel terror before so dire a fate. Death provides a release from these horrors. Every day we stand so much nearer the end, every hour urges us toward the bank from which we must fall. One should not be afraid to quit the present field of action (*Ep* 120). So far is death from being terrible that "by its grace all things lose their terrors." To Seneca it seems that it is life which is terrifying and death which provides release (*Ep* 24).

The events of earthly existence are insignificant, not worth any emotional involvement. Who wins the Battle of Pharsalus or who wins an election are insignificant (*Ep* 71). One may leave the world if he feels that he has overstayed his welcome (*Ep* 120). The human body is an unpleasantness to be endured only as long as one wishes, and when one thinks fit, let him dissolve his partnership with this puny clay (*Ep* 65:22).

The Stoic feels bound by necessity and seeks a sense of freedom and release. In this area, among others, Stoicism seems to suffer from some sort of constipation. One should make his escape from this life whenever he chooses, and to die when one wishes is in his hand. "Choose any part of nature and tell it to let you out," (*Ep* 117:23–24). One should pick the means by which to quit life. The option of suicide leaves open the road to freedom. To grumble at life is pointless for it holds no man fast. "Do you like life, then live on. Do you dislike it? Then you're free to return to the place you came from," (*Ep* 70:15). The philosopher may choose his own mode of death just as he chooses a ship or a house. He leaves life as he would a banquet—when it is time (*Ep* 70:11, *Plotinus on Suicide*, 1, 9).

Stoicism always emphasized duty and derogated pleasure and passion. Reason is good, emotion is evil. Pleasure is best deferred. Apples taste sweetest when they're going sour. The drinker drinks the last drought—the wave that drowns his senses, and puts the finishing-touch on his drunken bliss. Every pleasure defers its most intense thrill to the last (*Ep* 12).

Thus death is not to be viewed as an evil, and suicide is seen as a suitable act. However, suicide should not be an act of passion or emotion. To die badly or to die well in the manner of the philosopher is the important point (*Ep* 70:5–6). Seneca would not destroy himself merely to avoid pain, for the philosopher must be above pain. "I shall make my exit, not because of actual pain but because it's likely to prove a burr to everything that makes life worthwhile," (*Ep* 58:36). The man who dies because of pain is weak; the man who lives to suffer is a fool.

Finally, man is not trapped:

> You see that yawning precipice? It leads to liberty. You see that flood, that river, that well? Liberty houses within them. You see that stunted, parched, and sorry tree? From each branch, liberty hangs. Your neck, your throat, your heart are so many ways of escape from slavery . . . Do you inquire the road to freedom? You shall find it in every vein of your body. (*DeIra* III, 15:3–4)

Seneca (and his wife Paulina) put these thoughts into action, calmly cutting their wrists at the order of his former pupil, the Emperor Nero.

THE HEBREWS

Body and Soul

Judaism provides a much different view of the relationship between freedom and suicide. From the rabbinic point of view, body and soul should function together harmoniously. Though the body supports the soul in their joint service of God, there is none of the Platonic sense that the body must die to liberate the soul. Body and soul are different but need not be in conflict:

> Antoninus said to Rabbi: 'The body and the soul can both free themselves from judgment. Thus, the body can plead: The soul has sinned, [the proof being] that from the day it left me I lie like a dumb stone in the grave [powerless to do aught]. Whilst the soul can say: The body has sinned, [the proof being] that from the day I departed from it I fly about in the air like a bird [and commit no sin].' He replied, 'I will tell thee a parable. To what may this be compared? To a human king who owned a beautiful orchard which contained splendid figs. Now, he appointed two watchmen therein, one lame and the other blind. [One day] the lame man said to the blind, "I see beautiful figs in the orchard. Come and take me upon thy shoulder, that we may procure and eat them." So the lame bestrode the blind, procured and ate them. Some time after, the owner of the orchard came and inquired of them, "Where are those beautiful figs?" The lame man replied, "Have I then feet to walk with?" The blind man replied, "Have I then eyes to see with?" What did he do? He placed the lame upon the blind and judged them together. So will the Holy One, blessed be He, bring the soul, [re]place it in the body, and judge them together, as it is written. *He shall call to the heavens from above, and to the earth, that he may judge his people:*' *He shall call to the heavens from above*—this refers to the soul: *and to the earth, that he may judge his people*—to the body. (Babylonian Talmud, Sanhedrin, 91a–b).

Man must keep his body both physically and morally clean (Büchler 1922, 14–20). It is told that Hillel once left the house of learning with his students. They asked where he was headed, and he replied that he was going to perform a religious duty—to bathe in the bathhouse. A king appoints someone to keep his statue clean. Therefore, man, created in the divine image, must certainly keep his body clean (*Avot D'R Nathan*, 2:33). Hillel described the soul as a guest in the body; the body should keep itself fit in order to offer hospitality to so distinguished a guest. To Hillel, the body was neither an evil to be repressed nor a bastion of heroism to be glorified by Olympic victories. For him, both physical and spiritual activities were part of man's fulfillment of his obligation to God.

The modern Israeli scholar Ephraim Urbach has pointed to the fact that *nefesh*, the Hebrew word for soul, is used in a number of places in the Hebrew Bible to refer to the whole human being. Urbach has supplied a number of references to support this view (e.g. Exod. 4:19, 1 Kings 19:10) and specifically distinguished the term *nefesh* from the Greek word *psyche* or *anima*, which connotes a disembodied soul (Urbach 1979, 214–215).

Control over Death

In the Rabbinic system there is no thought of a decision required about suicide. Suicide is forbidden by the Torah. It is not at all the act of the Talmudic scholar. Indeed, it is a criminal act which should be punished by a court, were it possible. However, the criminal-victim is likely acting under at least a temporary insanity, and this may require pity and compassion more than persecution.

In Rabbinic thought the choice between life and death is not one to mull over daily, as talk of suicide so fills the letters of Seneca and other writings of Classical philosophers. It was a choice made once: "See I have put before you today life and death, blessing and curse and you shall choose life so that you and your seed shall live," (*Deut.* 30:19). The choice is not whether or not to destroy one's life but how to live it best. The Stoics saw fate as a powerful force controlling human destinies, typically in a capricious manner. Indeed necessity was so strong that they sought to escape it, and in particular they sought to escape from the inevitability of death in the illusion of gaining control over death through suicide. Knowing that he could bring death by slitting his wrist gave Seneca the "feeling of freedom in every vein." The option of bringing death seems to give the Stoic the illusion of control over death so as to prevent death from striking him by chance.

The Mishna is not concerned with fate and real freedom always exists in the human realm, i.e., the freedom to act righteously. However, the Mishna does not posit illusory freedom or choice in matters beyond human control. In this way the rabbis are the polar opposites of the Stoics. Where the Stoics felt overwhelmed by necessity or fate in all things except in the time and manner of their death, the rabbis argued that in such matters as death, there was in fact, no choice. "Against your will you are born, against your will you live, against your will you die. Against your will you shall in the future give account before the King of Kings," (*Avot* 4:29).

The Stoics desperately seek a feeling of freedom that offers them at least a temporary illusion of control. The rabbis accepted that God controls these matters of life and death. Feeling no need to take these impossibly difficult decisions from the hands of the one omnipotent and benevolent deity, the human being then gains the freedom to devote his attention wholly to those tasks which are peculiarly his, i.e., loving God and studying and fulfilling His commandments. The Mishna goes on to offer its own statement on freedom. The Ten Commandments were carved (*harut*) on stone. "Read not *harut* but *herut* (freedom). One is not free unless he devotes himself to study of the Torah," (*Avot* 6:2). Freedom here means freedom of the human spirit from fears and desires. When one's fears and desires run wanton then the person is dominated by them and there is no freedom. The Stoic seeks freedom from the terror of death by choosing his own means of exit. The rabbinic Jew acknowledges God's total power over birth, life, and death. In so doing he accepts the responsibility of his freedom to make moral choices. Birth and death are events beyond human understanding which God alone will handle. The individual is given freedom in terms of following the Torah.

The Stoic comparison of life to a banquet which one may depart at will meets a striking antithesis in a second century Mishnaic statement. "This world is like a portico before the world to come. Prepare yourself in the portico so that you may enter into the banquet hall," (*Avot* 4). That is, prepare yourself in the world by living righteously so that you may merit the rewards of the next world. The two worlds are dissimilar in function. In this world, good deeds and repentance are appropriate ends more beautiful than all the rewards of the next world. At the same time, the peace of spirit attainable in the next world is preferable to all of the joys of this world. Earthly life is thus not a banquet which must inevitably end. It is a time for work and preparation. The contrast with Stoic views carries on to a second point. One must not assume that the next world is some sort of refuge from this one. (*Avot*) There is still awareness, and one must come before the King of Kings for a final judgement which will be beyond anything earthly man can comprehend. Both Earth and Heaven are thus important—each in its own way.

THE ANOMALY OF MASADA

Why then is the mass suicide of the Jews defending Masada today held up as a model of Jewish martyrdom? The story of the defense of Masada against the Romans and the mass suicide of its Jewish defenders in 73 C.E. has gained new celebrity in our day, spurred on by the archaeological findings of Israeli Professor Yigael Yadin. Indeed, it has become a symbol of resistance to brutality. Yet the incident is never once mentioned in Rabbinic literature and for centuries was known to the world only through the Roman historian Josephus who had previously been a commander of the Jewish fighters.

In an attempt to shed some light on this topic, we concentrate on the actual account of Josephus. By now the speech of Eleazar ben Yair to his followers at Masada (as reported by Josephus) ranks as one of the famous orations of antiquity. Scholars debate whether ben Yair ever gave the speech at all or if he did, what he actually said. It is quite likely that Josephus followed the practice accepted by classical historians since Thucydides, of reporting not a verbatim account of the oration but rather an account of what could have or seemingly ought to have been said.

In his Masada speech, Josephus (*The Wars of the Jews*, VII, pp. 600–603) who hated the Sicarii (the militant nationalists who defended Masada), may well have put in ben Yair's mouth ideas that Josephus himself deplored. The speech contains several parts. In part one, ben Yair presents arguments more suitable to Greek fatalism and determinism than to Jewish thinking. First, God has given the Sicarii freedom to choose their own sort of death, i.e., to suicide en masse:

> And I cannot but esteem it as a favor that God hath granted us, that it is still in our power to die bravely, and in a state of freedom . . . (p. 600)

Secondly, the revolt against the Roman Empire has failed because God has sentenced the Jewish race to extinction:

The same God, who had of old taken the Jewish nation into his favour, had now condemned them to destruction . . . (p. 600)

Further, the situation is hopeless:

Consider how God hath convinced us that our hopes were in vain. (p. 601)

When his followers do not respond enthusiastically to this call for a mass suicide, ben Yair is portrayed as trying a second even more explicitly Greek argument which he attributes to Jewish tradition. We should not fear death, because it is not death, but life which is the calamity. Death gives freedom to the soul which then returns to a wonderful abode where it dwells with God. Death is much like sleep:

For the laws of our country, and of God himself, have continually taught us, and our forefathers have corroborated the same doctrine . . . that it is life that is a calamity to men, and not death; for this last affords our souls their liberty, and sends them by a removal into their own place of purity, where they are to be insensible to all sorts of misery; for while souls are tied down to a mortal body they are partakers of its miseries; and really, to speak the truth, they are themselves dead. (p. 601)

Here we have a curiosity. Ben Yair's argument reflects the thinking of Plato or Seneca rather than Jewish thinking. It is unlikely that a Judaean nationalist revolutionary like ben Yair knew much of Plato or Stoicism. However, Josephus probably did. Ben Yair goes on to cite the Indian Brahmins as a good example to the Sicarii. They bring on their own deaths with pleasure and courage in their desire for death and immortality:

We, therefore, who have been brought up in a discipline of our own, ought to become an example to others of our readiness to die; yet if we do not stand in need of foreigners to support us in this matter, let us regard those Indians who profess the exercise of philosophy; for these good men do but unwillingly undergo the time of life, and look upon it as a necessary servitude, and make haste to let their souls loose from their bodies . . . And not we, therefore ashamed to have lower notions than the Indians. (p. 601)

It is noteworthy than ben Yair is portrayed as using examples from a clearly non-Jewish philosophy to support his argument for suicide.

Ben Yair's harangue now enters a third stage. His references to freedom, imprisonment of the soul and the Brahmins have made no impression on his followers who are loyal Jews. He now speaks of the great suffering of the Jews during the war, the immense trauma of the destruction of Jerusalem, and reaches a peak of intensity in depicting a man watching his wife and children being carried off by heartless enemies:

Let us pity ourselves, our children and our wives, while it is in our power to show pity to them; for we are born to die, as well as those were whom we have begotten; nor is it in the power of the most happy of our race to avoid it. But for abuses and slavery, and the sight of our wives led away after an ignominious manner, with their children, these are not such evils as are natural and necessary among men; although such as do not prefer death before those miseries, when it is in their power to do so, must undergo even them, on account of their own cowardice. (p. 602)

At last ben Yair is portrayed as speaking in a Jewish idiom—love for homeland and family. His listeners are deeply moved, and according to Josephus, now carry through the mass suicide.

What are we to make of all this in terms of our thesis? Much of Josephus' account of Masada is highly problematic. He puts non-Jewish arguments for suicide, first Graeco-Roman and then Indian, in ben Yair's mouth. This anomaly is made all the more striking in the light of two more pieces of historical evidence: first, the glaringly different speech by Josephus himself in a mass suicide at Jotapata earlier in the war; second, the absence of any reference to suicide in a Jewish version of Josephus known as Josippon. Let us now turn to these two points.

Earlier in the Roman-Jewish war Josephus was commander of the Jewish garrison of the town of Jotapata in Galilee. As Josephus describes it, he saw little chance of holding out against the powerful Roman army of Vespasian and urged his people to surrender. However, the defenders would not give up. They held out against the

Romans for some weeks. Ultimately the city fell, and when it did, Josephus fled to a cave where he found forty of his soldiers already in hiding. Soon the Romans too found the cave and demanded that the men surrender. The Jewish soldiers favored the mass suicide but Josephus strongly disagreed (*The Wars of the Jews*, III, pp. 514–516). In his speech he sought to dissuade the other fighters from suicide, offering a traditional Jewish argument that contradicted the Graeco-Roman philosophical thinking attributed to ben Yair at Masada on several points. In contrast to the Platonic doctrine, body and soul are the best of friends, and they should remain together:

> O my friends, why are we so earnest to kill ourselves and why do we set our soul and body, which are such dear companions, at such variance. (p. 515)

It may be glorious to die for freedom in battle but not to die at one's own hand. Suicide is an act not of bravery but of the utmost cowardice and foolishness:

> I confess freely that it is a brave thing to die for liberty; but still so that it be in war, and done by those who take that liberty from us; but at present our enemies do neither meet us in battle, nor do they kill us. Now, he is equally a coward who will not die when he is obliged to die, and he who will die when he is not obliged so to do. (p. 515)

Self-murder is contrary to natural instinct, but more it is impiety to God, who is angry when he sees His gift of life treated with contempt. Only God can decide when to end life:

> Now self-murder is a crime most remote from the common nature of all animals, and an instance of impiety against God our creator . . . And do you not think that God is very angry when a man does injury to what He hath bestowed on him? For from him it is that we have received our being; and we ought to leave it to his disposal to take that being away from us. (p. 515)

The body is entrusted to the soul by God for safe-keeping:

> The bodies of all men are indeed mortal, and are created out of corruptible matter; but the soul is ever immortal, and is a portion of the Divinity that inhabits our bodies. (p. 515)

Josippon, a medieval Jewish historian who drew on Josephus as well as other sources tells a story similar to Josephus' account of Masada. However, instead of a mass suicide, the men kill their wives and children, to save them from prostitution and slavery, and then fight to the death against the Romans (Ch. 87). At the same time, Josephus' account does correspond to a number of examples in Graeco-Roman literature of collective suicides where men slaughtered their families and then themselves. Cohen (1982) provides a list of sixteen Graeco-Roman accounts of mass suicide in the ancient world.

Thus, Josephus' attempts to cast Masada as a Jewish prototype are problematic for four reasons. First, he gives ben Yair Graeco-Roman and then Brahmin pro-suicide arguments. Second, Josephus himself gives Jewish arguments against suicide at Jotapata. Third, there is no mention of suicide at Masada in Josippon, a Jewish reconstruction of Josephus. Finally, Josephus' portrayal follows a typical pattern of a Graeco-Roman collective suicide.

The question arises as to Josephus' motives. He seems interested in portraying himself positively and ben Yair negatively. He goes about this in several ways: (1) Josephus portrays ben Yair as both anti-Jewish and anti-Roman. He is anti-Roman in that he refuses to surrender to Rome. He is anti-Jewish in that he argues for suicide on non-Jewish grounds. (2) Josephus, in contrast, portrays himself as loyal both to Judaism and to Rome. He finds favor with Rome in his argument for capitulation and accommodation rather than pointless resistance against it. At the same time, Josephus is also the good Jew who has strongly defended his people's abhorrence of suicide.

It can be concluded that traditional Judaism has continuously taken a life-oriented stand. It was the Graeco-Roman world which flirted with suicide. Early suicidal behavior by certain Christian sects and heresies (e.g., the Donatists and the Circumcelliones) picked up this Graeco-Roman rather than Jewish strain. The mass suicide at Masada does not seem to represent a Jewish way of thinking, even at the time of Josephus, and great care must be taken by suicidologists in references to this event.

REFERENCES

Aristotle (1976). *The Ethics of Aristotle: The Nichomachean Ethics.* Trans: J.A.K. Thomson. New York: Penguin.
Athenaeus of Naucratis (1927). *The Deipnosophists.* C. B. Gulick (Tr.) London: W. Heinemann Ltd.
Avot D'R. Nathan (1887) S. Schechter (Ed.), Vienna, n.p.
Babylonian Talmud (1975). New York: Rom Edition.
Ben Gurion, Y. (1956) *Sefer Yosippon.* Jerusalem: Hotsaat Hominer.
Büchler, A. (1922) *Types of Jewish-Palestinian Piety from 70 B.C.E. to 70 C.E.* London: Jews' College, Publication # 8.
Cicero (1914). *De Finibus Bonorum et Malorum.* H. Rackham (Tr.) New York: The Macmillan Company.
Cicero (1945). *Tusculan Disputations.* J. E. King (Tr.) Cambridge, Mass: Harvard University Press (The Loeb Classical Library).
Cohen, S. J. D. (1982). Masada, literature tradition, archaeological remains, and the credibility of Josephus. *Journal of Jewish Studies.* 33, 385–405.
Diogenes Laertius (1972). *Lives of Eminent Philosophers* (Vols. 1 and 2). R. D. Hicks (Tr.) Cambridge, Mass: Harvard University Press (The Loeb Classical Library).
The Holy Scriptures (1955). Philadelphia: The Jewish Publication Society of America.
Jerusalem Talmud (1966). New York: Krotoschin Edition.
Josephus, F. (1985). *Complete Works,* W. Whiston (Tr.) Grand Rapids, MI: Kregel Publications.
Plato (1954). *The Last Days of Socrates (Including Euthyphro, The Apology, Crito, Phaedo).* Middlesex, England: Penguin Classics.
Plato (1970). *The Laws.* Middlesex, England: Penguin Classics.
Plato (1955). *Phaedo.* R. Hackforth (Tr.) Cambridge, England: Cambridge University Press.
Plato (1955). *The Republic.* Middlesex, England: Penguin Classics.
Plotinus (1918). *Complete Works.* K. S. Guthrie (Tr.) London: George Bell and Son.
Seneca, L. A. (1979). *Seneca.* Cambridge, Mass: Harvard University Press (The Loeb Classical Library).
Shulchan Aruch, Yorah Deah (1977). Tel Aviv.
Urbach, E. E. (1979) *The Sages: Their Concepts and Beliefs.* I. Abrahams (Tr.). Jerusalem: The Magnes Press, The Hebrew University of Jerusalem.

2

Maimonides, and Freud, on Self-Destructiveness

DAVID BAKAN, PH.D.

This paper compares Freud's conception of "repression" with Maimonides' conception of "interference with intellectual apprehension." Maimonides' view suggests that the resultant vacuity in consciousness may play a role in the psychodynamics of suicide. A second factor in suicide for both Freud and Maimonides may be the internalization of the angry God imposed by the angry Moses.

I

Suicide, in the Jewish tradition, is presumed to be the consequence of some mental failure or duress (Maimonides, Mishnah Torah, Sanhedrin, 18:6).

Thus, to attempt to ascertain what Maimonides' thought with respect to the psychological dynamics of suicide might have been—he did not write on them directly—we would want to consider what his expressed views with respect to normal and abnormal mental functioning were.

Various psychological observations are to be found throughout Maimonides' writings. His views on normal and desirable human functioning are particularly to be found in his descriptions of the psychological conditions associated with prophecy. He deals extensively with prophecy in *The Guide of the Perplexed* (1963); see also Bakan (1992). For Maimonides prophecy is the highest stage of human development. It entails the fullest cultivation of the human intellectual and imaginative faculties. It is a higher stage than philosophy, which involves only the cultivation of the intellectual faculty.

His views on mental abnormality are particularly associated with an attempt to understand wrong-doing. His most extensive treatment is to be found in a work that is commonly referred to as The Eight Chapters (1966).

The latter work is especially important because in it Maimonides openly expresses himself as both a legalist and a physician. The Eight Chapters is, in the first place, aimed at providing psychological knowledge to judges involved in court proceedings. Maimonides indicates that judges in particular have to be understanding of the psychological processes of the people who come before them. Maimonides indicates that judging is best which entails the least use of coercion; and it is for this reason that psychological knowledge is desirable. In the pages of The Eight Chapters Maimonides further proposes the adoption of the perspective of a physician, a physician of the soul. He describes the practice of medicine in this sense as itself a religious activity.

I would like to highlight two aspects of Maimonides' thought that might perhaps illuminate the psychodynamics of suicide, and juxtapose them with some Freudian contributions. The first is with respect to the human intellectual faculty. The second is with respect to an unfortunate larger social condition which he links to a failing in the character of Moses. Both of these tie in with some of the things which are prominent in Freud's writings. And both of them bear on the question of human self-destructiveness.

II

One of the most fundamental notions in Maimonides' writing is that misconduct interferes with intellection, and that failure in intellection leads to misfortune. This truth is expressed in the notion that God provides for the righteous, and withholds providence from the unrighteous. But this is only metaphorical. For God, according to Maimonides, does not intervene in such a direct way in the events of the world that transpire.

Positively, studying Torah—which includes the study of nature as the fulfillment of the commandment to love God—and following Torah—which is following the commandments and their traditional explanations, the latter being grounded in an understanding of the constraints and opportunities provided by nature—keeps all things in balance, promoting the welfare of society, the welfare of the body, and the welfare of the mind. The last promotes the study of Torah, completing the loop.

Positively, this all can lead to intellectual and moral perfection, which is the necessary condition for prophecy, and which, in this sense, is possible for all human beings. And positively this can ultimately lead to an enlightened death by the "kiss of God."

The essence of the process is intellectual apprehension. And if the loop is not maintained the critical negative consequence is interference with intellectual apprehension.

Thus, Maimonides interprets the meaning of the garden of Eden story as follows. When Adam engaged in misconduct, he did not gain in intellectual apprehension. Quite the contrary, Adam "was punished by being deprived of that intellectual apprehension" (1963, p. 24). All evils derive from the absence of intellectual apprehension. For evil, for Maimonides, is essentially blindness and the stumbling that results from it.

All of this is a natural process. The world, for Maimonides, always follows its natural course. The punishment for wrong-doing is, as indicated above, intrinsic, and not extrinsic. Punishment for wrong-doing is part of the natural world as the world was created by God. It is not by particular divine intercession. And the mechanism is simple. It is the obstruction to intellectual apprehension.

Maimonides comes to the example of hysteria as a result of wrong-doing. It is interesting that Maimonides exemplifies this natural effect of wrong-doing precisely with the neuroses, the loss of normal voluntary control, and especially the hysterias. The examples he gives are precisely hysterical paralysis, and hysterical blindness, quite the phenomena that Charcot was demonstrating when Freud was in Paris, and to which Freud gave his first psychoanalytic attention. Maimonides' case material, as it were, is from Scripture. He cites:

> . . . the instance in which a man's hand [is] prevented from working so that he can do nothing with it, as was the case of Jeroboam . . . [I Kings, 13:4], or a man's eyes [are prevented] from seeing, as happened to the Sodomites who had assembled about Lot [Genesis 19:11] (1966, p. 95).

to make the point.

We can readily identify Freud's repression with Maimonides'

interference with intellectual apprehension. What might have been conscious is not. That is, what might have been conscious—using Freud's word—is repressed into the unconscious, and is unreachable.

But in a certain sense, Maimonides' notion is more embracing than Freud's. And the difference between Freud and Maimonides may have particular significance in connection with the psychodynamics of suicide.

Freud tended to concentrate on the ongoing effects of intellectual content which had been pressed, repressed, from consciousness to unconsciousness. Maimonides' view leads to consider as well the vacuity, the emptiness that is left in consciousness, which is associated with repression. I suspect that this vacuity itself plays a role in the psychodynamics of suicide. I offer it as an hypothesis. The relationship between depression, and the painful vacuity that is often present, and suicide is suggestive with respect to the hypothesis.

III

The second item is Maimonides' concern with a defect in the character of Moses. This was Moses' irateness, his tendency to become very angry quickly. Maimonides' opinion of Moses in this respect is important as background with respect to the Freudian hypothesis of self-destructiveness as associated with the introjected father/God/Moses in the super-ego.

Freud conceptualized the neurosis as existing not only on the individual level, but also on the trans-individual level. He saw close connections between religion and neurosis. In connection with the Jewish religion, which he recognized as the core of virtually all religion in Western Civilization, he fixed his eye critically on the figure of Moses.

A lifelong preoccupation with the figure of Moses characterizes both Freud and Maimonides. In a way the life intellectual projects of both Freud and Maimonides were the same. They both were involved in a struggle to keep the civilizing feature of religion and eliminating the coercive features in it. Essentially, both converged on the irateness of the Moses figure.

When Freud studied the statue of Moses by Michelangelo he sought to extract an intention of an anger which would never express itself in aggressive conduct. When he wrote about Moses in that last work that he carried to England under his arm when he was expelled from Austria, he sought to undermine his authority and credibility by making him out to be a deposed Egyptian official who, in his own desperation, imposed himself on a hapless group of slaves.

Maimonides also saw great damage done to the people by Moses. God, Maimonides says, does not get angry. God is not a person. Maimonides sometimes allows that there might be some pedagogical value in personifying God. But under no circumstances is that to be taken as permission to attribute vices to God. And anger is a vice.

Moses, Maimonides explains, by his own irateness, misled the people into believing that God could get angry. The belief in an angry God is the all too common form of idolatry that resulted from this. And all ills are ultimately connected to idolatry.

The elaboration of the explanation of self-destructiveness in terms of the interiorization of the angry God, imposed by the angry Moses, is one of the great contributions that Freud made.

REFERENCES

Bakan, D. (1992). *Maimonides on Prophecy*. Northvale, New Jersey: Jason Aronson.

Maimonides, Moses. *The Eight Chapters* (1966). J. Gorfinkle (ed. and trans.). New York: AMS Press.

Maimonides, M. *The Guide of the Perplexed* (1963). S. Pines (ed. and trans.). Chicago: University of Chicago Press.

Maimonides, M. *Mishnah Torah* (6 vols.) (1962). New York: M. P. Press.

3

Fatalism and Suicide in Greek and Biblical Thought

KALMAN J. KAPLAN, PH.D., AND CONSTANTINO V. RICCARDI, M.A.

This essay explores the interrelationship of fatalism and suicide. Two basic world views are presented. The first is the Graeco-Roman view, as exemplified in the Promethean myth in which the ultimate power controlling the world is unrelenting fate: a power so all-embracive that not even the gods can escape the dictates of fate. The second world view is that of the biblical tradition, which contends that the ultimate power of the universe is a purposeful, redemptive, and loving God: a personal force experienced even in the depths of human anguish.

Both world views have addressed the problem of human suffering for over 2,000 years. Yet the Greek and Roman world has multitudinous examples of suicide in its history and literature while the biblical world has very few. We suggest that belief in a personal loving God offers a wealth of spiritual and psychological resources not available to someone who simply accepts "fate" with suicidal resignation.

It has been said that Freud's greatest discovery was the Oedipus complex. Its central role in psychoanalysis is unquestioned. It represents the third stage in Freud's view of psychosexual development and is critical to explaining how the individual identifies with his same-sex parent and how the superego is formed. Indeed it is an adage of psychoanalytic theory that "the superego is heir to the Oedipus complex".

Yet over the past forty years, the question has emerged as to what the implications would be of substituting a narrative from the Hebrew Bible for this Greek story. Erich Wellisch (1954) was the first to raise this question in his pioneering work "Isaac and Oedipus." As the title of the book implies, Wellisch proposes a biblical approach to psychotherapy wherein "the Akedah" (Abraham's binding of Isaac and his ultimate non-sacrifice) is offered as an alternative to the legend of Oedipus. For Wellisch, the biblical story offers a resolution of the father–son relationship not available to the Greek civilization. A covenant of love replaces the cold peace between father and son emerging out of the incomplete resolution of the Oedipus complex.

Much the same argument has been made by Kalman Kaplan and his associates (Kaplan, Schwartz, and Markus Kaplan, 1984, Kaplan, and Schwartz, 1993) and has been suggested by Yosef Yerushalmi (1991) in his superb book *Freud's Moses.* and by James Grotstein (1994) in his essay "Why Oedipus and not Christ?" Kaplan and Schwartz (1993) have specifically applied this argument to suicide and to self-destructive behaviors. Basically, Kaplan and Schwartz argue that the unresolved Oedipus complex carries within it the germ of parental nonacceptance of the child, which places the child in the impossible position of continuously attempting to gain parental approval through achievement. This lack of acceptance occurs in Greek thought, in the relationship between gods and humans and within the human family itself. Biblical narratives, in contrast (for example, the Akedah in Judaism, Golgotha in Christianity), present the vision of a loving God who accepts and treasures the human being unconditionally. Human achievements are seen not in the context of earning God's love, an impossible task, but developing it and expressing it within a social context. This sense of acceptance exists both in the realm of relations between God and the human beings and within the human family itself. This provides a strong message of hope that is suicide-preventive. This paper focuses on another point of this contrast: the comparative role of fatalism in Greek and biblical thought and the relationship of fatalism to self-destructive behavior.

This paper explores contrasts between Greek and biblical thought with regard to fatalism and self-destructive behavior. In the Greek theogony, nature exists before the gods. Sky (the male) marries Earth (the female) and produces, first the hundred-handed monsters, and then the Cyclopes.

> First sky ruled over the entire world. He married Earth and produced Briareus, Gyes, and Cottus, the so-called, Hundred-Handed, who possessed a hundred hands and fifty heads and were unsurpassed in size and strength. After these Earth bore him the Cyclopes: Arges,

Steropes, and Brontes, each of whom has one eye in his forehead (*Apollodorus*, 1:1–2).

The family pathology begins immediately, the father taking the children away from the mother:

> Sky tied them (the Cyclopes) up and threw them into Tartarus, a dark and gloomy place in Hades as far from earth as earth is from the sky and again had children by Earth, the so-called Titans (*Apollodorus*, 1:3).

Such action of course breeds reaction, and Earth repays Sky in spades:

> Grieved at the loss of the children who were thrown into Tartarus, Earth persuaded the Titans to attack their father and gave Cronus a steel sickle. They all set upon him, except for Ocean, and Cronus cut off his father's genitals and threw them into the sea . . . From the drops of the spurting flood were born the Furies: Alecto, Tisiphone, and Megaera. Having thus eliminated their Father the Titans brought back their brother who had been hurled to Tartarus and gave the rule to Cronus (*Apollodorus*, 1:4).

Thus, the Oedipal conflict is born and, indeed, ingrained through the Furies into the fabric of the natural world. The Oedipal conflict seems to be an unchanging law of nature, foretold by Earth and Sky:

> When Earth and Sky foretold that Cronus would lose the rule to his own son, he devoured his offspring as they were born (*Apollodorus* 1:5).

The infant Zeus is saved through a ruse; Cronus was misled by being given a stone wrapped in swaddling clothes instead. When Zeus reaches adulthood he makes war on Cronus and the Titans (*Apollodorus* 2:1), fulfilling the prophecy of Earth and Sky.

This same Hellenistic focus on fate and necessity as being greater than the gods is portrayed eloquently in Aeschylus' tragedy *Prometheus Bound* (1942). At the play's beginning, Prometheus is being nailed and chained to a barren and desolate crag in the Caucasus by Might, a demon and servant of Father Zeus, and Hephaestus, the Greek god of the forge. Prometheus's sin was to steal fire from heaven because he had a "human-loving" disposition. In addition to being nailed and chained to the rock, an iron wedge is driven through Prometheus's chest, and iron bands are placed around his chest and legs. Prometheus, a god known for his cunning and knowledge of the future, envisions his sufferings lasting 10,000 years. Once Might and Hephaestus leave him, Prometheus, in agony, accepts his fate:

> So must I bear, as lightly as I can,
> The destiny that fate has given me;
> for I know well against necessity,
> against its strength, no one can fight and win. (p. 206)

At this point the ultimate source of power in Aeschylus's world-view is seen. The ultimate source of power is fate or necessity. It is an impersonal force that no one, not even the god Father Zeus, the enemy and persecutor of Prometheus, can control. This is exemplified in the following lines:

CHORUS: Who then is the steersman of necessity?
PROMETHEUS: The triple-formed fates and the remembering furies.
CHORUS: Is Zeus weaker than these?
PROMETHEUS: Yes, for he, too, cannot escape what is fated. (p. 221)

Toward the conclusion of the play, Hermes, the messenger of Zeus, comes to Prometheus and demands to know who will overthrow Zeus and when this will occur. Prometheus sneers at Hermes, refers to him as Zeus's footman, the "fetch and carry" messenger, and the "lackey of the gods."

Prometheus refuses to yield to any requests of Hermes or Zeus unless he is first unshackled. The exasperated Hermes says to Prometheus:

> You are a colt new broken, with the bit
> clenched in its teeth, fighting against the reins,
> and bolting. You are too strong and confident
> in your weak cleverness. For obstinacy
> standing alone is the weakest of all things
> in whose mind is not possessed by wisdom.

> Think what a storm, a triple wave of ruin
> will rise against you. First this rough crag
> with thunder and lightning bolt the Father
> shall cleave asunder, and shall hide your body
> wrapped in a rocky clasp within its depth;
> a tedious length of time you must fulfill
> before you see the light again, returning.
> Then Zeus's winged hound, the eagle red,
> shall tear great shreds of flesh for you, a feaster
> coming unbidden, every day your liver
> bloodied to blackness will be his repast. (p. 242)

Even the threats of being thrown into hell and an eagle tearing out his liver on a daily basis will not thwart or subdue Prometheus's rage. His response to Hermes and his message to Zeus is "there is no disgrace in suffering at an enemy's hand, when you hate mutually."

The final lines of the tragedy are spoken by Prometheus:

> Now it is words no longer: now in very truth
> the earth is staggered: in its depths the thunder
> bellows resoundingly, the fiery tendrils
> of the lightning flash light, and whirling clouds
> carry the dust along: all the winds' blasts
> dance in a fury one against the other
> in violent confusion: earth and sea
> are one, confused together: such is the storm
> that comes against me manifestly from Zeus
> to work its terrors. O Holy mother mine,
> O Sky that circling brings the light to all,
> you see me, how I suffer, How unjustly. (p. 244–5)

The ultimate power in the Greek world of Aeschylus is "fate." In the plays of Aeschylus the human being is not the chief problem. The human being "is merely the vehicle of destiny and that destiny is the real problem."

If we use the word *fate* or the word *destiny* in Aeschylus's sense, we are describing an impersonal yet ultimate force that totally dominates the human condition. Prometheus may have foreknowledge of his deliverance, but he must await the prescribed time. He can do little more than rage. Unlike his biblical counterparts,

Prometheus rebels rather than submit, but to no avail. What does this disclose concerning human nature and its stories about the gods? Aeschylus's tragic view (a major expression of public religion) states simply that "the highest knowledge can be reached only through suffering." But what is the cause of this suffering? Certainly one cause is a predetermined and impersonal ultimate power that is indifferent to the plights of gods and mortals. Fate or destiny simply *is* and in its infinite irrational silence there is only the drama of passion and rage.

Consider the implications of Fate or Necessity for self-destruction. A woman spurns an adolescent male. He feels that he is "fated" to live in lonely melancholy, with the image of the woman haunting him. Not considering that there is the possibility of another woman or that, in fact, the future is open-ended, he becomes tunnel-visioned and suicidal. In other words, the adolescent male transforms a single event, as unpleasant as it may be, into an archetype, a law of necessity, a general rule that enslaves him—"All women will reject him." The same scenario could apply to business. A person loses a company or a fortune and feels he is "fated" to poverty. Again, he has foreclosed on the future, transforming a singular occurrence into a general rule. Without a belief in an eternal Creator, affirming the possibility of redeeming an individual loss, the individual will be left in despair and may begin suicidal thought processes.

Consider in contrast, the Hebrew version of creation and the Creator. Here, God exists before nature and in fact creates the heaven and the earth:

In the beginning God created the heaven and the earth (Gen. 1:1).

God then proceeds to create order out of chaos. First, light is divided from darkness (Gen. 1:24). God then divides water from the land (Gen. 1:9). At this point, God begins to prepare this world for the entrance of man. First He has the earth bring forth vegetation (Gen. 1:11). He then places living creatures in the sea and fowls in the air (Gen. 1:20). Now God places living creatures on the earth: cattle, creeping things, and other beasts (Gen. 1:24).

The world is now ready for man in God's plan. God creates man, His ultimate handiwork, in His own image and gives him dominion over all in nature He has created:

And God created man in His own image, in the image of God created He him; male and female, created He them. And God blessed them; and God said unto them: "Be fruitful, and multiply and replenish the earth, and subdue it; and have dominion over the fish of the sea, and over the fowl of the air, and over every living thing that creepeth upon the earth. And God said: "Behold, I have given you every herb yielding seed, where is upon the face of all the earth, and every tree, in which is the fruit of a tree yielding seed—to you it shall be for food (Gen. 1:27-29).

In a second creation story, some lines further ahead, man is specifically described as being formed from the dust of the ground (Gen. 2:7). Woman in turn is described as being taken from the rib of man (Gen. 2:22). And the man said: "This is now bone of my bone, and flesh of my flesh. She shall be called woman because she was taken out of man" (Gen. 2:23).

Certainly there is no sign of an Oedipus complex here nor the same sense of fatalism as it exists in the Greek story of creation. God supersedes nature and gives to each human individual freedom to act. Yet Western man shies away from this freedom, turning the biblical proclamation that God created the heaven and the earth into its obverse. God becomes a psychological projection, the creation of man and subject to the very nature and material laws He has created.

In his great work, *Athens and Jerusalem*, Lev Shestov puts it as follows: "The Creator of the world has Himself become subordinate to Necessity which He created and which, without at all seeking or desiring it, has become the sovereign of the universe" (1966, p. 85). In other words, the radical conception that God created nature and is thus able to change what seem to be immutable natural laws has deteriorated into that much more deterministic view that nature creates the gods and in fact governs them. Secure parenting deteriorates into insecure parenting (Ainsworth, 1979).

Such a disempowered god, of course, cannot help the human being withstand individual misfortune. Unlike Job, the Greek man seems unable to protect himself from the overwhelming laws of fate and necessity. Thus he becomes suicidal. A radical transformation in human consciousness to accept the freedom offered by the God of the Hebrew Bible seems essential to empower the human being and provide him with the resilience necessary to withstand the traumas of life without converting them into the fatalistic sense of doom emerging from the Greek tragic vision.

REFERENCES

Aeschylus. (1942). Prometheus Bound. Trans. and intro: D. Greene. In *The Complete Greek Tragedies*, vol. 1. New York: Random House (The Modern Library).

Aeschylus. (1961). *Promethus Bound and Other Plays*. Trans. and intro: P. Vellacott. Baltimore, Maryland: Penguin Books.

Ainsworth, M.D.S. (1979). Infant-mother attachment. *American Psychologist*, 34:932–937.

Apollodorus. (1976). *The Library*. Trans: M. Simpson. Amherst: University of Massachusetts Press.

Grotstein, J. (1994). Why Oedipus and not Christ? Presented at the 102nd Annual Meetings of the American Psychological Association. Los Angeles, California, August, 1994.

The Holy Scriptures. (1917). 2 vols. Philadelphia: Jewish Publication Society of America.

Jaeger, Werner. (1945). *Paideia: The Ideals of Greek Culture*. Trans. from the Second German Edition: G. Highet. vol. 1. New York: Oxford University Press.

Kaplan, K. J., Schwartz, M. W. and Markus-Kaplan, M. (1994). *The Family: Biblical and Psychological Foundations*. New York: Human Sciences Press.

Kaplan, K. J. and Schwartz, M. W. (1993). *A Psychology of Hope: An Antidote to the Suicidal Pathology of Western Civilization*. Westport, Connecticut: Praeger.

Kereny, C. (1963). *Prometheus: Archtypal Image of Human Existence*. Trans: R. Manheim. New York: Pantheon Books.

Shestov, L. (1966). *Athens and Jerusalem*. Trans: B. Martin. New York: Simon and Schuster.

Wellisch, E. (1954). *Isaac and Oedipus: Studies in Biblical Psychology of the Sacrifice of Isaac*. London: Routledge and Kegan Paul.

Yerushalmi, Y. (1991). *Freud's Moses. Judaism: Terminable and Interminable*. New Haven, Connecticut: Yale University Press.

4

The Fatalism of "Aher"

MATTHEW B. SCHWARTZ, PH.D.

This article analyzes the response of the Mishna to the pessimism endemic to Greek and Roman stoicism. The tragic case of Aher is discussed.

"R. Yaacov says 'This world is like a waiting room (*prozdor*) before the next world. Prepare yourself in the *prozdor* so that you may enter into the banquet hall (*traclin*).' He used to say, 'One hour of repentance and good deeds in this world is better than the whole eternal life. And one hour of blissfulness of spirit in the world to come is better than the whole of this world.'" (Mishnah Avot 4:16-17) The tragic figure of Aher, Elisha ben Avuyah, the second century rabbi who turned violently against the Torah and the Jewish People during the Hadrianic persecution, continues to fascinate scholars and even novelists, e.g. Milton Steinberg's *As A Driven Leaf*. This essay shall argue that these Mishnaic statements may have been a direct response to Aher's Hellenizing philosophy. For while rabbinic Judaism deplores fatalism and suicide, Greek thinkers often found them congenial and Aher had accepted the Greek view.

Three questions arise in regard to this Mishna. (1) Who was R. Yaacov? (2) Is there any significance in the image of a waiting room and a banquet hall? (3) Why does the Mishna use Greek and Latin words instead of a Hebrew equivalent?

(1) Parallel statements to the Mishnah (Leviticus R. 3:1 and Kohelet R. 4:6) use the name R. Yaacov ben Korshoi. Thus R. Yaacov is one and the same with R. Yaacov ben Korshoi, who is referred to (BT Kiddushin 39a) as a grandson of Aher. Aaron Heiman in his *Toledot Tanaim Veamorain* (II:170) does argue that the text in Kiddushin is questionable and that we in fact have no direct statement linking R. Yaacov and R. Yaacov ben Korshoi. However, the texts of Avot and the two midrashim would seem to substantiate the fact of R.

Yaacov and R. Yaacov ben Korshoi being one and the same and also of his being probably a grandson of Aher.

(2) Aher had, of course, studied Greek literature carrying Greek books under his garment even into the house of study and constantly singing Greek songs and poems. Surely then, he was familiar with the ideas of Seneca, the famed Stoic philosopher and advisor to the Emperor Nero. A favorite theme in Seneca's writings is suicide and he often argues at length in its praise. One of his widely cited images was that life is like a banquet and one may leave it whenever he wishes (Ep. 77:8). R. Yaacov, a devout Jew, was perhaps seeking to refute directly this parable of Seneca's, which he had heard from his grandfather, Aher. To the Jew, not this world is a banquet but the next world. However, one must not rush to enter the world to come by suicide, for both worlds are a part of divine creation and each has its own singular beauty and special purpose.

(3) The words *prozdor* and *triclin* are drawn from the Greek or Latin. Perhaps R. Yaacov was responding to Aher by using the Greek or Latin words because it was those exact words in which Aher had cited to him the passage from Seneca many years before.

It is clear that Aher's general view of the world was gloomy and indeed outright fatalistic. He accepted other-worldly voices telling him that he could never repent, he seemed taken with the notion that people's ability to learn declines with age and he seems to have set himself unrealistic goals in scholarship that were beyond the reach of even his brilliant mind (JT Hagigah 2:1).

REFERENCES

Babylonian Talmud (1975). New York: Rom Edition.
Heiman, A. (1964). *Toledot Tanaim Veamoraim*. Jerusalem: Kiryah Ne'emanah.
The Holy Scriptures (1955). Philadelphia: The Jewish Publication Society of America.
Jerusalem Talmud (1966). New York: Krotoschin Edition.
Midrash Rabbah (1961). Jerusalem Vilna Edition.
Mishnah (1969). New York: M. P. Press.
Seneca, L. A. (1979). *Seneca*. Cambridge, Mass.: Harvard University Press (The Loeb Classical Library).
Steinberg, M. (1939). *As a Driven Leaf*. New York: Behrman House.

5

The Death of Jesus and Anti-Semitism

KALMAN J. KAPLAN, PH.D.

A question largely ignored by current students of religion and suicide is the degree to which major Christian theologians have stressed that the death of Jesus was voluntary. This chapter examines the effect of this viewpoint on the emotions of believing Christians as survivors of an "altruistic suicide" and, specifically, how this may have affected the sad historical phenomenon of outbreaks of theological anti-Semitism.

THE VOLUNTARY DEATH OF JESUS AND THE CHRISTIAN KERYGMA

There can be no question that the death of Jesus is essential to the central *kerygma* (message) of Christianity. Indeed, the Gospel of John in the Christian New Testament emphasizes the mystery and passion of the sacrificial death of Jesus as part of a divine plan to save mankind. "For God so loved the world that He gave His only begotten son, that whoever believes in Him should not perish but have eternal life" (John 3.16). Furthermore, this act is seen as representing the epitome of love: "Greater love has no one than this, that one lay down his life for his friends" (John 15.13). In fact, in New Testament letters, the death of Jesus is offered as a standard of behavior for others: "We know love by this that He laid down his life for us and that we ought to lay down our lives for the brethren." (John 3.16).

Is Jesus' Death Voluntary?

Significantly, Christian thinkers, both early and late, have insisted upon the voluntary aspects of the death of Jesus Christ. Tertullian, for example, held that Jesus Christ on the cross gave up the ghost freely and of his own volition before death by crucifixion overtook him (*To the Martyrs*, 4). Origen supported this point of view (*Exhortation to Martyrdom*). A more mainstream Christian thinker, St. Augustine himself, particularly stressed the voluntary aspects of the death of Jesus: "His soul did not leave His body constrained, but because He would and where He would and how He would" (Augustinus, *The Trinity*, 4).

Centuries later, another central Christian theologian, St. Thomas Aquinas took great pains to argue that Christ was not slain by another, but gave up his life voluntarily (*Summa*, 3.47.1). Aquinas begins by offering three objections to the idea that Christ was slain by another. First, he offers the citation from John: "No man takes my life from Me, but I lay it down of myself" (John 10.18). Second, he cited Augustine: "Those who were crucified were tormented with a lingering death." This did not happen in Christ's case, because "crying out, with a loud voice, He yielded up the spirit" (Matthew 27.50). Third, Aquinas again cited Augustine's view that Christ willed His soul to leave His body. At the same time, Aquinas pointed to a seemingly contradictory passage in Luke (18.33): "After they have scourged Him, they will put Him to death." Aquinas attempted to resolve this seeming contradiction by distinguishing between *direct* and indirect causes. Christ's persecutors were a *direct* cause of His death. Christ was an *indirect* cause of his death by not preventing this: "Therefore, since Christ's soul did not repel the injury inflicted on His body but willed His corporeal nature to succumb to such injury, He is said to have laid down His life, or to have died voluntarily'" (*Summa*, 3.47.1).

Jesus as Martyr, Jesus as Suicide

What kind of death are we talking about here? It should be noted that Durkheim defines suicide in his classic study *Le Suicide* (1897/1951) as "all cases of death resulting directly or indirectly from a positive or negative act of the victim himself, which he knows will produce this result." The inclusion of the term "indirectly" in Durkheim's definition of suicide suggests that martyrs be classified generally as suicides. Specifically, Durkheim's definition argues that Jesus' death be classified as a suicide, albeit an altruistic suicide, indeed the very epitome of an altruistic suicide. Further it suggests that the believing Christian be seen as the survivor of a suicide, left with a suicide note that Jesus died for his sins.

To be sure, Augustine and Aquinas back away from this conclusion, each condemning suicide while affirming the voluntary nature of Jesus' death. Augustine, for example, strongly condemned suicide in *The City of God* as a "detestable crime and a damnable sin" (1:27). He based this prohibition on his interpretation of Deuteronomy 5.17: "Thou shalt not kill" (1.20). Augustine goes on to portray Jesus as urging flight from persecution rather than self-murder (1.22).

A similar argument is offered centuries later by Aquinas, who, it should be remembered, stressed that Jesus was the voluntary *indirect* cause of his own death (*Summa*, 3.47.1). At the same time, Aquinas (2.2.64.5) reiterated Augustine's argument associating murder with suicide (*The City of God*, 1.20). Aquinas then adds three of his own arguments against suicide. First, it is unnatural and uncharitable toward oneself, and thus a mortal sin. Second, suicide is antisocial. Third, life is the gift of God. Though given, it remains His property, so only God can pronounce the sentence of life and death: "I will kill and I will make to live" (Deut. 32.39).

Martyr-Suicides Among Early Christians

Augustine and Aquinas tried to have it both ways, condemning suicide while affirming Jesus' voluntary martyrdom. However, such subtle distinctions often seemed lost on early Christians, who, to be sure, were often facing a martyr's death. However, mixed with the acceptance of death as unavoidable, there was also a desire and, indeed, an active pursuit of death. The most striking group example was the waves of martyr-suicides engaged in by the heretical Donatists and Circumcelliones. Whole companies of Donatists, for example, threw themselves from rocks. The Donatists, however, did not kill themselves if they could persuade the authorities to do it. One device was to attack magistrates on the road. Sometimes the Donatists stopped ordinary travelers on the road and threatened them with being murdered themselves if the travelers did not agree to kill the Donatists (Willis, 1950).

Church Legislation Against Suicide

The strength of the suicide urge within early Christians led to the harsh attempts of the church to control it: first, in the writings of Augustine and later Aquinas discussed previously; second, in the specific anti-suicide legislation passed by Church Councils. The first anti-suicide legislation in canon law was passed at the Council of Arles in 452. It repeated earlier Roman economic legislation forbidding the suicide of slaves. The second Council of Orleans (533) denied funeral rites to suicides accused of crimes. The Council of Braga (563) extended this law to all suicides. In 590, the Council of Antisidor forbade the church to accept offerings for the souls of suicides.

John Donne's Defense of Suicide

Despite this formidable army of legislation against suicide, a lingering sense of the suicidal implications of Jesus' death remained. In 1600 the English poet John Donne brings this implicit connection out into the open in his brilliant and controversial work *Biathanatos*. Donne offers a Christian defense, or at least tolerance, of suicide on the grounds that Christ's death was brave and voluntary: "It is a heroic act of fortitude, if a man when an urgent occasion is presented, exposes himself to a certain and assured death as he did" (*Biathanatos*, 3.4.5). Donne viewed Christ as an altruistic suicide. He was a martyr who willingly gave his life to redeem man and thus served as a model for many of the early Christian martyr-suicides: "And that Apollonia and others who prevented the fury of the fire, did therein imitate this act of our Savior, of giving up his soul, before he was constrained to do it."

Jewish, Christian, and Greek Martyrs

The glorification of death significantly differentiates the Christian martyr from the Jewish martyr. For some Christian martyrs, voluntary death is an ideal to be imitated; for the Jewish martyr, in contrast, death is something to be avoided in a way that does not compromise his faith. To put it another way, the death of Jesus is essential for the Christian idea of salvation. Some Christian martyrs court death and must transform it psychologically into a voluntary act, in a manner similar to many of the Greek altruistic suicides portrayed in Euripides (Oates and O'Neill, 1938).

For example, in *Iphigenia in Aulis*, Euripides gives Iphigenia the following lines, "I have chosen death: it is my own free choice. I have put cowardice away from me. Honor is mine now" (1375–1377). In Euripides' *The Heracleidae*, Macaria rejects a lottery as a method of choosing who will be sacrificed. "My death shall no chance lot decide, there is no graciousness in that peace, old friend. But if ye accept and will avail you of my readiness, freely do I offer my life, and without constraint" (541–543).

In contrast, the death of Jesus (or any other figure, for that matter) is totally irrelevant to the message of Judaism. The untimely death of anyone is sad, but it is not linked logically or psychologically to any idea of Jewish redemption. The Jewish martyr does not court death, nor must he make it a voluntary act. The paradigmatic Jewish martyr is Rabbi Akiba, who was tortured cruelly by the Romans when they found him teaching the Torah during the period of persecution that followed the Bar Kochba War (135 C.E.). As the story is told in the Babylonian Talmud (*Berachot*, 61b), a Roman officer saw Rabbi Akiba smiling and asked him why. Rabbi Akiba responded he was in great agony, and he knew he would soon die. He was glad only that in his last moment, he could still sanctify God's name by reciting the Shema: "Hear Oh Israel, the Lord our God, the Lord is one." Rabbi Akiba did not seek martyrdom and he felt no beatific joy in his pain. He did not try to convert his death into a voluntary act. Rather he continued to express his faith in God.

THE CHRISTIAN AS SURVIVOR OF A SUICIDE, AND CHRISTIAN ANTI-SEMITISM

We are thus faced with a peculiar and outrageous paradox. It is the Christian who gains from the death of Jesus (it being essential to the Christian idea of redemption: John 3:16) and not the Jew. Yet the Jewish people, historically, have been blamed as the *direct* cause of Jesus' death; this despite the undeniable fact that Jesus is simultaneously seen as voluntarily giving up his life to redeem mankind, and thus the *indirect* cause of his own death. And this despite the fact that Christianity is the daughter of Judaism. How did this come to be? Many thinkers, both Jewish and Christian, have attempted to tackle this extremely serious problem. The remainder of this paper will attempt to examine it from the vantage point of suicidology.

The Gospel of John as a Suicide Note

The believing Christian can be seen as the recipient of a suicide note: the Johanine Gospel (i.e., the Gospel of John). It is an unmistakable message, loud and clear, albeit written by a third party and long after Jesus' death. *Jesus died for man* to erase the sin brought into the world through Adam violating God's commandment not to eat of the tree of knowledge.

The note begins: Jesus died to conquer death, which came into the world as a result of this sin and to restore the believer to eternal life. Further, this sacrifice is an expression of the love of God for the world, "For God so loved the world that He gave His only begotten son, that whoever believes in Him should not perish but have eternal life" (John 3.16).

The suicide note continues: Jesus died voluntarily. He was not forced to do this against his will. "No man take my life from Me, but I lay it down myself" (John 10.18).

The note concludes: Jesus' voluntary death represents the epitome of love. "Greater love has no one than this, that one lay down his life for his friends" (John 15.13).

The Christian as Survivor of a Suicide

The believing Christian thus finds himself in a difficult position. He is the beneficiary of a great sacrifice on the part of a figure, Jesus, he believes to be innocent and loving. It is a sacrifice the believing Christian did not solicit but it is clear, unmistakably clear, that the sacrifice was done for the believer's own salvation.

Without this sacrificial act the Christian remains in sin and thus condemned to death. Yet with this act, he experiences the loss of a parental figure who loved him enough to die for him. Like other survivors of suicide, the believing Christian must experience some ambivalence, his gratitude toward Jesus mixed with anger toward Him for abandoning him and a tremendous sense of loss. This tendency must be especially strong for those branches of Christianity emphasizing the sacrificial aspect of his death rather than his resurrection.

Potential Responses of the Christian Survivor

What are the potential responses of the Christian survivor to the death of Jesus? (a) He may choose to die as a martyr-suicide himself. This brings him close to Jesus Christ in two ways: (1) through imitation of the death of his savior and (2) through offering a reunion with Jesus Christ in the next world. (b) He may choose to live, benefiting from Jesus' sacrificial death. He must feel a mixture of guilt and anger. This may manifest itself in two ways: (1) through internalization, leading to self-blame or (2) through externalization, leading to blame of others, specifically to Jesus' family of origin—the Jewish people. Let us consider each of these possibilities in turn.

The Death Alternative. The death alternative was exercised by many early Christians. The mass suicides of the heretical Donatists and Circumcelliones have already been mentioned. Consider now the death of the early Christian martyr, Ignatius of Antioch. His desire for martyrdom was active and uncompromising. "I am yearning for death with all the passion of a lover" (Ignatius, *Epistles*, 9). He seems to feel nothingness. "Pray leave me to be a meal for the beasts, for it is they who can provide my way to God . . . ground fine by the lion's teeth to make pure bread for Christ. Let them not leave the smallest scrap of my flesh" (Ignatius, *Epistles*, 4).

Another example can be found in the writings of the Bishop Cyprian of Carthage. Jesus' crucifixion brought salvation to the world. His act of self-sacrifice and suffering was so immense, however, that it must now be "a great matter to imitate him who in dying convicted the world" (*On the Glory of Martyrdom*, 29); "what He exhorts man to suffer, He Himself first suffered for us" (Cyprian, *Letters*, 55.3). The crucifixion set the example of the highest moment toward which man must strive, because the world of the body is evil and should be scorned. "Consider what glory it is to set aside the lusts of life . . . What then is martyrdom, the end of sins, the limit of dangers" (*On the Glory of Martyrdom*, 54). Moreover, "Death makes life more complete, death rather leads to glory."

Yet the ordinary Christian survivor is blocked in this alternative. On the one hand, he is exhorted to give up his life voluntarily, imitating his savior. "we know love by this that He laid down His life for us and we ought to lay down our lives for the brethren" (1 John 3.16). Further he should not be attached to this world. "Do not love the world nor the things in the world. If anyone loves the world, the love of the Father is not in him" (1 John 2.15). This message is stated even more succinctly in the Gospel of John, "He that hates his life in this world, shall keep it onto life eternal" (John 12.25).

Nevertheless, the Christian survivor is dissuaded from taking his own life by several factors. First, the church officially condemned suicide, differentiating it from a martyr death. The arguments of Augustine and Aquinas have already been cited in this regard as have the decrees of the Church Councils at Arles, Orleans, Braga, and Antisidor. Second, the New Testament itself, while acknowledging the desire for reunion with Jesus Christ in the next world, also stresses the importance of doing one's duty in this world. Paul, for example, specifically writes this in his epistle to the Phillipians. The epistle states that Jesus will "change our vile body that it may be fashioned into His glorious body" (3.21) and Paul will stay at his appointed post, though he longs to depart: "For I am in a strait betwixt the two, having a desire to depart, and to be with Christ, which is far better. Nevertheless to abide in the flesh is more needful for you" (Phil. 1.23.24). Thirdly, with the success of Christianity, martyrdom, or dying for the faith, becomes much less of an issue. Situations in which to martyr oneself become infrequent. Finally, it is a very difficult decision to take one's life, an act that by its very nature is ambivalent and one that very few people are up to. For all these reasons, the first alternative of suiciding has not been taken by that many modern Christians.

The Life Alternative. The life alternative may put the Christian survivor in a difficult psychological position. Like any survivor of a suicide, he feels a mixture of sadness and anger. The specific suicide note he received, that Jesus had died for him, brings guilt into the equation as well. In the internalizing coping mechanism, the Christian survivor may blame himself for Jesus' death. He reproaches himself for his own sinfulness, necessitating the death of his savior. There is great irony in this resolution. The sacrificial death of Jesus Christ, intended to free the believing Christian from sin, may leave him feeling more sinful than ever. His sin now is not simply eating of the fruit of the tree of knowledge, but instead, to paraphrase Aquinas, becoming the *direct* cause (*Summa*, 3.47.1) as well as the *direct* beneficiary of the death of Jesus Christ. To put it another way, Jesus' death has become necessary to erase sin because the believing Christian has already sinned.

Such an internalizing resolution is inherently unstable. It may lead to a depression that may degenerate into the death resolution described above. It may also transform into the far more sinister external coping mechanism that we turn to now. In the externalizing coping mechanism, the Christian survivor projects his guilt 180 degrees outward, into anger toward the other. His depression is transformed into aggression; but against whom? Sadly, the historical evidence is all too clear on this point. The guilt of the Christian survivor has been transformed into anger toward the Jew. The Christian self-blame for the suicide of Jesus has been transformed into other-blame of the Jews.

Passages in the Gospels, especially the Gospel of John, seem to blame the entire Jewish people for the death of Jesus. "And for this reason the Jews were persecuting Jesus, because he was doing these things on the Sabbath" (John 5:16). "For this course therefore the Jews were seeking all the more to kill Him, because He not only was breaking the Sabbath but also was calling God His own father, making himself equal to God" (John 5:18). "They (the Jews) therefore cried out, 'Away with Him, away with Him, crucify Him.' Pilate said to them, 'Shall I crucify your King'? The chief priests answered 'We have no King but Caesar.'" (John 19:15).

We have specified the dynamic underlying these inflammatory comments. Externalizing the blame for Jesus' death relieved the Christian of his own guilt as the beneficiary of this act. To paraphrase Aquinas, Jesus remains the *indirect* cause of His death, by not preventing it. Now however, the Jews replace the Christians as the *direct* cause of His death, even though the Jew did not gain from His death as did the Christian. Despite the poison contained in certain New Testament references toward the Jews, there were large passages of time in which Jews and Christians lived in relative harmony, often side by side. This is what made the anti-Semitic attacks even harder to bear when they did occur. These pogroms on Jews were often tolerated, if not initiated, by erstwhile Christian neighbors and acquaintances.

Externalizing the blame for Jesus' death relieves the Christian of his own guilt as the beneficiary of this act. To paraphrase Aquinas, Jesus remains the *indirect* cause of his death, by not preventing it. Now however, the Jews replace the Christians as the *direct* cause of his death, even though the Jew does not gain from this death, while the Christian does.

Why are the Jews Blamed? A Family Therapy Explanation

Why have the Jews historically been chosen as the particular target for blame for the death of Jesus? Why has Christianity, which itself emerged from Judaism, projected its guilt regarding the death of Jesus on the collective Jewish people? There have been of course, many explanations offered for this heinous phenomenon over the centuries: economic, political, sociological, and theological. One powerful explanation is that of "displacement theology," wherein the Church attempted to displace the Jewish people as "Israel." Our approach in this paper is to focus on the Jewish people as the "family of origin" of Jesus and to argue by analogy from the clinical setting.

Consider a survivor of suicide who comes into therapeutic treatment. To make the case more concrete, let us suppose the patient is a young person in his late teens who is attempting to cope with the suicide of his best friend. Further, the patient brings in a suicide note he received from his friend indicating that his friend loves the patient so much that he has decided to take his own life and leave the patient a large inheritance to take care of him financially for the rest of his life. Nevertheless, the suicide is partially experienced as an aggressive act. The patient–survivor manifests a great amount of emotional turmoil. He feels angry at his best friend for leaving him. He doesn't understand why. At the same time he naturally feels happy that he has received an inheritance for the rest of his life. He feels tremendously guilty that he may have been the cause of his friend's death. The patient maintains that he didn't want his friend to die or to leave him an inheritance. He stresses vehemently that although he is the beneficiary of his best friend's suicide, he did not ask for it and was not the cause of it.

The patient–survivor continues to wrestle with this problem. Slowly, he seems to arrive at a resolution. His friend's family of origin treated his friend very badly. They were rejecting, abandoning, and hostile to his friend. They misunderstood his friend and made his life miserable. They were the ones who are really responsible for his death. This resolution miraculously gets the patient–survivor off the hook. Even though he benefits from his friend's death the friend's family of origin was the *direct* cause. The analogy to the Church's historical blame of the Jewish people for the death of Jesus is direct. The Christian, as survivor, benefits from Jesus' death. Yet he is able to blame Jesus' family of origin, the Jewish people, for his death, thus getting himself off of the hook, while reaping the benefits of Jesus' sacrifice!

Easter Week as the Anniversary of a Suicide: Outbreaks of Christian Anti-Semitism

The patient–survivor described in the previous section remains in treatment for several years. What becomes evident is that the patient becomes more agitated each year as the anniversary date of his friend's suicide approaches. First the patient becomes depressed, then he becomes angry at his friend's family of origin. As the anniversary date passes, the patient calms down—until the next anniversary date.

It takes no great leap to make the analogy to the Christian Holy Week as the anniversary of Jesus' suicide. The history of the Jewish experience in Eastern Europe is replete with stories of anti-Jewish pogroms and other outrages, often occurring in conjunction with "Passion Plays" performed during the Christian Holy Week preceding Easter.

a. Ritual Murder Charges: The Host Desecration Slander and the Blood Libel. Two linked allegations against the Jews were central to this process: the Host desecration slander and the blood libel. Both of these charges emerged from the Fourth Lateran Council of 1215, in which the Roman Catholic Church asserted the Doctrine of Transubstantiation. This doctrine decreed that the flesh and blood of Christ became present in the consecrated Host and wine (originally, the matzo and wine of the Passover Seder). As a result, the Eucharist cult acquired concrete character. The Host desecration slander maintained that the Jews, in reenactment of the crucifixion, stabbed, tormented, and burned wafers, out of which the blood of Christ spurted (Roth, 1973, pp. 1040–1043). The blood libel, in distinction, maintained that Jews murdered Christians, usually children, in order to obtain blood to make the matzo for Passover (Slutsky, 1973, pp. 1120–1132).[1]

b. Easter Persecutions in Medieval England, France, and Spain. The first distinct case of blood libel against Jews in the Middle Ages occurred in Norwich, England, in 1144, where it was alleged that the Jews had "bought a Christian child (the 'boy-martyr' William) before Easter and tortured him with all the tortures wherewith our Lord was tortured, and on Long Friday hanged him on a road in hatred of our Lord." This charge of torture and murder of Christian children in imitation of the Passion of Jesus persisted with slight variations throughout the twelfth century (for example, in Gloucester, England, 1168; Blois, France, 1171; and Saragossa, Spain, 1182) and was repeated in many libels of the thirteenth century.

The English harassment of Jews reached its climax in 1255 in the case of "Little St. Hugh" of Lincoln. The chronicler Matthew Paris relates "that the Child was fattened for ten days with white bread and milk and then . . . almost all the Jews of England were invited to the crucifixion." According to the forced confession of a Jew, Copin, the Jews of Lincoln appointed one of their own as a judge, to take the place of Pilate. The boy was subject to diverse tortures. The Jews beat him till blood flowed, crowned him with thorns, derided him, and spat upon him. They crucified him and pierced his body with a lance. After the boy expired, they took his body down from the cross and disemboweled it (Slutsky, 1973, p. 1121). As a result of this utter fabrication, 100 Jews were arrested, of whom 19, including Copin, were hanged without trial, and St. Hugh was enshrined in the

---

1. Both of these charges emerged from ancient, almost primordial, concepts concerning the potency and energies of blood and were patently ridiculous with regard to the Jewish people. Blood sacrifices were practiced by many pagan religions; however, they were expressly forbidden by the Torah. Indeed, the Jewish law of salting meat (*melihah*) is designed to prevent the least drop of avoidable blood remaining in food. Yet both of these charges emerged in medieval Christian thought, reflecting its paranoid delusion that the Jews were fabricating a criminal conspiracy against Jesus, himself a practicing Jew, and the Christians.

The psychiatrist Ernest Rappaport suggests that the Host desecration charge is more efficient than the blood libel in that it does not require waiting for a dead child as a stand-in for the murdered Christ (1975, p. 97).

church. Some 35 years later (1290), the Jews of England were expelled summarily (Hay, 1950, pp. 124–125; Rappaport, 1975, p. 96).

Allegations against the Jews during the Christian Holy Week were common throughout the next three centuries. The crucifixion theme raised in the Hugh of Lincoln case was generalized in the Siete Partidas law code of Spain, 1263. "We have heard it said that in certain places on Good Friday the Jews do steal children and set them on the cross in a mocking manner." On the eve of expulsion of the Jews from Spain, the blood libel case of the Holy child of LaGuardia arose during the Passover season (1490–1491). Conversos (forced Jewish converts to Christianity) were made to confess under torture that with the knowledge of their chief rabbi, they had assembled in a cave, crucified the child, and abused him and cursed him to his face, as was done to Jesus (Slutsky, 1973, p. 1122).

c. Easter Persecutions in Medieval Germany and Poland. The blood libel charge emerged in medieval Germany as well. In 1283 a Christian child was found dead during Easter near the town of Mainz on the Rhine. A relative gathered a crowd and accused the Jews of having killed the child in a ritual murder. Jewish houses were broken into and looted and ten Jews were murdered. The stolen Jewish goods were confiscated by Emperor Rudolf I (Wiesenthal, 1987, p. 95). In a dirge lamenting the Jews massacred at Munich because of blood libel in 1286, an anonymous poet supposedly quotes the words of the Christian killers. "These unhappy Jews are sinning, they kill Christian children, torture them in all their limbs, and took the blood cruelly to drink" (Slutsky, 1973, pp. 1121–1122).

By 1400 the ritual murder charge had spread to Poland, where crowds were whipped into a frenzy by the Roman Catholic clergy. Despite the attempts of King Casimir IV to reassure the Jewish communities, the clergy linked Jews to the new heresies that were sweeping the West. Host desecration charges were leveled against the Jews, and the first organized anti-Jewish pogroms broke out in Poland around 1500.

d. Easter Persecutions in Later Russia. The blood accusation charges reached another climax in the nineteenth and twentieth centuries, this time largely in Russia. The first blood libel case in Russia occurred in the vicinity of Seine, south of

Vitebsk on the eve of Passover, 1799. When the body of a woman was found near a Jewish tavern, four Jews were arrested on the ground of the "popular belief that the Jews require Christian blood" (Slutsky, 1973, p. 1129). Large-scale waves of pogroms, typically linked to Passover or Easter, occurred subsequently in Russia between the years 1859 and 1921.

The Odessa pogroms of 1859 and 1871 follow this paradigm. The 1859 pogrom erupted during the Christian Holy Week, when rumors swept through the city that Jews had hurled insults at Christians during the rituals of Holy Thursday and that a young Christian had been tortured by the Jews. The attackers were quoted as shouting at the Jews: "You drink our blood, you rob us." The shape of the 1871 pogrom was disturbingly similar. Disorders broke out during Holy Week on March 28 and lasted until April 1. Quarreling had broken out between Jewish and Christian children, which escalated into a riot when foreign soldiers intervened and began to vandalize the Jewish quarter. In the crowds of Christians, there were often heard the words: "The Jews offended our Christ, they grow rich and they suck our blood" (Klier and Lambroza, 1992, pp. 18–21).

A similar pogrom took place in Yelisavetgrad, a large city in New Russia. On the eve of the Greek-Orthodox Easter in 1881, local Christians spoke to one another of the fact that "the Zhyds are about to be beaten." The Jews naturally became alarmed. The police maintained public order during the first days of the Greek-Orthodox Passover. However, when the troops were inexplicably removed from the streets on the fourth day of the festival, the pogrom began. The instigators began by sending a drunken Russian into a saloon kept by a Jew. When the saloon keeper pushed the troublemaker out into the street, the Russian crowd began to shout: "The Zhyds are beating our people" and threw themselves upon the Jews who happened to pass by (Dubnow, 1975, vol. II, p. 249).

A pogrom on a more comprehensive scale was allowed to take place in the city of Nicholayev, the South-Russian port of entry. It was arranged in honor of the Easter festival and lasted for three days (April 19–21, 1899). Bands of rioters, to the number of several thousand, including many newly arrived laborers led by a few "intellectuals," fell upon Jewish stores and residences, keeping with the established pogrom ritual, while the police and

Cossack forces proved to be strangely "powerless" (Dubnow, 1975, vol. III, pp. 34–35).

Perhaps the most well-known of the modern Easter pogroms in Russia was organized by the authorities in Kishinev on April 6–7, 1903. Agents of the Ministry of the Interior were involved in its preparation, evidently with the backing of the Minister of the Interior. The pogrom was preceded by a poisonous anti-Jewish campaign led by P. Krushevan, the director of the Bessarabian newspaper *Bessarebets*, who incited the population. When the body of a Christian child was found and a young Christian woman patient committed suicide in the Jewish hospital, the mob became violent. A blood libel, circulated by the *Bessarebets*, spread like wildfire, despite evidence that the child had been murdered by his relatives and that the young woman was in no way connected to the Jews. According to official statistics, 49 Jews lost their lives and more than 500 were injured; 700 houses were looted and/or destroyed and 600 businesses and shops were looted. The material loss amounted to 2,500,000 gold rubles and about 2,000 Jewish families were left homeless. Both Russians and Romanians joined the riots, often sent in from other cities. The garrison of 5,000 soldiers stationed in the city of Kishinev itself could easily have held back the mob. However, it took no action (Neusner, 1973, pp. 1064–1068).

The early years of the twentieth century brought to public attention the infamous trial of Mendel Beillis, a Jewish employee in a Kiev brick factory, who was charged with having murdered a Christian boy, Andrei (Andryusha) Yuschinsky, to use his blood for Passover matzo. Although Beillis was finally acquitted, the trial revealed the ubiquitousness of the blood libel accusation into the twentieth century and its link to Passover, the Christian Holy Week, and the death of Jesus. Mimeographed leaflets were circulated along Andryusha's funeral route on March 27, 1911. They read:

> Orthodox Christians! The Yids have tortured Andryusha Yuschinasky to death! Every year before their Passover, they torture to death several dozens of Christian children in order to get their blood to mix with their matzos. They do this in commemoration of our Savior, whom they tortured to death on the cross. The official doctors found that before the Yids tortured Yuschinsky,

they stripped him naked and tied him up, stabbing him in the principal veins so as to get as much blood as possible. They pierced him in 50 places. Russians! If your children are dear to you, beat up the Yids! Beat them up until there is not a single Yid left in Russia. Have pity on your children! Avenge the unhappy martyr! It is time! It is time! (Samuel, 1966, p. 17).

e. Ritual Murder Slanders in Contemporary Passion Plays. The themes of ritual murder reemerged in Julius Streicher's Nazi newspaper, *Der Steurmer*, (May 1, 1934) and have been emphasized with a vengeance in the contemporary Passion Plays held during the Christian Holy Week throughout parts of Europe. One famous version, *Sanguis Christi*, (Boon, 1947) has been performed in Brugge, Belgium since 1938, and another even more well-known one has taken place in Oberammergau in Bavaria (Oberammergau Passion Play, 1910). *Sanguis Christi* places Jesus on trial before Pilate, the Roman procurator in Jerusalem, who appears on a balcony. The Jews stand below and are portrayed as an infuriated mob who shout and rant at a kind and well-meaning Pilate.

PILATE: What does this people want of me?

JEWISH PEOPLE: Blood, blood, the Law, Jesus of Nazareth, blood, false prophet, blood! Law! Death! Death! Death! Hail Pilate!

PILATE: I find no fault in this man.

JEWISH PEOPLE: Ah! Woe!

PILATE: What must I do with your Jesus of Nazareth?

JEWISH PEOPLE: Crucify Him! Crucify Him! Crucify Him!

PILATE: You shed innocent blood.

JEWISH PEOPLE: His blood be upon us and our children.[2]

---

2. The portrayal of Pontius Pilate as a basically kind man, reluctant to crucify the Jew Jesus but pushed to do so by a hostile Jewish mob stands

The psychological power of the Passion Play was not lost on Adolph Hitler. In July, 1942, he underscored the importance of the Oberammergau play, a seven-hour marathon, to the Nazi movement: "It is vital that the passion play be continued at Oberammergau, for never has the menace of Jewry been so convincingly portrayed . . . There one sees in Pontius Pilate, a Roman racially and ethnically superior, there he stands out like a firm, clean rock in the middle of the whole muck and mire of Jewry!"

The undeniable evidence that hatred and persecution of Jews occurred again and again in conjunction with the Christian Holy Week and the Jewish Passover serves to support our major thesis. The Christian experiences survivor guilt regarding the suicide of Jesus. This phenomenon is intensified during the anniversary date of Jesus' death, the Christian Holy Week. The guilt during this period become intensified and is often displaced, with the help of ritual reenactments (such as the charges of Host desecration, blood libel, and contemporary Passion Plays) into aggression against the Jewish people.[3]

SUMMARY

In summary, history reveals a peculiar and outrageous paradox. It is the Christian who gains from the death of Jesus (it being essential to the Christian idea of redemption: John 3:16) and not the Jew. Yet the Jewish people, historically, have been blamed as the *direct* cause of Jesus' death; this despite the undeniable fact that Jesus is simultaneously seen as voluntarily giving up his life to redeem mankind, and thus the *indirect* cause of his own death, which according to the

---

truth on its head. It flies clearly in the face of historical evidence regarding the great cruelty of Pilate. As procurator of Judea, Pilate was probably responsible for hundreds if not thousands of Jewish deaths—by crucifixion. They were, sadly, an everyday occurrence under his regime. From his Roman perspective, Pilate was interested in one thing—keeping order! There is no evidence that he ever hesitated to crucify a Jew.

3. Perhaps those branches of Christianity that emphasize the sacrificial death of Jesus (e.g., Eastern Orthodoxy) rather than his resurrection are especially prone to this phenomenon. It is probably no coincidence that Eastern Europe has represented the setting for many of these outrages.

Christian interpretation greatly resembles Durkheim's definition of an altruistic suicide. The Easter week in particular has provided the occasion for the acting out of this blame. Historical records point to many occurrences of theologically inspired attacks against the Jews during this period of the year and in the pernicious effects of two particular allegations, the blood libel and the Host desecration charge.

This paper offers a suicidological approach to this historical phenomena. Specifically, it suggests a number of essential elements: (1) Christian insistence that the death of Jesus is a voluntary martyrdom, if not a suicide, (2) simultaneous Church condemnation of suicide, (3) Christian experience of guilt as being the survivors of a suicide, (4) Christian projection of guilt into anger against Jesus' people, the Jews, and, (5) the outbreak of Christian-inspired persecutions against Jews during the Christian Holy Week, the anniversary date of Jesus' suicide. All this horror has occurred despite the fact that Christianity is the daughter of Judaism and that specifically, Jesus (Yeshua) was undeniably a practicing Jew who would have been persecuted by the various mobs and militia acting in his name. One only wonders what the response of Jesus would have been to such conduct.

REFERENCES

Aquinas, Thomas. (1981). *Summa Theologica*. 5 vols. Trans: Fathers of the English Dominican Province. Westminster, Maryland: Christian Classics.

Augustinus, Aurelius. (1957–1972). *The City of God Against the Pagans*. 7 vols. Trans: William M. Green. Cambridge, Massachusetts: Harvard University Press.

Augustinus, Aurelius. (1963). *The Trinity*. Trans: S. McKenna. Washington, DC: The Catholic University of America Press.

Boon, J. (1947). *Sanguis Christi: The Play of the Holy Blood of Brugge, in Three Parts*. Trans: M. Swepstone. Leuven: Opbouwen.

Cyprian. (1951). In *The Ante-Nicene Fathers*, vol. 5. Eds: A. Roberts and J. Donaldson. Grand Rapids, Michigan: Wm. B. Eerdmans.

Donne, J. (1608/1984). *Biathanatos*. Ed: Ernest W. Sullivan II. Cranbury, New Jersey: Associated University Press.

Dubnow, S. M. (1975). *History of the Jews in Russia and Poland from the Earliest Times until the Present Day*, vol. II. Trans: I. Friedlander. New York: KTAV Publishing House, Inc.

Dubnow, S. M. (1975). *History of the Jews in Russia and Poland from the Earliest Times until the Present Day*, vol. III. Trans: I. Friedlander. New York: KTAV Publishing House, Inc.

Durkheim, E. (1897/1951). *Suicide*. Trans: J. A. Spaulding and G. Simpson. Glencoe, Illinois: Free Press.

Hay, M. (1950). *The Foot of Pride: The Pressure of Christendom on the People of Israel for 1900 Years*. Boston: The Beacon Press.

The Holy Scriptures. (1955). Philadelphia: The Jewish Publication Society of America.

Ignatius. (1968). *Epistles. Early Christian Writings*. Ed: B. Radice. Baltimore, Maryland: Penguin Books.

Klier, J. D. & Lambroza, S. (1992). *Pogroms: Anti-Jewish Violence in Modern Russian History*. Cambridge: Cambridge University Press.

NASB Interlinear Greek-English New Testament. (1984). Grand Rapids, Michigan: Zondervan.

Neusner, J. (1972). "Kishinev." In *Encyclopedia Judaica*, vol. 10, pp. 1064–1068. Jerusalem: Keter.

Oates, W. J., and O'Neill, Jr., E., Eds. (1938). *The Complete Greek Drama*, 2 vols. New York: Random House.

Oberammergau Passion Play. (1910). *The Passion Play at Ober Ammergau*. Trans: W. T. Stead. Munich: C. A. Seyfried and Company, and London: Steads Publishing House.

Origen. (1954). *Prayer. Exhortation to Martyrdom*. Trans: John J. O'Meara. Ancient Christian Writers, no. 19. London: Longmans, Green.

Poliakov, L. (1972). "Anti-Semitism." In *Encyclopedia Judaica*, vol. 3, pp. 87–111. Jerusalem: Keter.

Rappaport, E. (1975). *Anti-Judaism: A Psychohistory*. Chicago: Perspective Press.

Roth, C. (1972). "Persecution of the Host." In *Encyclopedia Judaica*, vol. 5, pp. 1040–1044. Jerusalem: Keter.

Samuel, M. (1966). *Blood Accusation: The Strange History of the Beillis Case*. New York: Alfred A. Knopf.

Slutsky, Y. (1972). "Blood libel." In *Encyclopedia Judaica*, vol. 4, pp. 1120–1132. Jerusalem: Keter.

Slutsky, Y. (1972). "Pogroms." In *Encyclopedia Judaica*, vol. 13, pp. 694–701. Jerusalem: Keter.

Tertullian. (1959). "To the Martyrs" (Ad Martyres). In *Disciplinary, Moral and Ascetical Works*, vol. 40, Trans: R. Arbeshann, E. J. Daly, and E. A. Quain. Ed: R. J. Deferrari. New York: Fathers of the Church.

Wiesenthal, S. (1987). *Every Day Remembrance Day: A Chronicle of Jewish Martyrdom*. New York: Henry Holt and Company.
Willis, G. C. (1950). *Saint Augustine and the Donatist Controversy*. London: S.P.C.K.

II

Suicide and Euthanasia in Jewish and American Law

The six papers in the second section of this volume deal with the issue of suicide and euthanasia in Jewish law. The first paper, "Suicide in Jewish Law" by physician Fred Rosner presents systematically the subject of suicide as found in Jewish religious and legal literature. Human life is held to be infinitely valuable and suicide is seen as abhorrent. Nevertheless, both the Hebrew Bible and the Talmud recount stories of suicide. The Codes and other commentators seek to define what suicide is considered willful and what is not and how each case is to be tested. Rabbinic responsa are sparse on suicide, but the same pattern of thought is found. One writer argues that suicide is a greater sin than even murder. In the second paper in this section, Kalman Kaplan compares Edwin Shneidman's definition of suicide with that emerging in Jewish law. Both systems caution against too loose a definition of suicide, insisting that the intention to destroy oneself must be clear and unambiguous to be so classified. Such caution is warranted for both religious and scientific reasons.

In "Euthanasia as a Halakhic Option," Rabbi Dr. Byron Sherwin seeks a Jewish basis for justifying certain acts of euthanasia. He begins by distinguishing four types of euthanasia: active voluntary, passive voluntary, active involuntary, and passive involuntary. He then cites rabbinic sources that argue in support of passive euthanasia, that is, not prolonging the process of dying. Several further rabbinic opinions, although clearly a minority, discuss the issue of active euthanasia, that is, hastening the process of dying.

The next paper in this section is by Rubbi Dr. Reuven Bulka, the editor-in-chief of *The Journal of Psychology and Judaism*. It focuses on the attitude of Jewish law to the question of doctor-assisted suicide and euthanasia, as symbolized by Dr. Kevorkian and the general position of suicide and euthanasia within Jewish law. The entire issue of euthanasia is weighed against the Jewish attitude toward life and death. Implications of life-affirming therapeutic approaches are stressed. The following paper is a historical note by Dr. Matthew Schwartz chronicling the reaction of members of the Detroit rabbinic community and Christian clergy to D. Kevorkian's 1996 trial for assisted suicide and to the ensuing comments by Kevorkian's attorney, Geoffrey Feiger.

The final paper in this section is by Dr. Joseph Richman, Professor Emeritus at the Albert Einstein College of Medicine, a faculty member of the New York Center for Psychoanalytic Training, and a member of The American Association of Suicidology since its inception in 1968. He is the author of many seminal works in the area of treatment of depression and prevention of suicide among older adults, with a concentration on family factors. Dr. Richman compares the respective position papers on the issue of legalization of euthanasia and assisted suicide by the American Association of Suicidology and the New York Task Force on life and the law. While the New York State Task Force came out firmly against legalization of these procedures, the American Association of Suicidology took no position. Dr. Richman discusses his own clinical experience, which turned him from a supporter to an opponent of rational suicide and euthanasia.

6

Suicide in Jewish Law

Fred Rosner, M.D., F.A.C.P.

The medical, psychological, psychiatric, legal, and social literatures are replete with articles, monographs, symposia, and other publications on suicide. Factors such as age, sex, marital status, day of week, month of year, method, religion, race, motivation, living conditions, repetitive attempts, medical and psychiatric histories of patients attempting and committing suicide are amply covered in these writings as well as the many books published on this subject.

Several salient features of the problem deserve mention. Suicides are three times as frequent in men as in women, although there are more attempts by women than men. Twice as many white Americans commit suicide as do black Americans, and twice as many single people kill themselves as do married individuals. College students have a suicide rate 50 percent higher than non-college students of comparable age, sex, and race. In industrialized countries, physicians, dentists, and lawyers have a higher rate of suicide than other professionals. Although the suicide rate has remained relatively constant in the United States over the past decade or so, poisoning by drugs, especially barbiturates, and diazepam and its congeners has become popular as a method of choice. The age group with the highest suicide rate is that above 65 years. Suicide ranks third as a cause of death among teenagers. It has also been estimated that the ratio of suicide attempts to actual successes in adolescents is 100 to 1.

One phase of suicide hardly discussed at all is the religious aspect. This essay attempts to organize and present in a systematic fashion the subject of suicide as found in Jewish sources. The closely related topic of martyrdom is discussed briefly at the end.

ABHORRENCE OF SUICIDE IN JUDAISM

The fundamental prohibition of suicide in Judaism is based on two biblical sources: "Thou shall not commit murder" (Exodus 20:13; Deuteronomy 5:17) and, "And surely the blood of your lives will I require . . ." (Genesis 9:15). The latter phrase clearly refers to one who strangulates himself (Genesis Rabbah 34:13; Baba Kamma 91b). A person who commits suicide is a shedder of blood, has committed the crime of murder, and is liable for death at the hand of Heaven (Maimonides, *Mishneh Torah, Laws of the Murderer* 2:2).

The Hebrew word *ma'al* meaning trespass, in the phrase, *If anyone sin and commit a trespass against the Lord* (Leviticus 5:21) is homiletically said to consist of the initials of the Hebrew term for suicide: *me'abed atzmo lada'at*. Some Rabbis write that a person who commits suicide is worse than a killer because all sins are atoned for at the time of death but a suicide sins with his death (Responsa *Hatam Sofer, Even HaEzer* #69 and *Yoreh Deah* #326; *Gesher Hahayyim*, Part 1, Chapt 25:1; Responsa *Tzitz Eliezer*, Vol 10 #25, Chapt 6:4).

The value of human life is infinite in Judaism. To preserve a life, all biblical and rabbinic commandments are suspended except for murder, idolatry and forbidden sexual relations such as incest. One's life must be guarded and protected. A person is not the owner of one's body to allow one to take one's own life or harm oneself. A person's body is the property of God and is entrusted to the person by the Holy One, blessed be God (Maimonides, *Mishneh Torah, Laws of the Murderer* 1:4).

A person who commits suicide denies the fundamental Judaic belief in reward and punishment (*Hizkuni* commentary on Genesis 9:5 and *Ibn Ezra* on Deuteronomy 32:39). Such a person cannot repent and the death is not an atonement for that person (Responsa *Teshuva Me'Ahavah* #355). One who commits suicide has no portion in the world to come (commentaries of *Tosafot Yom Tov* and *Tiferet Yisrael* on Sanhedrin 10:1. So, too, *Yad Hamelekh's* commentary on Maimonides, *Mishneh Torah, Laws of Mourning* 1:11. See also Responsa *Maharsham*, Part 6, *Yoreh Deah* #49, Responsa *Rav Paalim, Yoreh Deah*, Part 3 #29, and other rabbinic sources).

SUICIDE IN THE BIBLE

In the Bible, a number of people are described who committed suicide by various methods: a) Samson; b) Saul and his armor bearer; c) Ahitophel; and d) Zimri, king of Israel.

a) During the period of the Judges, in approximately the eleventh or twelfth century B.C.E., lived Samson of the tribe of

Dan, whose story is known to all. Samson's final effort in bringing down the Philistine temple upon himself as well as his enemies is vividly described.

> And Samson said: "Let me die with the Philistines." And he bent with all his might; and the house fell upon the lords, and upon all the people that were therein. So the dead that he slew at his death were more than they that he slew in his life (Judges 16:23–32).

b) Elsewhere in the Bible, we read of King Saul's final battle against the Philistines on Mount Gilboa in the eleventh century B.C.E. (I Samuel 31:1–7). Here, Saul saw his three sons Jonathan, Abinadav, and Malkhishua and most of his army slain. Not wishing to flee or to be taken prisoner and exposed to the scorn of the Philistines, King Saul entreated his armor-bearer to kill him. The latter refused, and so the king fell upon his own sword. The biblical passage concludes: "And when his armor-bearer saw that Saul was dead, he likewise fell upon his own sword and died with him" (ibid 31:5).

From these events it would appear as if Saul committed suicide. However, later on when David is informed of Saul's death, the Bible states:

> And David said unto the young man that told him: "How knowest thou that Saul and Jonathan his son are dead?" and the young man that told him said: "As I happened by chance upon Mount Gilboa, behold, Saul leaned upon his spear; and lo, the chariots and the horsemen pressed hard upon him. And when he looked behind him, he saw me, and called unto me. And I answered: Here am I. And he said unto me: Who art thou? And I answered him: I am an Amalekite. And he said unto me: Stand, I pray thee, beside me, and slay me, for the agony hath taken hold of me because my life is just yet in me. So I stood beside him and slew him, because I was sure that he could not live after that he was fallen . . ." (II Samuel 1:5–10).

Biblical commentators differ in their interpretation of this passage. Rabbi David Kimchi, known as *Radak*, explains that Saul did not die immediately when he fell on his sword but was mortally wounded. In his death throes, Saul asked the Amalekite to render the final blow of mercy to hasten his death. Rabbi

Solomon ben Isaac (*Rashi*), Rabbi Levi ben Gerson (*Ralbag*), and Rabbi David Altschul (*Metzudat David*) all agree with Kimchi and consider the death of King Saul as a case of euthanasia. Others view the story of the Amalekite as a complete fabrication.

In any event, Saul attempted suicide. Only the question of his success or failure is debated. As to Saul's armor bearer, no one disputes that he committed suicide. There is an extensive rabbinic literature in regard to whether or not Saul acted within the bounds of Jewish law or *halakhah*. Most writers justify his action and vindicate him (Genesis Rabbah 34:19; *Radak*, I Samuel 31:4; *Yalkut Shimoni* on Samuel #141; *Ramban's Torat HaAdam*; *Sefer Hasidim* #315; *Rosh*, Moed Katan, Chapt 3 #94; *Tur*, *Shulhan Arukh*. *Yoreh Deah* 345:3; *Bet Joseph* commentary on *Yoreh Deah* #157; *Radvaz* commentary on Maimonides, *Mishneh Torah*, *Laws of Mourning*, 1:11; *Yam Shel Shlomo*, Baba Kamma, Chap 8, #59). A minority of rabbis state that Saul's act was not to the liking of the Sages (commentary *Daat Zekenim Baale Hatosafot* on Genesis 9:5 and *Orhot Hayyim*, Part 2, p. 26. See also Responsa *Mishpat Cohen* #144:4 and Responsa *Yabiya Omer*, part 2, *Yoreh Deah*, 22).

c) King David's faithless counselor, Ahitophel, committed suicide by hanging himself in his native town of Giloh. One of several reasons probably prompted suicide. First, he knew that Absalom's attempt to overthrow David was doomed and that he would die a traitor's death. Second, and less likely, is the disgust of Ahitophel at Absalom's conduct in setting aside his counsel, thus wounding Ahitophel's pride and disappointing his ambition (Graetz, Vol. 1, p. 143). Finally, David's curse may have prompted Ahitophel to hang himself (Talmud, Makkot 11a).

> And when Ahitophel saw that his counsel was not followed, he saddled his ass and arose, and got himself home unto his city, and set his house in order, and strangled himself: and he died and was buried in the sepulchre of his father (II Samuel 17:23).

d) King Baasha of Israel reigned from 888 B.C.E. and was succeeded by his son Elah. The latter was addicted to idleness and drunkenness and passed the days drinking in his palace while his warriors were battling the Philistines at Gibbethon (Graetz, op. cit., p. 192). Zimri, a high-ranking officer, took advantage of the situation, assassinated Elah, and mounted the throne. His reign, however, lasted only seven days. As soon as the news of King

Elah's murder reached the army on the battlefield, General Omri was elected king and laid siege to the palace. When Zimri saw that he was unable to hold out against the siege, he set fire to the palace and perished in the flames. The Bible records: "And it came to pass, when Zimri saw that the city was taken that he went unto the castle of the king's house, and he burnt the king's house over him with fire, and he died" (I Kings 16:18).

Some biblical commentators, notably *Radak* and *Metzudat David*, to whom the thought of suicide was abhorrent, state that Omri burned the house over Zimri. Most commentators, however, interpret the biblical passage literally.

In addition to Saul, several other prominent people are described in the Bible who attempted suicide. These include Elijah (I Kings 19:4), Jonah (Jonah 4:3), and Hananiah, Mishael and Azariah (Daniel 3:1ff). The latter three committed these acts to sanctify the name of God (Talmud, Pesahim 53b).

SUICIDE IN THE APOCRYPHA

In the Second Book of Maccabees, two acts of suicide are recorded. The first occurred when King Demetrius I of Syria (162–150 B.C.E.) escaped from his imprisonment in Rome and returned home as an invader (Graetz, op. cit., pp. 482–485). Attempting to put down a rebellion of his Judean subjects, King Demetrius sent Nicanor, one of the warriors who had escaped with him from Rome, to Judea, to treat the insurgents with the utmost harshness. Nicanor, in order to induce surrender from the Judeans, ordered that the most respected man in Jerusalem, Ragesh (Razis) be seized. When the arresting soldiers were forcing open the courtyard door to Ragesh's house, "he fell upon his sword, preferring to die nobly rather than to fall into the wretches' hands" (II Maccabees 14:41–42). The ghastly tale of his lack of success in the first suicide attempt, his subsequent attempt by throwing himself down from a wall, and his final success by self-disembowelment is vividly described (ibid. 14:43–46).

The second act of suicide is that of Ptolemy, an advocate of the Judeans at the Syrian court, who was called a traitor before King Antiokhus Eupator. Unable to maintain the dignity of his office, Ptolemy poisoned himself (ibid. 10:12).

OTHER SUICIDES AND NEAR SUICIDES IN ANCIENT JEWISH WRITINGS

All the suicides mentioned in the Bible and Apocrypha are psychologically understandable. Each knew what lay ahead if he remained alive, namely a prolonged, torturous martyrdom and/or disgrace to the God of Israel. All were prominent people. Except perhaps for King Saul, none could be accused of having experienced temporary insanity to excuse his act of self-destruction. Perhaps Ragesh and Ptolemy were influenced by the Greek philosophy of their times, in which suicide was highly acceptable.

There are several individuals mentioned in the Bible, Apocrypha, and other ancient Jewish writings who considered suicide and perhaps wished to attempt it, but did not.

Job, during his quest for an explanation of his wretchedness, speaks of suicide: "And my soul chooseth strangling and death rather than these my bones" (Job 7:15). He did not attempt suicide, perhaps out of either love or fear of God, as he himself states: "Though He slay me, yet will I trust in Him" (ibid. 13:15). Possibly Job did not mean to even consider suicide but was remarking that he would prefer death to life. This question remains unresolved.

One of the most famous "near-suicides" is Flavius Josephus, who failed to commit suicide at Jotapata in the year 69 C.E. when all the other zealots there did so in a mass-suicide pact. Flavius Vespasian, successor to Nero as emperor of Rome, had come to conquer Judea. Strong resistance was offered at the fortress of Jotapata. After a forty-day siege, the fortress fell. Many chose suicide by flinging themselves over the walls or falling on their weapons. Josephus, however, sought concealment in a huge cistern in which he found forty of his own soldiers. They all swore to die by their own hand in a mass-suicide pact. When his turn came Josephus reneged and surrendered to the Romans (Graetz, op. cit., pp. 276–290). In Josephus' *Antiquities of the Jews* and his *Wars of the Jews* there are numerous examples cited of suicide, including the mass suicide at Massada (F. Josephus, *Wars of the Jews* 7:320). For the Jewish legal view about the suicides of Massada see the essays by Rabinowitz in *Sinai*, Vol. 55, 1965, pp. 329ff; Goren and Neriya in *Or Hamizrach*, Tamuz-Elul 5720 (1960) and Tevet 5721 (1961); and Ben Zimra in *Sinai*, Vol. 80, 1977, pp. 173ff.

SUICIDE IN THE TALMUD

The Talmud is replete with stories concerning suicide and martyrdom as well as discussions relating to the laws of burial and mourning for the deceased. Among the most renowned examples is the story of Rabbi Hanina ben Teradyon's death by burning at the hands of the Romans (Abodah Zarah 18a). He was wrapped in a Scroll of the Law, bundles of branches were placed around him, and these were set ablaze. The Romans also brought tufts of wool which they had soaked in water, placing them over his heart to prevent a quick death. When his disciples pleaded with him to open his mouth so that the fire would consume him more quickly, he replied that one is not to accelerate one's own death. The executioner asked him: "Rabbi, if I raise the flame and remove the tufts of wet wool from your heart, will I enter the world-to-come?" "Yes," was the reply. The executioner did as he proposed, and the rabbi died speedily. The executioner then jumped into the fire and was burned to death. A voice from heaven exclaimed that Rabbi Hanina ben Teradyon and his executioner had been assigned to the world-to-come.

Another case of suicide is related of Herod, who was a slave of the Hasmonean house of the Maccabees and had set his eyes on a certain maiden of that house (Baba Batra 3b). One day he heard a voice from heaven saying that every slave that rebelled now would succeed. So he killed the entire household but spared the maiden. When she saw that he wanted to marry her, she ran up to the roof and cried out: "Whoever comes and says that he is from the Hasmonean house is a slave, since I alone am left of it, and I am throwing myself down from this roof." Herod loved her so much that he preserved her body in honey for seven years.

The suicide of a Roman officer who saved the life of Rabban Gamliel is portrayed as follows: When Tinneius Rufus the wicked destroyed the Jewish Temple, Rabban Gamliel was condemned to death. A high officer came to the house of study to search for him, but Rabban Gamliel hid. The officer found him and asked him secretly: "If I save you, will you bring me into the world-to-come?" The answer was affirmative. After making Rabban Gamliel swear to it, the officer mounted the roof and threw himself down and died. The Romans annulled the decree against Rabban Gamliel, according to their tradition that the death of one of their leaders (i.e., the officer's suicide) was a punishment for an evil decree. Thereupon a voice from heaven was heard saying that this high officer was destined to enter the world-to-come (Taanit 29a).

Nearly identical stories are told in the Talmud in two separate discussions (Hullin 94a and Derekh Eretz Rabbah, ch. 9, 57b). Because of an incident that once occurred, it was decreed that guests might not give any of the food that was set before them to the host's son or to his servant or deputy unless they had received the host's permission to do so. The incident was that in a time of scarcity a man invited three guests to his house and only had three eggs which he set before them. When the host's hungry child entered and stood before them, one of the guests took his portion and gave it to him; the second guest did the same, and so did the third. When the father came in and saw his son with one egg in his mouth and holding two in his hands, he picked him up to his full height and flung him to the ground, so that he died. When the mother saw her child dead, she went up to the roof, threw herself down, and died. On seeing this, the father also went up to the roof, threw himself down, and died. Rabbi Eliezer ben Jacob said: "Because of this, three souls perished."

A related incident that terminated in suicide concerns a man who had sent his friend a barrel of wine and there was oil floating at the mouth of the barrel, leading the recipient to believe that the whole barrel contained oil. He invited some guests to partake of it. When he came and found that it was only wine, he went and hanged himself out of shame because he had nothing else prepared to set before his guests. As a result, it was decreed that a man should not send his neighbor a barrel of wine with oil floating on top of it.

Another talmudic episode of suicide is found in the commentary of *Rashi* (Abodah Zarah, 18b). Rabbi Meir is said to have fled to Babylon. One of the reasons given is "because of the incident of {his wife} Beruryah." The incident concerns the fact that Rabbi Meir's wife once taunted him regarding the rabbinic adage that women are temperamentally lightheaded. He replied that one day she would testify to this truth. Subsequently she was enticed by one of her husband's disciples, proving she was too weak to resist. She then committed suicide by strangulation.

A mass suicide is described in the Talmud, where four hundred boys and girls are said to have been carried off for immoral purposes (Gittin 57b). They guessed what they were wanted for and said to themselves that if they drowned in the sea they would attain the life of the future world (as portrayed in Psalms 68:23). The girls leaped into the sea first and the boys followed.

Elsewhere in the Talmud is related the story from the Second Book of Maccabees of the woman and her seven martyred sons (Gittin 57b). The sons were killed one by one by Emperor Antiokhus Epiphanes for refusing to serve an idol. As the last son was being led away to be killed, his mother said to him: "My son, go and say to your father Abraham: Thou didst bind one {son to the altar, i.e., Isaac}, but I have bound seven altars." A voice thereupon came forth from heaven saying: "A joyful mother of children" (Psalms 113:9).

Another incident relates to a certain student who once left his phylacteries in a hole on the side of the road before entering a privy (Berakhot 23a). A harlot passed by and took them. She came to the house of learning and said: "See what so-and-so gave me for hire." When the student heard this, he went to the top of a roof and threw himself down and killed himself.

The rules and regulations governing suicide are discussed in at least two places in the Talmud (Baba Kamma 61a and 91b). "No *Halakhah* {Law} may be quoted in the name of one who surrenders himself to meet death for the words of the Torah." Later in the same tractate we find: ". . . who is the *tanna* that maintains that a man may not injure himself? It could hardly be said that he was the *tanna* of the teaching 'And surely your own blood of your souls will I require' (Genesis 9:5) which Rabbi Eleazer interpreted to mean 'I {i.e., God} will require your blood if shed by the hand of yourselves {i.e., suicide},' for murder is perhaps different." *Rashi* interprets this scriptural verse to mean that even though one strangles oneself so that no blood flows, still "I {God} will require it."

The major talmudic discussion of the rules governing suicide states that we do not occupy ourselves at all with the funeral rites of someone who committed suicide willfully (Semahot 2:1ff). Rabbi Yishmael said: We exclaim over him, "Alas for a lost {life}. Alas for a lost {life}." Rabbi Akiva said of him: "Leave him unmourned; speak neither well nor ill of him." Further, "we do not rend garments for him, nor bare the shoulder [as signs of mourning], or deliver a memorial address over him. We do, however, stand in a row for him {at the cemetery after the funeral} to offer condolences and recite the mourner's benediction for him because this is respectful for the living {relatives}. The general rule is that we occupy ourselves with anything that is intended as a matter of honor for the living."

The Talmud defines an intentional suicide (ibid. 2:2). It is not one who climbed to the top of a tree and fell down and died, nor one who ascended to the top of a roof and fell down and died, as these may have been accidents. Rather, a willful suicide is one who calls out: "Look, I am going to the top of the roof or to the top of the tree, and I will throw myself down that I may die." When people see him go to the top of the tree or roof and fall down and die, then he is considered to have committed suicide willfully. A person found strangled or hanging from a tree or lying dead on a sword is presumed not to have committed suicide intentionally, and none of the funeral rites are withheld from him.

The Talmud next relates two childhood suicides and considers neither an intentional suicide (ibid. 2:4–5). One case concerns the son of Gornos of Lyddda who ran away from school, and the other case is that of a child in Bene-Berak who broke a bottle on the Sabbath. In each case, the father threatened to punish the child, and out of fear each child destroyed himself in a pit. Rabbi Tarfon in the former case and Rabbi Akiva in the latter case ruled that these were not willful suicides and therefore none of the funeral rites should be withheld.

SUICIDE IN THE MIDRASH

In the Midrash the story is told of Rabbi Akiba walking barefoot to Rome when met by a eunuch officer of the emperor riding on a horse (Ecclesiastes Rabbah 10:7:26b). The officer asked him whether he was the famous rabbi of the Jews and he answered yes. In order to embarrass Rabbi Akiba, the eunuch said three things: "He who rides on a horse is a king, he who rides on a donkey is a free man, and he whose feet have shoes on is a human being; he who has none of these is worse than a dead person." Rabbi Akiba replied saying three things: "One's beard is one's majestic countenance, happiness of heart is one's wife, and the inheritance of God is to have children; woe is the man who is lacking all three. Not only that but Scripture states, 'I have seen servants upon horses and princes walking as servants upon the earth'" (Ecclesiastes 10:7). When the eunuch officer heard these words, he knocked his head against a wall until he died.

Another case of intentional suicide is that of Yakum of Tzerorot, nephew of Rabbi Yose ben Joezer of Tzeredah (Genesis Rabbah 65:22:130b). Yakum taunted Rabbi Joseph Meshita and, as self-punishment, subjected himself to the four modes of execution inflicted by the courts: stoning, burning, decapitation, and strangulation. He took a post, implanted it in the earth, raised a wall of stones around it, and tied a cord to it. He made a fire in front of it and fixed a sword in the middle of the post. He hanged himself on the post, and before the cord burned through, he was strangled. Then the sword caught him, while the wall of stones fell upon him and he was burned.

SUICIDE IN THE CODES OF JEWISH LAW

In the *Mishneh Torah*, Maimonides states:

> For one who has committed suicide intentionally we do not occupy ourselves at all with the funeral rites, and we do not mourn for him nor eulogize him. However, we do stand in a row for him, and we recite the mourner's benediction, and we do all that is intended as a matter of honor for the living (Maimonides, *Mishneh Torah*, Laws of Mourning 1:11).

Maimonides then defines an intentional suicide exactly as defined in the Talmud. The commentators on Maimonides' code, Rabbi David ben Zimra, known as *Radvaz*, Rabbi Joseph Karo, known as *Keseph Mishneh*, and Rabbi Abraham Boton, known as *Lehem Mishneh*, all point out that Maimonides considers mourning an honor for the dead and, therefore, prohibited.

Rabbi Jacob ben Asher, known as *Tur*, codifies the section on suicide of the Talmud nearly verbatim (*Tur, Shulhan Arukh, Yoreh Deah* 345). He states that we do not rend garments, bare the shoulder, or eulogize the willful suicide victim. However, we do stand in a row to offer condolences to the family at the cemetery, and we utter the mourner's benediction, for these are intended as a matter of honor for the living relatives. *Tur* then continues by saying that the prohibition of rending the garments refers only to distant relatives, but the immediate relatives who have to mourn the deceased should rend their garments as a sign of mourning. This is diametrically opposed to Maimonides. Rabbi Joseph Karo, in his *Shulhan Arukh*, follows Maimonides.

Tur defines a willful suicide as it is defined in the Talmud (Semahot 2:1ff). However, a child who committed suicide even willfully is not considered to have attained his full measure of intelligence. Similarly, he continues, anyone who commits suicide in unusual circumstances, such as King Saul, is not considered a willful suicide and is entitled to all funeral rites. According to Rabbi Joel Sirkes, known as *Bet Hadash*, and Rabbi Joseph Karo, known as *Bet Joseph*, in their commentaries on Jacob ben Asher, the latter statement by *Tur* is based on Nahmanides' work entitled *Sefer ha-Adam*.

In his *Shulhan Arukh*, Rabbi Joseph Karo seems to combine the talmudic and Maimonidean regulations regarding suicide. He states that we do not occupy ourselves at all for anyone who has committed suicide willfully (Karo, *Shulhan Arukh, Yoreh Deah* 345). We do not mourn for him (contrary to Jacob ben Asher but in agreement with Maimonides) nor eulogize him nor rend garments for him nor bare the shoulder. However, all that is in honor of the living, such as standing in a row to offer condolences to the relatives of the deceased, is performed.

Several commentators on Karo, including Rabbi Zekhariah Mendel of Cracow, known as *Ba'er Hetev*, Rabbi Abraham Tzvi Hirsh Eisenstadt, known as *Pithei Teshuvah*, and Rabbi Shabtai ben Meir Hakohen, known as *Siftei Kohen* or *Shakh*, point out that Jacob ben Asher's code differs from Karo's in that the former requires garment rending and mourning of close relatives of the deceased. *Siftei Kohen* also quotes Rabbi Solomon ben Abraham Adret, who explains that the phrase "we do not occupy ourselves at all," as cited from the Talmud and Maimonides, does not refer to burial itself. Rather, only the rites surrounding the funeral are withheld but the deceased must be buried (Responsa *Rashba* #763).

SUICIDE IN RECENT RABBINIC WRITINGS

Responsa literature on suicide is rather sparse. Rabbi Moses Schreiber was asked concerning a person found drowned in a river (Responsa *Hatam Sofer, Yoreh Deah* #326). Rabbi Schreiber concludes that laws of mourning, including the recitation of the *Kaddish* prayer, are observed even for an intentional suicide victim.

Rabbi Yehiel Mikhel Tukazinsky devotes an entire chapter to a discussion of suicide (*Gesher Hahayyim*, Ch. 25). The person who commits willful suicide is considered a murderer. It matters not whether he kills someone else or himself, since his own soul is not his, just as someone else's soul is not his. Were we able to bring this man to justice in this world, he would be adjudicated as any murderer. In fact, he may be so judged in heaven above.

Rabbi Jekuthiel Judah Greenwald discusses the definition of a willful suicide and all the laws pertaining thereto (*Kol Bo Al Avelut*, pp. 318–321). He reviews the talmudic sources and codes of Jewish law dealing with suicide. He also points out that the adage "He who willfully destroys himself has no share in the world to come" is not found in the Talmud or the writings of the early rabbinic decisors (*rishonim*). It is a folk saying first quoted by the later rabbinic decisors (*aharonim*) but based on talmudic discussions of suicide.

The most extensive recent rabbinic writing about suicide in Judaism is a twenty-six chapter work edited by Rabbi Yehiel Mikhel Stern. The interested reader is referred to this source for details. It may be a graver sin to commit suicide than to murder someone else, for several reasons. First, by killing himself, a person removes all possibility of repentance. Second, in most circumstances death is the greatest atonement for one's sins (Yoma 86a). However, in a suicide's death there has been committed a cardinal transgression rather than expiation. A third reason why Judaism abhors suicide is that the person who takes his own life asserts by this act that he denies the Divine mastery and ownership of his life, his body, and his soul. The willful suicide further denies his Divine creation. Our sages compare the departure of a soul from a human body to a Torah scroll which has been consumed by fire. Thus, a person who commits suicide can be likened to one who burns a *Sefer Torah*. Finally, he who takes his own life is also one who denies the Judaic teaching of the immortality of the soul and the eternal existence of Almighty God.

MARTYRDOM IN JUDAISM

The subject of suicide is intertwined with the topic of martyrdom, since many suicides are committed as an act of martyrdom. The Jewish attitude toward martyrdom is based upon the following biblical passage. "Ye shall therefore keep My ordinances and My judgments, which if a man do, he shall live in them: I am the Eternal"

(Leviticus 18:5). The rabbis deduced from the words "he shall live" that martyrdom is prohibited save for idolatry, forbidden sexual relations, and murder (Talmud, Sanhedrin, 74a). All other commandments may be transgressed if life is in danger in order that "he shall live." Martyrdom includes both the ending of one's own life for the sanctification of the name of God and allowing oneself to be killed in times of religious persecution rather than transgress biblical commandments. Perhaps the best known examples of martyrdom in Jewish life are the ten famous Torah scholars executed or martyred by the Roman state at different times for their insistence on teaching the Torah.

SUICIDE AND MODERN PSYCHIATRY

The preponderance of modern psychiatric thinking on the pathology of suicide is that, with rare exceptions, the act of suicide, whether or not successful, is *prima facie* evidence of mental illness. Most often the illness is depression or despondency but occasionally may manifest itself as a psychosis or schizophrenia. The rare exception can be illustrated by a person who has lived a full and good life and who feels he/she has nothing to look forward to. If this type of person attempts or commits suicide, it is not a sign of despondency.

Suicide may represent an act which expresses the fantasy reunion of a person with a departed loved one or a fantasy reunion with God. Such a psychiatric aberration of a person's mind cannot be classified as anything other than pathological. Suicide can accompany virtually all psychiatric illnesses or may occur during periods of life crisis and stress in persons without discernible mental illness.

Although physicians daily witness profound despair and tragedy in their patients, suicide attempts are an unusual event, and successful suicide is rarer still. The clinician should recognize the painful states of bitterness and desperation which so often raise the suicidal impulse.

At the other extreme of modern psychiatric thought is the American psychiatrist Thomas Szasz, who claims that suicide is rarely, if ever, a sign of mental illness. He further asserts that a person should have the right to commit suicide just as a person has many civil rights. *Halakhah* (Jewish Law) would not condone such an approach because Judaism believes that the human body does not belong to man to do with as he pleases. Man was created in the image of God and was entrusted with his body, to guard it and to watch over it. This is the philosophy behind Judaism's abhorrence of suicide. Since the vast majority of suicides are assignable to emotional stress or psychiatric illness, lenient rabbinic rulings are usually enunciated.

Certain recent writers have totally distorted Judaism's view toward suicide. Droge and Tabor categorically state that "there is no biblical prohibition against taking one's life, neither in legal materials nor in attitudes reflected by the various accounts of self-killing in the Hebrew Bible" (Droge & Tabor, p. 98). This erroneous assertion is negated by the authors' own citation of ancient and medieval Jewish sources which clearly point to the biblical sources upon which the prohibition of suicide is based. These include Genesis 9:5, Exodus 20:13 and Deuteronomy 5:17. These authors also distort the talmudic material they survey by saying that it is read "backward." It is unfortunate that they conclude that *halakhah* is "uncompromising" and "dogmatic" (ibid., p. 106). The rabbinic view sees the oral and written laws as an integrated whole and the "backward" interpretation distorts the rabbinic tradition. Droge and Tabor also misinterpret Sanhedrin 74a–75a when they assert that "instead of a focus on when one is *allowed* to choose death . . . {the Talmud} deals with the opposite problem: when one is *required* to choose death rather than violate the commandments of God." It is true that one is required to let oneself be killed rather than violate the three cardinal rules. Otherwise, however, one is not allowed to choose death. Jews are obligated to choose life (Deuteronomy 30:19). One cannot serve God when one is dead. The only condoned death choice is one in which one sanctifies the name of God by choosing a martyr's death when faced with no other alternative whatsoever. Judaism is a religion of life. Every moment of life is precious. To save a life, all laws except the cardinal three are suspended. He who saves a life is as if he saved a whole world (Sanhedrin 4:5). One does not usually choose death in Judaism except in a rare case of martyrdom, as aforementioned, namely to avoid transgressing the three cardinal rules. Otherwise, it is the choice of life, not death as espoused by Droge and Tabor, in the service of God, that serves as an entry into eternal life.

SUMMARY AND CONCLUSIONS

Judaism regards suicide as a criminal act and strictly forbidden by Jewish law. The cases of suicide in the Bible as well as those in the Apocrypha, Talmud, and Midrash took place under unusual and extenuating conditions.

In general a suicide is not accorded full burial honors. The Talmud and codes of Jewish law decree that rending one's garments, delivering memorial addresses, and other rites of mourning which are an honor for the dead are not to be performed for a suicide victim. The strict definition of a suicide for which these laws apply is one who had previously announced his intentions and then killed himself immediately thereafter by the method he announced. Children are never regarded as deliberate suicides and are afforded all burial rites. Similarly, those who commit suicide under extreme physical or mental strain, or while not in full possession of their faculties, or in order to atone for past sins are not considered as willful suicides, and none of the burial and mourning rites are withheld.

These considerations may condone the numerous acts of suicide and martyrdom committed by Jews throughout the centuries, from the priests who leaped into the flames of the burning Temple to the martyred Jews in the time of the Crusades, form the Jewish suicides during the medieval persecutions to the martyred Jews in more recent pogroms. Only for the sanctification of the name of the Lord would a Jew intentionally take his own life or allow it to be taken as a symbol of his extreme faith in God. Otherwise intentional suicide would be strictly forbidden because it constitutes a denial of the Divine creation of the human, of the immortality of the soul, and of the atonement of death (see also Abodah Zarah 17b, Taanit 29a, Berakhot 61b, Pesahim 50a, Baba Batra 10b, Sanhedrin 11a, 14a, 74a, 110b; I. Y. Unterman, pp. 38ff; and I. Jakobovits, pp. 52–54).

REFERENCES

Babylonian Talmud (20 vols.) (1965). New York: Otzar Hasefarim.

Droge, A. J. & J. D. Tabor (1992). *A Noble Death: Suicide and Martyrdom Among Christians and Jews in Antiquity*. San Francisco: Harper.

Graetz, H. *History of the Jews* (1956). Philadelphia: Jewish Publication Society.

Greenwald, J. J. (1965). *Kol Bo Al Avelut*. New York: Feldheim.

The Holy Scriptures (2 vols.) (1985). Philadelphia: Jewish Publication Society.
Jakobovits, I. (1959). *Jewish Medical Ethics*. New York: Bloch.
Karo, J. (16th cent.). *Shulhan Arukh* (10 vols.) (1985). New York: M. P. Press.
Maimonides, M. (12th cent.) (1962). *Mishneh Torah* (6 vols.). New York: M. P. Press.
The Midrash (10 vols.) (1961). H. Freedman & M. Simon (Eds.). London: Soncino Press.
Mikraot Gedolot (10 vols.) (1951). New York: Pardes Publishing House.
Stern, Y. M. (1985). Harefuah Leor Hahalakhah. Jerusalem: Institute for Research in Medicine and Halakhah, Vol. 4, part 2, 1–138.
The Talmud (18 vols.) (1961). I. Epstein (Ed.). London: Soncino Press.
Tukazinsky, Y. M. (1960). *Gesher Hahayyim*. Jerusalem.
Unterman, I. Y. (1955). *Shevat Mi-Yahudah*. Jerusalem.

7

Shneidman's Definition of Suicide and Jewish Law

A Brief Note

KALMAN J. KAPLAN, PH.D.

In his 1985 book *Definition of Suicide,* Edwin Shneidman argues for a tightening of the term suicide in modern usage. He offers the following definition of suicide: "Currently in the Western world, suicide is a conscious act of self-induced annihilation, best understood as a multidimensional malaise in a needful individual who defines an issue for which suicide is perceived as the best solution," (p. 203). The word "conscious" limits suicide to human acts, while the word "act" calls for a narrowing of our usage of the term suicide to a particular behavior that leads to death. The last part of this definition focuses on the intention of the individual to die.

Shneidman suggests that the words "completed suicide" and "attempted suicide" should be used only for those events in which there has been a conscious effort to end one's life. Shneidman calls other self-destructive acts such as self-mutilations, excessive dosage of drugs, and other events of this type as "quasi-suicidal attempts" or "parasuicides," (pp. 17–22). Thus, Shneidman limits the term "attempted suicide" to those individuals who have "committed suicide" and fortuitously survived. For example, an individual who holds a fully loaded gun to his temple and pulls the trigger which does not fire can be termed a suicide attempt. Likewise, an individual who jumps from a high building but is saved by a ledge. Or a person who sets himself on fire who is accidently saved by a bystander.

In contrast, a number of deaths which typically have been classified as suicide would not be by Shneidman's criterion. Consider, for example, a death which occurred in our Chicago Followup Study at Michael Reese Hospital and Medical Center. A woman drowns in the Chicago River on her third attempt to baptize herself. Her intent, at least on the conscious level did not seem to be to die even though her behavior is quite likely to lead to death. Shneidman would in all probability classify this a subintentioned death rather than as an intentioned suicide. A subintentioned death is one in which the victim has played a covert, partial, latent, unconscious role in hastening his own death.

Shneidman's attempt to fix stringent criteria for the suicidal act finds an echo in Jewish law. The Talmud (Semahot 2:2) defines an intentional suicide as follows. It is not one who climbed to the top of a tree and fell down and died, nor one who ascended to the top of a roof and fell down and died, as these may have been accidents. Rather, a willful suicide is one who calls out "Look, I am going to the top of the roof or to the top of the tree, and I will throw myself down that I may die." When people see him go to the top of the tree or roof and fall down and die, then he is considered to have committed suicide willfully. A person found strangled or hanging from a tree or lying dead on a sword is presumed not to have committed suicide intentionally, and none of the funeral rites forbidden to a suicide are withheld from him. (Rosner, 1994, p. 221). Significantly, the Talmud relates two childhood suicides and considers neither one an intentional suicide. One case involves the son of Gornos of Lydda who ran away from school and the other involves a child in Bene-Berak who broke a bottle on the Sabbath. In each case, the child who out of fear of his father, destroyed himself in a pit. Rabbi Tarfon in the former case and Rabbi Akiba in the latter ruled that these were not willful suicides and that none of the funeral rites should be withheld.

It is clear that ancient Jewish law and the contemporary Edwin Shneidman are both warning us against too loose a definition of suicide. The intention to destroy oneself must be clear and unambiguous for both. Otherwise, it is more prudent not to classify the event as an intentioned suicide *per se*. Such caution is warranted for both religious and scientific reasons.

REFERENCES

Babylonian Talmud (20 vols.) (1965). New York: Otzar Hasefirim.
Rosner, F. (1994) Suicide in Jewish Law. *Journal of Psychology and Judaism*. 18(4), 283–297.
Shneidman, E. (1985). *Definition of Suicide*. New York: John Wiley and Sons.

8
Euthanasia as a Halakhic Option

RABBI BYRON L. SHERWIN, PH.D.

The accelerating collision of longer life expectancy and advanced developments in medical technology makes the problem of euthanasia ever more pertinent. An extensive, well-developed discussion of euthanasia exists in classical Jewish religious-moral-legal literature. While this essay presents the traditional position that permits passive euthanasia and that prohibits active euthanasia, the unique contribution of this study is an attempt to present, to justify, and to defend a position within the context of classical Jewish religious-moral-legal literature that would permit active euthanasia in certain situations.

Scripture says: "You should love your neighbor as yourself" [Lev. 19:18]; therefore choose an easy death for him. B. *Talmud, Pesahim* 75a.

THE PROBLEM OF EUTHANASIA: AN INTRODUCTION

The "miracles" of modern medicine have engendered the complexities of modern medical ethics. Advances in medical technology have exacerbated moral decision making in medical settings. One of the most compelling issues confronting contemporary bioethics is euthanasia. A problem for the patient, for the patient's family, for the physician, for the nurse, for the social worker, for the clergy, etc., the choice of prolonging or ending life is no longer left solely to God. As patients, as potential patients, as families of potential patients, or perhaps as physicians and nurses, the choice may one day be our own. If and when any of us might be compelled by circumstances to make such decisions, what would we do? One place where we might look for guidance is in Jewish tradition. As will be shown, classical Jewish sources have confronted the problem of euthanasia throughout the centuries. These ancient, medieval and modern reflections on the problem may be helpful in decision-making, in helping one think through the issue with Jewish tradition.

Modern philosophers often distinguish between two kinds of euthanasia: active and passive. Active euthanasia refers to an action that causes or accelerates death. An example of active euthanasia would be the administering of a powerful pain-killing drug to a terminal cancer patient which, besides easing the pain, would also bring about the patient's death. Passive euthanasia refers to the withdrawal of life supports. An example of passive euthanasia might be the removal of "artificial" life-support systems such as a heart-lung machine that helps sustain the life of a patient who might otherwise die. In addition, a distinction is also often made between "voluntary" and "involuntary" euthanasia. In voluntary euthanasia, the individual whose life is in question takes an action that brings his or her own life to an end. In involuntary euthanasia, an action to end the patient's life is taken without his or her explicit consent to end his or her life. Thus, euthanasia may take a variety of forms:

1. Active-voluntary
2. Passive-voluntary
3. Active-involuntary
4. Passive-involuntary

An example of "active-voluntary" euthanasia would be where the patient wills to end his or her own life and actively implements this decision. For instance, if a person with terminal cancer makes a conscious decision to end his or her life by swallowing an overdose of pain-killing medicine which, besides alleviating pain, may also accelerate death, this would be a case of active-voluntary euthanasia.

"Passive-voluntary" euthanasia would be where the patient chooses to remove the means that are prolonging his or her life, without which he or she *might* die. For example, if a patient who may not be able to breathe normally removes a respirator and/or I.V., which then brings about his or her death, this would be an example of passive-voluntary euthanasia.

"Active-involuntary" euthanasia would be when a party *other than the patient* takes deliberate action to accelerate the patient's death. "Passive-involuntary" euthanasia would be when a party other than the patient removes certain life-support systems without the patient's knowledge or consent—for example, if a patient has a flat EEG and is in an irreversible coma, but his or her heart and lungs are operating because of mechanical assistance, then "pulling the plug" would be an example of passive-involuntary euthanasia. To be sure, the distinction amongst these four forms of euthanasia is helpful, but it is sometimes hazy. For instance, is "pulling the plug" passive or active euthanasia; does it remove an action, i.e., the introduction of "heroic measures," or is it an action aimed at accelerating death? Indeed, contemporary *halakhists* are divided on the question of whether "pulling the plug" is a form of withholding treatment (i.e., passive euthanasia), and therefore probably permitted, or an overt act of intervention designed to shorten life (i.e., active euthanasia), and therefore prohibited. (See e.g., discussion and sources in J. D. Bleich, "The Quinlan Case: A Jewish Perspective," in eds., Rosner and Bleich, *Jewish Bioethics*, p. 275, no. 2).

Having stated some of the questions and problems that euthanasia forces us to confront, it is now appropriate to review some classical and modern Jewish sources on the problem in order to see how Jewish tradition deals with euthanasia.

Though as a rule Judaism condemns murder and suicide, there are exceptions to the rule. For example, martyrdom—killing oneself or others, or allowing oneself and others to be killed—for "the sanctification of God's Name" (*Kiddush ha-Shem*) is not considered murder or suicide by Talmudic and subsequent Jewish tradition. Indeed, much of classical Jewish literature considers *Kiddush ha-Shem* to be the highest possible human expression of divine worship and service. The martyrdom of Rabbi Akiva served as a model to be emulated by future generations (see *Berakhot* 61b). Furthermore, killing in self-defense and other forms of "justified homicide" have been sanctioned as "necessary evils" by rabbinic tradition (see e.g., Exod. 22:1, *Sanhedrin* 72a–b). Neither were all examples of manslaughter considered murder; rabbinic tradition required conditions such as premeditation and malicious intent before defining an act of killing as murder (see e.g., Rashi to Exod. 21:4).

Since martyrdom is one of the exceptions to suicide and murder, it is interesting that post-Talmudic Jewish sources found a precedent for euthanasia in a Talmudic text that discusses martyrdom (*Avodah Zarah* 18a):

> It was said that within but few days Rabbi Jose ben Kisma died and all the great men of Rome went to his burial and made a great

lamentation for him. On their return, they found Rabbi Haninah ben Teradion sitting and occupying himself with the Torah, publicly gathering assemblies, and keeping a scroll of the Law in his bosom. Straightaway they took him, wrapt him in the scroll of the Law, placed bundles of branches around him and set them on fire. They then brought tufts of wool, which they had soaked in water, and placed them over his heart, so that he should not expire quickly. His daughter exclaimed, "Father, that I should see you in this state!" He replied, "If it were I alone being burnt it would have been a thing hard to bear; but now I am burning together with the Scroll of the Law. He who will have regard for the plight of the Torah will also have regard for my plight." His disciples called out, "Rabbi, what seest thou?" He answered them, "The parchments are being burnt but the letters are soaring high." "Open then thy mouth" [said they] "so that the fire enter into thee." He replied: "Let Him who gave me [my soul] take it away, but no one should injure oneself." The executioner then said to him, "Rabbi, if I raise the flame and take away the tufts of wool from over thy heart, will thou cause me to enter into the life to come?" "Yes," he replied. "Then swear unto me" [he urged]. He swore unto him. He thereupon raised the flame and removed the tufts of wool from over his heart, and his soul departed speedily. The executioner then jumped and threw himself into the fire. And a *bath kol* [a heavenly voice] exclaimed: "Rabbi Haninah ben Teradion and the executioner have been assigned to the World to Come." When Rabbi heard it he wept and said: "One may acquire eternal life in a single hour, another after many years."

This Talmudic text (i.e., *Avodah Zarah* 18a) was interpreted by later authorities as establishing the following principles:

1. Martyrdom is not to be considered self-murder, i.e., suicide.
2. An individual's life belongs not to oneself but to God.
3. Active-voluntary euthanasia is prohibited, but passive-voluntary euthanasia may be permitted. When the rabbi is encouraged to open his mouth so that the fire may enter and end his agony (i.e., active-voluntary euthanasia), he refuses. But, when the executioner offers to remove the soaked tufts of wool artificially prolonging his life (i.e., a life-support system), the rabbi gives him permission (i.e., passive-voluntary euthanasia).

As will be discussed further below, views on euthanasia which are drawn from this Talmudic text (i.e., *Avodah Zarah* 18a) are reiterated in subsequent Jewish literature.

ACTIVE EUTHANASIA IS PROHIBITED

The thirteenth-century work of the Jewish pietists of Germany, *Sefer Hasidim, the Book of the Pious* (no. 315 in ed. Wistinetzki, p. 100) states:

> If a person is suffering from extreme pain and he says to another: "You see that I shall not live [long]; [therefore,] kill me because I cannot bear the pain," one is forbidden to touch him [the terminal patient].

The text continues and proscribes the terminal patient from taking his or her own life:

> If a person is suffering great pain and he knows that he will not live [long], he cannot kill himself. And this principle we learn from Rabbi Haninah ben Teradion who refused to open his mouth [to allow the fire to enter and take his life].

In one of the "minor tractates" of the Talmud, *Tractate Semahot* (1:1, 1:4) we read:

> A dying man [*goses*] is regarded as a living entity in respect to all matters in the world. Whosoever touches or moves him is a murderer [if by so doing his death is accelerated]. Rabbi Meir used to say: He may be compared to a lamp which is dripping [i.e., going out]; should one touch it, one extinguishes it. Similarly, whoever closes the eyes of a dying man [thereby accelerating his death] is considered as if he had taken his life.

This prohibition against practicing active euthanasia expressed here is reiterated, almost verbatim, by the medieval codes of Jewish law (see also, *Shabbat* 151b and Rashi there; note Solomon Luria, *Yam Shel Shelomo*, "Perek ha-Yovel" no. 59; *Responsa Hatam Sofer—Yoreh Deah*, no. 326). This prohibition extends to the patient, the attending physician, the family and friends of the patient, and to all other individuals as well. In his legal code, the *Mishneh Torah* (Book of Judges, "Laws of Mourning," 4:5), Maimonides wrote:

> One who is in a dying condition is regarded as a living person in all respects. . . . He who touches him [thereby accelerating his death]

is guilty of shedding blood. To what may he [the dying person] be compared? To a flickering flame, which is extinguished as soon as one touches it. Whoever closes the eyes of a dying person while the soul is about to depart is shedding blood. One should wait a while; perhaps he is just in a swoon.

The fourteenth-century code of Jacob ben Asher is called the *Four Rows (Arba'ah Turim)*. In many ways, it served as the model for Joseph Karo's sixteenth-century code, *The Set Table (Shulhan Arukh)*. Echoing the discussion in *Semahot* and Maimonides' code, Jacob ben Asher wrote *(Yoreh Deah* no. 339):

> A dying man is to be considered a living person in all respects . . . [therefore] anyone who hastens the exiting of the person's soul is a shedder of blood.

The *Shulhan Arukh (Yoreh Deah* no. 339:1) reads:

> A patient on his deathbed is considered a living person in every respect . . . and it is forbidden to cause him to die quickly . . . and whosoever closes his eyes with the onset of death is regarded as shedding blood.

In his gloss on this text, Moses Isserles writes, "To do anything that causes death to be accelerated is forbidden."

The nineteenth-century *Abridged Shulhan Arukh (Kitzur Shulhan Arukh)* by Solomon Ganzfried *(Yoreh Deah* 194:1) embellishes a bit on the earlier sources:

> Even if one has been dying for a long time, which causes agony to the patient and his family, it is still forbidden to accelerate his death.

The premises upon which classical Jewish views regarding active euthanasia are based are:

1. An individual's life is not his or her own "property," but God's, and therefore God has the final disposition over it. In other words, each serves as God's steward for the life given into his or her care. As Haninah ben Teradion put it *(Avodah Zarah* 18a), "Let Him who gave me my soul take it away."
2. Jewish law does not dwell on the issue of quality of life.

Rather, Jewish law maintains that each moment of life is intrinsically valuable in and of itself, independent of its "quality." Therefore, life being sacred—each moment of life being intrinsically valuable—every effort must be made to preserve each moment of life, even to the moment of death. For example, according to Jewish law, "even if they find a person crushed [under a fallen building] so that he can live only for a short time, they must continue to dig," and if this has occurred on the Sabbath, one is *required* to violate the Sabbath even if it means granting the victim only "momentary life" (see *Yoma* 84–85; *Shulhan Arukh—Orah Hayyim* 329:4).

3. An individual is prohibited from inflicting self-injury (*Baba Kamma* 91b), particularly the ultimate self-injury—suicide (*Avodah Zarah* 18a, *Genesis Rabbah* 34:13, *Mishneh Torah—Book of Torts*, "Laws of Murder," 2:3), which is generally defined as self-homicide (e.g., *Pesikta Rabbati* 24:1).
4. Since "there is no agency for wrongful acts" (*Kiddushin* 42b), and since murder is a wrongful act, one cannot act as the agent of a person who desires death and bring about or accelerate that person's death, even at that person's explicit request (see sources noted above and *Genesis Rabbah* 34:14). In this regard, the physician is explicitly enjoined from employing medical intervention for the intention of accelerating death (e.g., *Siftei Kohen* to *Shulhan Arukh—Yoreh Deah* 336:1).

PASSIVE EUTHANASIA MAY BE PERMITTED

The Talmudic case of Haninah ben Teradion is used by some post-Talmudic sources as a precedent for the permissibility of passive euthanasia. The rabbi permitted the tufts of wool which were "artificially" sustaining his life to be removed. This would seem to permit both voluntary and involuntary passive euthanasia, either on the part of the patient (i.e., voluntary) or on the part of another party (i.e., voluntary or involuntary), such as a physician. To be sure, Jewish law would not permit the removal of any and all life-support mechanisms. For example, it generally would not permit withholding insulin from a diabetic. The text of the story of Haninah ben Teradion clearly relates to an individual who has no chance of survival in any case, i.e., to a terminal patient.

In many of the same sources noted above proscribing active euthanasia, one finds material that permits passive euthanasia. The *Book of the Pious* observes (ed. Wistinetzki, no. 315, p. 100):

> One may not [artificially] prolong the act of dying. If, for example, someone is dying and nearby a woodcutter insists on chopping wood, thereby disturbing the dying person so that he cannot die, we remove the woodcutter from the vicinity of the dying person. Also, one must not place salt in the mouth of a dying person in order to prevent death from overtaking him.

This view is adapted and is quoted almost verbatim in subsequent codes of Jewish law. In his gloss to the *Shulhan Arukh*, the sixteenth-century Polish rabbi, Moses Isserles, observed (*Yoreh Deah* 339:1):

> It is forbidden to cause one's death to be accelerated, even in the case of one who has been terminally ill for a long time . . . however, if there is some factor which is preventing the exit of the soul such as a nearby woodchopper or salt placed under his tongue—and these things are impeding his death—it is permissible to remove them because in so doing one actively does nothing but remove an obstacle [preventing his natural death].

Again, echoing the *Book of the Pious* (ed. Wistinetzki, no. 316, p. 100), the *Shulhan Arukh* states (*Yoreh Deah* no. 234):

> One must not scream at the moment at which the soul [of another] departs, lest the soul return and the person suffer great pain. That is to say, it is not simply permitted to remove an obstacle to one's [natural] death, but one cannot lengthen the pain and suffering of the patient.

In this regard, Moses Isserles, in his commentary to the *Arba'ah Turim* (*Darkkhei Moshe to Yoreh Deah* 339:1) interpreted the view of the *Sefer Hasidim* as meaning that "it is certain that for one to do anything that stifles the [natural] process of dying [of a dying person] is forbidden." Similarly, the sixteenth-century Italian rabbi, Joshua Boaz, referred to the *Sefer Hasidim* as being the basis of his own view that "it is permissible to remove any obstacle preventing [death] because so doing is not an action in and of itself" [see his commentary on Al-Fasi—The Rif—*Shiltei Ha-Gibborim* to *Moed Katan* 16b; see also Zevi Hirsch ben Azriel of Vienna's commentary *Beit Lehem Yehudah* on *Shulhan Arukh—Yoreh Deah* 339:1). Furthermore, in a responsum by Jacob ben Samuel, the author takes the controversial view that any medical or pharmacological intervention that impedes the natural process of dying should not be introduced (*Beit Ya'akov*, no. 59. For a discussion of this and competing views see, e.g., Solomon Eger, *Gilyonei Maharshah* to *Shulhan Arukh—Yoreh Deah* 339:1).

Commenting on the phrase in Ecclesiastes (3:2), "There is a time to die," the *Sefer Hasidim* (ed. Margaliot, no. 234, p. 208) observes that Ecclesiastes does *not* also state that "there is a time to live." The reason for this, according to the *Sefer Hasidim*, is that, when the "time to die" arrives, it is not the time to extend life. Consequently, the *Sefer Hasidim* prohibits efforts to resuscitate a terminal patient who has died on the grounds that extending the process of dying by resuscitation would cause the patient continued unnecessary anguish and pain. This text might serve as the basis for justifying a "Do Not Resuscitate" (DNR) order for terminal patients whose condition has reached the point of death and whose resuscitation through "heroic" measures would only prolong their death and extend their agony. Just as some sources consider active euthanasia to be a presumption of God's authority over life and death, the *Sefer Hasidim* insists that extending the process of dying, when the terminal patient is in severe pain, is also a presumption of God's authority over life and death and a presumptive rejection of the scriptural view that "there is a time to die."

It should be noted, however, that the specific removal of natural hydration and of feeding of a terminal patient to hasten death is specifically proscribed, probably because such withdrawal is considered cruel (see, e.g., *Sanhedrin* 77a; Maimonides, *Mishneh Torah—Torts*—"Laws of Murder," 3:10). According to a text in the *Sefer Hasidim* (ed. Margaliot, no. 234, p. 208), however, removal of nutrition and of hydration are required in two kinds of cases. One is in the case in which nutrition or hydration will harm the patient. The second is in the case of a terminal patient where death is imminent. Such a patient must be made comfortable, e.g., by keeping his or her lips and mouth moist, but such a patient must not be fed, lest the process of dying be prolonged and painful agony be unduly lengthened.

From the literature reviewed to this point, it would appear that the Jewish view of euthanasia is that active euthanasia is prohibited, but passive euthanasia may be permissible and even desirable; for while classical Jewish sources place great value on saving and prolonging human life, they put no premium on needlessly prolonging the act of dying (see e.g., Moses Feinstein, *Iggrot Moshe, Yoreh Deah* II 174). However, the sources seem uncompromising in the view that active euthanasia, under any circumstances, is a form of suicide and/or murder and is therefore prohibited. Indeed, a number of contemporary Jewish scholars, after reviewing the relevant sources, have come to this conclusion. For example, Rabbi Immanuel Jakobovits, in his authoritative work *Jewish Medical Ethics*, summarizes the Jewish position on euthanasia as follows (pp. 123–124):

> It is clear, then, even when the patient is already known to be on his deathbed and close to the end, any form of *active euthanasia* is strictly prohibited. In fact, it is condemned as plain murder. In purely legal terms, this is borne out by the ruling that anyone who kills a dying person is liable to the death penalty as a common murderer. At the same time, Jewish law sanctions, and perhaps even demands, the withdrawal of any factor—whether extraneous to the patient himself or not—which may artificially delay his demise in the final phase.

Despite this apparent consensus on the matter, a number of contemporary scholars have attempted to discover and to formulate a basis for active euthanasia under certain circumstances. This reevaluation of the sources has been prompted by certain contemporary medical and pharmacological developments and by the present proliferation of terminal cancer cases brought about by the lengthening of the average human life span.

ACTIVE EUTHANASIA RECONSIDERED

As was noted above, there seems to be a unanimity of opinion in Judaism that life is intrinsically precious, even "momentary life." This assumption makes moot any discussion regarding "life vs. the quality of life." This claim also serves as a formulation for the condemnation of murder and suicide, of killing and self-killing. However, as was also noted above, exceptions to the prohibition against killing and self-killing were condoned by classical Jewish tradition, such as in cases of martyrdom and cases of "justifiable homicide." These exceptions to the rule lead one to the conclusion that the value of life itself is not *always* considered absolute. The permissibility, even the desirability, of martyrdom assumes that there are occasions where life itself may be set aside because the preservation of life is not always an absolute moral imperative.

While it is true that the dominant view of Jewish tradition is that life itself is of intrinsic value, there exists an alternative view that relates both to cases of martyrdom and to cases of pain and anguish. For example, one Talmudic text maintains that a life of unbearable pain, a life coming to an inevitable and an excruciating end, is not a life worth continuing, that such a life is like having no life at all.

A Talmudic passage describes an individual who is overcome with a severe physical affliction as one "whose life is no life" (*Betzah* 32b). Similarly, a nineteenth-century commentary on the Mishnah (*Tiferet Yisrael* to *Yoma* 8:3) observes that "great pain is worse than death." And while "a dying person [*goses*] is like a living person in all respects" (*Semahot* 1:1), the Mishnah in effect "devalued" the monetary worth of a dying person who wished to vow the equivalent of his monetary worth as a donation to the sanctuary. The Mishnah (*Arakhin* 1:3) reads, "One at the point of death [*goses*] . . . cannot have his worth vowed, not be subject to valuation." On this text, the Talmud comments, "It is quite right that one at the point of death cannot have his worth vowed, because he has no monetary value; nor can he be made the subject of a valuation because he is not fit to be made subject of a valuation (*Arakhin* 6b). Thus, the imperative "Choose Life" (Deut. 30:19) is not as absolute as is often assumed.

A further examination of classical Jewish sources related to martyrdom reveals that life in and of itself was not always considered of ultimate value. Such an examination also reveals precedents for taking one's own life and allowing for oneself to be killed rather than to endure the physical torture that often was a martyr's fate. In such cases, taking one's own life was often not considered suicide. What proves intriguing is the pertinence and the applicability that instances in which martyrs chose death to physical suffering, chose to accelerate their own death rather than to withstand physical agony, may have to the problem of euthanasia in general, and to the problem of active euthanasia in particular. For example, the case of King Saul's death provoked considerable discussion in classical Jewish literature that concerned itself with suicide. Wounded in battle, Saul asked to be killed, rather than to be handed over to his enemies. According to one version, Saul killed himself by falling on his sword (1 Samuel 31:1–6). According to a second version, he asked a youth to kill him: "Stand over me and finish me off, for I am in agony and barely alive" (II Samuel 1:9), and the Amalekite youth complied. Saul was found justified in his action by some rabbinic authorities because he chose death, i.e., martyrdom, rather than to be abused by the enemies of Israel, a precedent followed throughout Jewish history. What is particularly relevant to euthanasia is the comment of David Kimhi (Radak) on this episode. Kimhi commented (on II Samuel 1:9) that Saul's statement means: "I suffer so severely from my wound, and my soul is yet in me; therefore, I want you to accelerate my death." Thus, according to Kimhi, Saul's motive was to choose death rather than to continue to suffer. If both Saul's action and his motive (according to Kimhi) are considered justifiable, then this text would serve as a precedent for active euthanasia. (On Saul's action, see the lengthy discussion of Joel Sirkes' *Bayit Hadash* and Joseph Karo's *Beit Yosef* on *Arba'ah Turim—Yoreh Deah* 157).

Talmudic literature records many instances of martyrdom. One, noted above, was the case of Rabbi Haninah ben Teradion. Another text describes how four hundred Jewish children drowned themselves at sea, rather than submit to rape at the hands of Romans (*Gittin* 57b and *Tosafot* there). In a medieval commentary to the tale of the children, a reference is made to the case of Haninah ben Teradion. The two cases taken together are interpreted by the twelfth-century Rabbenu Jacob Tam as meaning that in order to avoid sufferings certain to result in death, it is permitted to take one's own life, and in such an instance it is required, rather than prohibited, to injure oneself by choosing death (*Tosafot* to *Avodah Zarah* 18a; see also, *Pithei Teshuvah* to *Shulhan Arukh—Yoreh Deah* 345:2 and the lengthy discussion in Leopold Greenwald, *Kol Bo Al-Aveilut* 1:10, p. 21). Furthermore, it is noteworthy in this regard that the language of the deathbed confessional of a dying person is remarkably reminiscent of that of a martyr. In one version of the confessional, the patient says, "I surrender my life, my body and my soul for the unification of the Divine Name" (see Abraham Danzig, *Hohmat Adam* 151:12). Here there is a clear parallel between the martyr and the dying person.

While suicide is proscribed by Jewish law, the prohibition against suicide was clearly set aside in the cases of martyrdom just noted. In other sources, "suicide" was redefined so that killing oneself was not always defined as suicide. With reference to euthanasia, consider, for example, the view that one finds in the Talmud (*Avodah Zarah* 27b) and in the medieval codes (*Shulhan Arukh—Yoreh Deah* 155: 5–7 and *Pithei Teshuvah* there), that it is sometimes preferable, particularly in the case of a terminal patient, to choose death rather than to be treated by a Gentile physician who may try to entice the Jewish patient to apostasy or who may use "idolatrous" practices to effect a cure. In such instances, extending "momentary life is not considered." This clearly indicates that the preservation of life in itself was not always of paramount importance or consideration. A further source to be considered in this regard is a controversial nineteenth-century responsum by Rabbi Saul Berlin (*Responsa Besomim Rosh* in first edition, Berlin, 1793 but eliminated in many subsequent editions).

In Berlin's responsum, the author maintains that an individual who takes his or her own life because of mental or physical pain and anguish is not to be considered a suicide. According to Berlin, the earlier halakhic regulations prohibiting suicide were primarily intended for cases where the act resulted from a pessimistic view of life. However, Berlin asserted, a person who takes his or her own life to avoid continued pain and anguish is not to be considered a suicide.

The controversial and unprecedented nature of Berlin's responsum and the possibly tenuous analogy between cases of martyrdom and cases of euthanasia, while suggestive, still do not adequately defend an option for active euthanasia within Jewish tradition. Consequently, it is necessary to look further.

In a late midrash on proverbs (*Yalkut Shimoni*, "Proverbs" no. 943), the text tells us:

> It happened that a woman who had aged considerably appeared before Rabbi Yose ben Halafta. She said: "Rabbi, I am much too old, life has become a burden for me. I can no longer taste food or drink, and I wish to die." Rabbi Yose answered her: "To what do you ascribe your longevity?" She answered that it was her habit to pray in the synagogue every morning, and despite occasional more pressing needs she never had missed a service. Rabbi Yose advised her to refrain from attending services for three consecutive days. She heeded his advice and on the third day she took ill and died.

This text may be interpreted as a reinforcement of the view that passive euthanasia is permitted by Jewish law, under certain conditions. The woman's withholding of her prayers removed the cause of the extension of her life. But, what about a case in which one actively prays for death rather than endure pain and suffering? (On praying for one's own death, see, e.g., I Kings 19:4, Jonah 4:3, *Ta'anit* 23a, and, on praying for the death of another, see e.g., *Baba Metzia* 84a.) In this case, the woman's withholding of her prayers eventuated in her own death, but what about a case where prayer is aimed at bringing about the death of another? It would therefore seem to reason that if the rabbis permitted one actively to pray for one's own death and even for the death of another, rather than have one endure pain and suffering, then a basis of an argument could be made for a rabbinic precedent as far as both voluntary and involuntary active euthanasia are concerned. In the Talmud one finds such a precedent (*Ketubot* 104a):

> On the day that Rabbi Judah was dying, the rabbis decreed a public fast and offered prayers for heavenly mercy [so that he would not die]. . . . Rabbi Judah's handmaid ascended to the roof and prayed: "The immortals [i.e., the angels] desire him [to join them] and the mortals desire him [to remain with them]; may it be the will [of God] that the mortals may overpower the immortals [i.e., that he would not die]." When, however, she saw how often he resorted to the privy, painfully removing and replacing his *tefillin* [i.e., in terrible agony], she prayed: "May it be the will [of God] that the immortals may overpower the mortals." The rabbis meanwhile continued their prayers for heavenly mercy. She took a jar and threw it down from the roof to the ground. [For a moment,] they stopped praying, and the soul of Rabbi Judah departed.

Some interpret this text to mean that the death of Rabbi Judah was caused by the rabbis' cessation of their prayers when they were startled by the noise of the shattering jar. Others interpret this text to mean that his death was caused by the handmaiden's active prayer aimed at bringing about Rabbi Judah's death in order to alleviate his substantiated suffering. It is in this latter sense that the text was interpreted by the medieval commentator, Rabbenu Nissim (to *Nedarim* 40a):

Sometimes one must request mercy on behalf of the ill so that he might die, as in the case of a patient who is terminal and who is in great pain.

The question of whether one may pray for the death of a patient in pain is discussed in a lengthy responsum by the nineteenth-century Turkish rabbi Hayyim Palaggi (*Hikkeke* Lev, no. 50, pp. 90a–91a). In this case, a woman has been suffering for many years with a degenerative terminal disease. She has been afforded the best available medical care. Her family has provided constant and loving care. Hope for a remission has been abandoned by the patient, by the family, and by the attending physicians. Her condition progressively has deteriorated. Her pain is constant and unbearable. Her illness has left her an invalid. She has prayed to God to die, preferring death to life as a liberation from pain. She has asked her family to pray for her death, but they have refused. Palaggi has been asked whether there are any grounds for prohibiting prayers that she might find rest in death.

In a long and complicated argument, the details of which need not be restated here, Palaggi ruled that, while family members (being possibly motivated by less than honorable motives) may not pray for her death, others may do so. In the course of reaching this conclusion, Palaggi quoted a number of earlier sources, including the previously quoted statement of Rabbenu Nissim (on *Nedarim* 40a). Thus, Palaggi reaffirmed the earlier view that active prayer for the death of a terminal patient in pain, whose life has become a self-burden, is both permissible and even desirable. It is noteworthy that Palaggi did not even question the woman's right to pray for death on her own behalf.

To be sure, Palaggi did not explicitly advocate active euthanasia in the sense of performing concrete medical or other intervention other than prayer to accelerate the death of a terminal patient in agony. Nevertheless, Palaggi did establish the viability of an attitude that would recommend active euthanasia in particular instances. And, while it was not his explicit intention to do so, his view might be extended a step further to serve as the basis for advocating active euthanasia in cases similar to that of the woman described in his responsum.

A further basis for a possible justification for active euthanasia from classical Jewish sources may be posited by combining related precedent with a form of argument characteristic of Jewish legal discourse. The precedent is the only Talmudic text in which the term *euthanasia*—an "easy," "good," or "quick" death—occurs (Hebrew: *mita yafa*). The form of argument is the inference *a fortiori* (Hebrew: *kal va-homer*, literally: "the light and the weighty").

The term *mita yafa* is used in the course of Talmudic discussion concerning the execution of criminals convicted of capital offenses. In one text, the verse "You should love your neighbor as yourself" (Leviticus 19:18) is interpreted to mean that the criminal is to be given a *mita yafa*; the pain usually inflicted by the various types of death sentences is to be reduced both in time and in degree by administering a pain-killing drug (*Sanhedrin* 45a, 52a; *Baba Kamma* 51a; *Pesahim* 25a). The terminal patient is compared by the Talmud to a criminal condemned to the death penalty, in that his or her case is hopeless (*Arakhin* 6b). From this equation one might argue that the terminal patient ought to be given at least the same consideration as a criminal about to be executed for having committed a capital offense.

According to some halakhic authorities, when conventional therapies have been exhausted, experimental therapy may be introduced by a competent physician. This approach is sanctioned even if death were to result from such experimental therapy, especially where a terminal patient is involved. Hence, as long as even the most remote possibility of remission exists, hazardous therapy, even life-threatening therapy, may be employed. Employing such therapy, though it is known in advance that it might immediately end the patient's life, would be a form of active euthanasia that would not be proscribed by Jewish law.

The prohibition against placing oneself in danger is also set aside in cases in which a medical or surgical procedure potentially endangers the life of a patient whose life is not clearly endangered by his or her medical condition. Specifically, in a case in which the purpose of the procedure is specifically aimed at reducing or at eliminating substantial pain, such a procedure is permitted, despite its potential threat to the life of the patient.

Not only may one make a case for active euthanasia in Jewish law, one may also argue that in certain circumstances the killer is not to be considered a murderer. In order to consider an act as murder, according to Jewish law, two conditions must be satisfied: premeditation and malice (see Exodus 21:14). Rabbinic literature specifically exonerates a physician who kills his patient, even if he acted with willfulness, when malice is not also present. Though the medieval codes link premeditation with malice, there is no logical or psychological reason to do so. The rabbinic precedent may stand on its own (*Mekhilta*, "Mishpatim," 4; Rashi to Exodus 21:14). Thus, under certain circumstances, according to this "minority" view, the physician may be legally (but not necessarily morally) blameless for practicing active euthanasia.

One specific case in which active euthanasia by patient, agent, or physician may be more justifiable than others, according to the literature, would be that in which the patient is afflicted with a terminal disease, such as cancer.

Talmudic law distinguishes between *goses*, that is, one terminally ill, and *terefah* (literally, "torn"), that is, one terminally ill as the result of irreparable organic damage. Apparently, in the former case, recovery is at least theoretically possible, whereas in the latter case, recovery is altogether impossible. One who kills a *goses* is considered a murderer by the Talmud and the codes. But one who kills a *terefah* may not be guilty of murder (*Sanhedrin* 78a; *Mishneh Torah*—*Damages*—"Laws of Murderers" 2:8).

Though the "majority" view found in classical and contemporary Jewish literature condemns active euthanasia, the present discussion and the sources noted therein indicate the viability and the defensibility of a "minority" view supporting voluntary euthanasia when the primary motive is to alleviate pain and suffering among the terminally ill. To be sure, Judaism enjoins us to "Choose Life" (Deut. 30:19), but Judaism also recognizes that "there is a time to die" (Eccles. 3:2). In each case in which the problem of euthanasia presents itself, each person involved must decide which verse applies and how the fulfillment of that verse may best be implemented.

REFERENCES

Cohn, Haim H. "Homicide." *Encyclopedia Judaica*.
Greenwald, Leopold, *Kol Bo Al-Aveilut*, New York: Moriah, 1947.
Haas, Peter J. "Toward a Semiotic Study of Jewish Moral Discourse: The Case of Responsa." *Semeia* 34 (1985).
Jakobovits, Immanuel. *Jewish Medical Ethics*. New York: Bloch. 1959.
Reines, Charles W. "The Jewish Attitude Toward Suicide." *Judaism* 10 (1961).
Rosner, Fred, and J. David Bleich, eds. *Jewish Bioethics*. New York: Hebrew Publishing Co., 1969.

Rosner, Fred, and Moses Feinstein. "Treatment of the Terminally Ill." *Judaism* 37 (1988).
Sinclair, Daniel. *Tradition and the Biological Revolution.* Edinburgh: Edinburgh University Press, 1989.

9

Kevorkianism—Judaic and Logotherapeutic Reactions

REUVEN P. BULKA, PH.D.

The issue of doctor assisted suicide, called Kevorkianism, is herein examined. The Judaic attitude to suicide is presented in concise form, as is the Judaic understanding of the doctor's mandate. This leaves no room for equivocation on the Judaic view of Kevorkianism. The secular system known as logotherapy, founded by Viktor Frankl, is then presented relative to this issue, and in the background of logotherapeutic discussion on the matters of life's meaning, suffering, death, euthanasia and suicide.

The issue of doctor assisted suicide presently occupies center stage in North America. In the United States, Dr. Jack Kevorkian, sometimes ingloriously called Dr. Death, gained fame and notoriety via his intervening to snuff out the lives of people who asked to be relieved of their suffering.

Under threat of prosecution, Kevorkian agreed to stop administering his suicide formula, but he continued to campaign for legalizing doctor assisted suicide. And the agreement notwithstanding, it did not take too long for Kevorkian to return to his actually helping in the suicides of patients.

In his campaign to legalize doctor assisted suicide, this doctor has articulated an approach to medicine which may be called Kevorkianism.

In Canada, the relatively recent case of Sue Rodriguez was a headline grabber. She carried her request for legal doctor assisted suicide all the way to the Supreme Court of Canada, where she lost her battle by one vote. But she won the war, because a few months later, a doctor who has still, after years, not been identified, quietly helped Sue Rodriguez end her life and the crippling pain of ALS, known to most as Lou Gehrig's disease.

This is an issue that will not go away. It is a gut-wrenching issue, the issue of why suffer, why live, why not suicide? And the role of doctors in this is another important facet of the debate. What is the physician's mandate, and how far does it extend?

These two concerns, suicide and the role of doctors, are herein approached from two perspectives, the Judaic and the logotherapeutic. Judaism has bequeathed to the world a profound appreciation of medical practice, sound medical theory and insight, and a complete value system surrounding the issue of life's sanctity.

The logotherapy of Viktor Frankl addresses the issues of suffering, death, euthanasia, and suicide, and is therefore quite pertinent to the present debate. In the end, there is hardly a life issue more important than the matter of death, and Kevorkianism is hardly the only alternative.

THE JUDAIC ATTITUDE

The traditional Jewish attitude to suicide begins with a wholesale condemnation of the act. "One who destroys oneself wittingly has no share in the world-to-come" is a popular Jewish saying. Interestingly, Greenwald (1965) as well as many others, point out that there is no Talmudic or Midrashic source for this adage. It is simply a folk-saying. The fact that the folk adopted such a saying undoubtedly had its roots in the tradition itself. The saying is expressive of a negative attitude to suicide.

The suicide is considered guilty of murder, albeit non-prosecutable murder, as killer and victim are the same. Life is seen as a gift from God entrusted to the person, who may not exercise the rights of ownership—to destroy, and instead must exercise the responsibilities of trusteeship.

The Talmud (Baba Kamma, 91b) interprets the scriptural words "And surely your blood of your lives will I require . . ." (Genesis, 9:5) as applying to one who sheds blood by one's own hands. Both the derivation and the law are codified by Maimonides (Mishnah Torah, Laws of the Murderer and Guarding One's Body, 2:3).

The suicide, in some respects, is considered even worse than the homicide. First, the suicide leaves no room for repentance from the act. Second, death, as a sentence from a legal tribunal, serves as a catalyst for Divine forgiveness, a process which is obviated in suicide. The suicide is also seen as radically rejecting the foundations of faith (Tukacinsky, 1960).

Within this perspective, the suicide is more than merely "equated with murder" (Alvarez, 1974, p. 68).

Included in the category of suicide are actions which lead to a person's death through negligence, such as inciting a fight which leads to being killed, or walking a dangerous path, for instance over ice in the winter and then falling into the water (Judah the Pious, 1970, para. 675). These actions are suicidal in outcome if not in intent.

The broadened scope of suicide to include such actions is even more far-reaching than Stengel's insistence on defining the suicidal act as "any deliberate act of self-damage which the person committing the act could not be sure to survive" (1971, pp. 82–83).

Stengel only goes so far as to include deliberate acts of self-damage, whereas the Judaic view would include even negligence. One must answer for negligence, since in negligence one has failed to maintain watchfulness over life, thereby failing to affirm the sanctity of life. The religious perspective extends further than scientific categorization.

In fact, the Rabbis have forbidden many things because of their potential danger to life. Failure to adhere to these prohibitions makes one liable to the punishment of "flogging for rebelling" (Maimonides, Mishnah Torah, Laws of the Murderer and Guarding One's Body, 11:5). The Rabbis, it may be said, tried to prevent even the passive suicide.

There is more in the Rabbinic attitude to suicide than this (Bulka, 1989, pp. 23–39), but the general approach is fully consistent with the Judaic obligation to be life affirming, and to be careful with how life is preserved and guarded.

THE DOCTOR'S MANDATE

Jewish tradition does not grant the physician carte blanche in the healing process. The physician has permission to heal, nothing more.

On the biblical statement alluding to the healing process in duplicate language, i.e.—"and heal, the doctor shall heal" (Exodus, 21:20), the Talmud states that this thereby conveys the authorization by God for physicians to heal.

Presumably, without this authorization, medical intervention would be considered problematic. In retrospect, it is difficult to imagine that God would have enjoined the practice of medicine, specially in light of the host of medically sensitive regulations in the Torah.

The message in this permission granting is most likely that all doctors must realize that their healing mandate comes from God. That mandate is to heal, not to kill. A physician who cannot heal, for whatever reason, including that the illness has advanced far beyond healing, has no right to take life, any more than any individual has the right to take life.

The biblical obligation to restore what someone has lost (Deuteronomy, 22:2), is the basis for the obligation to restore one's health (Talmud, Sanhedrin, 73a). Maimonides, in his Commentary on the Mishnah (Nedarim, 38b), quotes this verse about restoring what was lost, namely health, as the basis for the physician's obligation to heal.

First, the physician is granted permission. Then, permission having been granted, the doctor has the obligation to engage in the "healing" process, to restore health.

Suicide, as previously mentioned, is forbidden according to Jewish law. No one has the right to commit suicide, and by definition, no one has the right to assist others in a forbidden activity such as suicide; i.e., to assist others in carrying out a forbidden activity.

The doctor who so assists not only contravenes fundamental Jewish law, but also renounces the very mandate which allows for the practice of medicine in the first place. That is the limited mandate to heal, not a mandate to kill, or to help in the killing. Jewish law on Kevorkianism is quite clear and straightforward, with no room for equivocation. Kevorkianism is rejected. That comes as little surprise.

But it is worthwhile to further explore the matter, through a secular, meaning-oriented therapeutic system, the logotherapy of Viktor Frankl. Lest one argue that only religion renounces Kevorkianism, the study of logotherapy affords a somewhat more universal perspective on the issue, a perspective which yields a similar conclusion to the matter of doctor assisted suicide.

LOGOTHERAPY ON DEATH

Death, according to Frankl, belongs to the tragic triad of human existence, together with suffering and guilt.

Before analyzing the bearing of death on life, it is necessary to understand the nature of death in Frankl's thinking.

Death, besides being tragic, is also unavoidable. Everyone who lives must eventually die. The reality of imminent end, according to Frankl, is something one can live with. It terrifies only the person with a guilty conscience about his or her life; it frightens only the one who has not lived life to full capability (Frankl, 1967, p. 104).

Death marks the end of a lifetime. It is the paradigm of the irreversible event as well as the fixation of irreversibility, the time when everything becomes inflexible and cannot be changed. One no longer "has" anything; one merely "is" the self (Frankl, 1966, p. 365).

One of, if not the key notion of logotherapy, is that life contains unconditional meaning at all times, up to and including the fact and reality of death. Meaning is something which is never attained, in the sense of having climbed a mountain and reaching the peak. There is always one more challenge, one more meaning to be realized, one more peak. Were this not the case, were we able to attain full meaning, then the period subsequent to that attainment would be bereft of meaning. Life would then lose its unconditional meaningfulness.

Therefore, one can never be content with past achievement, with what has already been achieved. One must never rest on laurels, however laudable, since there are always new challenges, and one can never relax from them (Frankl, 1967, p. 105).

Every moment in life poses its challenge and affords the opportunity to realize values. Ignoring the challenges of the moment means for that moment to have died. That moment is no more, it is irretrievable. There is, then, the death of the human in time, and the death of time in the human. This concept forms the basis of Frankl's theory concerning the past as well as his theory of human guilt.

Besides being the end of a lifetime, death, according to Frankl, is the culmination of life, the final stroke in the picture of the person. Frankl is rigidly opposed to that process which would deny any individual the opportunity to round off life in each one's unique fashion, euthanasia. To die one's own death is to give meaning to life up to and including the very last moment, via the attitude with which one approaches life's terminus. The way a person dies is integral to life and rounds off life to a meaningful totality (Ibid., p. 37).

Death exists in two dimensions, the physical and the spiritual. The physical dimension is shared by humankind equally. The passing of humans in the spiritual dimension contains a personal quality peculiar to each individual. The mercy-killer cuts life off before one's essence, the spirit, has a chance to complete its natural course in conjunction with the body.

Frankl realizes that however we look at death, our perspective is a this-worldly one. What we say about the dead is relative to the living, but is hardly an absolute truth. As far as what death really is, Frankl declares that those who claim they can grasp a person's death are engaging in self-delusion (Ibid., p. 111).

Frankl senses a real possibility that our notion of death may be false, that we see death as akin to falling asleep. In reality, death is more akin to being wakened. This approach will help people appreciate the fact that death is beyond comprehension (Frankl, 1968c, p. 150).

Quite possibly, death may not be the tragedy we think it to be. Like an alarm clock, or a loving hand that awakens us from sleep into our real world, death awakens us to our true reality, yet we do not appreciate this, and are terrified of death (Frankl, 1966, pp. 365–366).

It should be noted that by admitting the incomprehensibility of death, Frankl precludes uncovering the true meaning of death. The meaning of that which is beyond perception cannot be realized. As in the case of suffering, the farthest Frankl can go is to give meaning to death, to make it meaningful in life.

LOGOTHERAPY ON THE MEANING OF DEATH IN LIFE

The process of death, according to Frankl, is not a severed fragment of the human biography. Death is part of life. "Without suffering and death human life cannot be complete" (Frankl, 1968a, p. 106).

The meaning of life includes suffering and dying, privation and death (Ibid., pp. 131–132). The thesis of logotherapy is that one is to live, and die, meaningfully.

So much for the moment of death. What bearing does the inescapability of death have on life itself?

Frankl believes that the fact of death is crucial to life, that only in the face of death is it meaningful to act (Frankl, 1968b, p. 30). If we could live forever, we could postpone all meaningful activity to the endless tomorrow. But the fact of death as absolute end places upon us the imperative not to let any moment die (Frankl, 1967, p. 52).

This concept traces its roots back to Frankl's notion of death as the fixation of irreversibility. Death of the human in time signifies irreversibility of life. Death of time in the human signifies irreversibility of a moment. Concurrently, proper utilization of time signifies a positive irreversibility, for that which has been accomplished remains as reality forever. Everything that is actualized is permanently stored, and remains forever in the most secure existence of "having been" (Frankl, 1968b, pp. 30–31).

Death poses a constant imperative to humans, an imperative which says that each moment, as life itself, is irrepeatable, and must be utilized. Death makes life meaningful. The challenge of life is how to use each moment, which values are to be actualized and which doomed to non-existence (Frankl, 1968a, p. 191).

Frankl's concept of one's past leads to the unavoidable paradox that one's past is one's true future, since the past is what is, and cannot be taken away (Frankl, 1966, pp. 365–366).

A key notion in Frankl's logotherapy is human responsibility. Responsibility and irreversibility are intimately linked together. If what has been done can forever be undone, virtue and vice would disappear in uncertainty, praise and blame would be unrealistic, and education unmanageable. Human beings would be free from the responsibilities which underlie their humanness.

Responsibleness is a responsiveness to the challenges posed by life, challenges which call for undelayed response.

The existence of the human in time Frankl calls temporality. The existence of time in the human Frankl calls singularity. And one's responsibility must be understood in the context of temporality and singularity (Frankl, 1967, p. 52).

This leads to what Frankl considers a fundamental maxim of existential analysis, that the person should "live as if you were living for the second time and had acted as wrongly the first time as you are about to act now" (Ibid.).

Irretrievability of a past moment, singularity, and of a past life, temporality, constitute the basis of human existence, and are the impetus for one's responsibleness to life.

Frankl thus sees death as an ongoing life process, not in the pessimistic sense, but in the positive sense. Just as total death, the death of the human in time, challenges one's life in its totality, so fragmentary death, the death of time in the human, challenges humans in each moment. The sum of these moments constitutes human existence.

The significance of the past, a direct derivative of Frankl's concept of death, has its therapeutic advantages. Frankl speaks of the unhealthy trend in the United States of fear of aging, and its diminished possibility. But the possibilities for the young are not nearly as secure as the achievements, the realities, of older people (Frankl, 1968b, p. 31).

If the fear of death abounds, according to Frankl, in one who has misused life, then fear of aging is found in one who has misused youth. A meaningful youth is the best medicine for old age, just as a meaningful life is the best preparation for death.

This concept of the past has its application in the face of life-stopping tragedy, wherein one can argue that the meaningfulness of love, however short, is preserved forever as a reality (Ibid., p. 32).

Frankl sees the fact of death as an argument against the pleasure principle, for a condemned person would see no value to a full course meal just before dying. Since we are all confronted with death, pleasure cannot be the main motif of life (Frankl, 1967, p. 30).

Frankl elicits infinite meaning from death, but the true meaning of death, or what death means, has not been uncovered.

LOGOTHERAPY ON HUMAN FINITENESS

Frankl, throughout his writings, closely associates death with guilt. He suggests that we must confront our three-tiered finiteness; that we have failed, that we are suffering, and that we will die (Frankl, 1968b, p. 24).

We are guilty because we have failed. We have failed because we are human, finite, imperfect, and never able to complete the life task. It is important to shoulder this burden, and acknowledge one's finiteness (Ibid., 47).

One must always strive. Just as the accomplishments of the past are no excuse for lackadaisicality, being that one is perpetually faced with an infinite, necessarily unfinished task, so the failures of the past constantly gnaw at the person, prodding people to remember the past by changing the present.

Death, besides indicating outer human finiteness, in time, also signifies inner human infiniteness, the human as mortal internally, subject to error, or imperfect. Every individual possesses some internal flaw, which constitutes one's uniqueness as a personal being, making that person different from others (Frankl, 1967, p. 58).

Being different, and hence necessary, makes each life meaningful, since if everyone were the same, by virtue of being perfect, they would be easily replaceable. It is the imperfections that make for uniqueness and inexchangeability (Ibid., p. 56).

It becomes a paradox of life that one strives for that very reality which, were it achieved, would make one replaceable, perhaps redundant. One's finiteness not only includes one's being imperfect, but also precludes the possibility of attaining perfection.

Perfection would leave nothing more to achieve, creating the existential vacuum so harmful to human existence. Perfection is an infinite, that which one strains to but will never reach. However, via understanding that finiteness, one also overcomes it (Frankl, 1968b, p. 86).

It is vital to fully understand the import of one's finiteness, as it is a precondition to progress, while the inability to accept it is characteristic of the neurotic personality (Ibid., 47).

Singularity and uniqueness are the two essentials which provide the imperative for responsibleness, which itself emanates from human finiteness (Frankl, 1967, p. 60).

Both singularity and uniqueness evolve directly from Frankl's concept of death.

Human finiteness and guilt, through abuse of time, establish different criteria for judging life. The meaningful question is not "what" but "how;" not what was accomplished, but how was life lived, how were the singular opportunities that total one's existence used? Life is also not judged by length of years; rather, it is judged by the quality of the life, however short (Ibid., p. 53).

Meaningful existence is a qualitative value. The human is a

finite creature, and can also, unlike animals, control the extent of finite existence by terminating it. One kills the past through lethargy, and the future through suicide (Ibid., pp. 62–63).

Frankl believes suicide can be averted by opening up to people the dynamics of self-transcendence, by pointing to a task to be fulfilled. Having a reason, a "why" for life, one can endure the most unbearable "how" (Frankl, 1968a, p. 127).

Frankl carefully examines the possibility of justifiable suicide. One potentially justified suicide is balance suicide, in which a person draws a balance sheet of life's credits and debits and decides, objectively, to take one's life. Frankl rejects this, questioning the objectivity of such judgment. Further, if in even one case a person will have turned out to be mistaken, this places into question whether suicide is ever justified, since everyone thinks this is the right course, but can be mistaken (Frankl, 1967, p. 40).

The other two possibilities are suicide as sacrifice and suicide as atonement. These are also dismissed as unjustifiable, since often these suicides are rooted in resentment. Frankl therefore concludes that suicide is never ethically justified (Ibid., pp. 40–41).

Frankl compares the suicide to a chess-player who, faced with a new problem, sweeps the pieces off the board. The problem has not been solved, it has been removed. The chess-player has violated the rules of chess. The suicide has violated the rules of life (Ibid., pp. 42–43).

The human, because of the unique ability to commit suicide, says yes to life every moment the person lives meaningfully. One who commits suicide is guilty, in a more extreme way, of the same crime as one who squanders time. Both look to life for something, failing to recognize that life confronts them, seeking to elicit responsibleness to life.

LOGOTHERAPY ON THE AFTERLIFE

Frankl recognizes the importance of future orientation in the life process. One needs a fixed point in the future (Ibid., p. 80).

Death, however, poses a different problem, for if life must eventually stop, what sense is there to all the strivings and sufferings of life? Frankl recognizes this problem, that we begin from nothingness and end in nothingness, thus placing into question life's meaning (Frankl, 1966, p. 361).

Frankl is thus led to the theory, mentioned previously, that one's past is one's true future. What has happened is and cannot be erased, even if it is forgotten. It remains a part of the world, an objective reality independent of subjective memory (Ibid., p. 363).

This approach of Frankl presents a twofold problem. It cannot be denied that what has happened becomes reality, but in the vacuum of total ignorance of past reality, the question is—what value does such reality have? It cannot affect the meaning of life or give it direction, for it remains a dead reality. It exists, but it does not exist meaningfully.

The second difficulty is that humanity is faced not only with the death of individuals and generations, but also with the end of the world. Even conscious reality is terminal by the very nature of the world. The problem is a universal one. If the world and life on earth will ultimately cease entirely, of what worth is the life of each individual? Frankl's personal approach will satisfy only one who does not see the ultimate emptiness of the universe.

Frankl admits that trust in an ultimate meaning is basic to life, that without it humans could not move a limb, could not breathe (Frankl, 1967, pp. 150–151). The fact of death is a reality which undermines the possibility of ultimate being. In death, what was possessed of life is robbed of life. That life has disappeared into nothingness. Projected over the whole of life, the fact of death is translated into the eventual disappearance of humanity.

This dilemma is founded on the view that death is disappearance, that what is comprehended of death is what death really is. Frankl, as previously indicated, rejects this common idea of death. Death is incomprehensible and cannot be viewed as disappearance. Instead, it is absence of manifestation of the person (Frankl, 1967, pp. 111–112).

And what if no one manifests the self anymore, or when no one is around to appreciate past memories?

The problem expresses itself not only in ultimate oblivion but also in existential oblivion. One who is alone, whose virtue or vice will be known to the self only, what drives that person positively? To one who is not religious, it must seem senseless (Joost A.M. Meerloo, quoted by Frankl, 1968c, p. 153).

For the religious person this problem is almost non-existent, since life is seen as a mission and the life task apprehended in the light of Transcendence (Frankl, 1958, p. 87).

The religious person is never alone. Life is a perpetual dialogue. Death is not the end, hopefully only the end of the beginning.

Frankl, trying to grab the best of both worlds, suggests a rational approach to eternity, a super-meaning, conveying the idea of a super-world that is beyond our grasp, much like the human world is beyond the grasp of animals (Frankl, 1967, pp. 25–26).

Frankl admits the possibility that a super-meaning, a meaning beyond the confines of this world, may or may not exist. One can never really know, but can hope or have faith in the meaningfulness of life, at the same time enduring the inability to rationally understand the notion of unconditional meaningfulness (Frankl, 1968a, pp. 187–188).

The human, then, is to complement physical finiteness with rational finiteness. One must admit that there is more to the world than what one perceives. On this intangible rests the impetus for human endeavor.

Frankl's concept of death and its application to life give rise to other problems. A key point of concern is the premium Frankl puts on dying courageously (Ibid., pp. 107–108).

One who accepts fate without flinching is lauded by Frankl as being a hero (Frankl, 1967, p. 93).

The point of death, in Frankl's system, would seem the least likely time for patients to hold their own. What purpose is there in being heroic at this time? Heroism at this time is tantamount to spiritual stagnation, as if to say—fate will not break me. Would it not be far more meaningful to use these last moments to transcend one's self by analyzing the totality of life, attitudinally rejecting the meaningless strivings of life whilst acknowledging honestly the meaningful essence of life?

Would not death be filled with more meaning if the patient met death in trepidation, tormented by failings to the extent that, were the patient to recover miraculously, the person's life would become a more meaningful one? In this way one would become, even in death, a different person than in life, scaling the heights of transcendence in a purposeful encounter. This, by the way, is precisely what unfolds in the *vidui*, the confession one makes when seriously ill.

Even the person who apparently has occupied an entire life

with meaning fulfillment does not hesitate to understand the challenge of death. That person meets death not as a hero, rather as a finite creature who has not reached the limits of potential but strives for the limit even at the last moment. Also, the person whose life has been devoid of meaning retains the ability to transmute life into a meaningful endeavor up to the last moment.

Frankl, to be sure, acknowledges the great potential death has, retroactively, on a heretofore meaningless life; that one can transcend one's past and die in a way that invests one's entire life with meaning (Ibid., p. 85).

It becomes more difficult to comprehend why Frankl does not put a greater stress on the meaning aspect of dying. The human being, according to Frankl, is guilty because of having failed, and has failed because of being a finite creature. No one can be sure of having found the right meaning and lived meaningfully. Frankl should thus be expected to emphasize how meaningful dying can be, but instead he seems to emphasize the value of courage.

In speaking of the incomprehensibility of death, Frankl asserts that death should not be compared with sleep but with being awakened. If death is being wakened, this implies a Waker, or a Being transcending the human world who controls the fate of the living and the dead.

Frankl deplores suicide. He insists there is no legitimate excuse for it. One is obligated to obey the rules of life; not to win at any cost, but never to give up the fight (Ibid., p. 43).

However, the question still remains—Why not suicide? If a person is living a miserable existence, why should that person not terminate it? Who set up the rules to which the unfortunate must adhere? If one is ruler of one's self, and possesses the power to commit suicide, why can one not make use of it?

The suicide usually sees life as being a failure. This judgment is motivated by a quantitative approach to human existence. The potential suicide is frustrated either because of not having given or because of not having received. Frankl tries to counter this attitude by insisting that life is not measured by social success, but by how one elicits meaning even from hopeless situations, via the attitude one takes even in a hopeless circumstance (Frankl, 1967, pp. 26–27). One's life is judged by what one makes of one's predicament.

Frankl contends that human responsibility springs from one's singularity and uniqueness. The question of to whom one is responsible Frankl leaves open.

However, it is difficult to conceive of true responsibility in a secular system. If one's responsibility springs from uniqueness and singularity, where do this uniqueness and singularity spring from?

Frankl admits the advantages of a religious person, who can function confidently even in apparent oblivion. There is no oblivion for the religious person. The religious person proceeds on the course of life through all contingencies, even in tragedy and despair. Does this not establish belief in God as necessary for human existence? Meaning is hallowed by Frankl for it gives thrust to the human endeavor through all conditions and circumstances. Yet Frankl himself admits that certain situations, lacking faith, suspend the meaningfulness of life, rendering suspect the insistence on unconditional meaning.

Perhaps the most acute problem in Frankl's system is the concept of afterlife. Recognizing that a transient world threatens the basis of life, but unwilling to make logotherapy a purely religious system, Frankl proposes two alternatives. For the religious person he offers a providential afterlife, for the non-religious he offers super-meaning (Frankl, 1967, pp. 26–27).

Ultimately, the logotherapeutic system stands or falls depending on its concept of afterlife. However, speaking of afterlife as a metaphysical concept is inadequate. It is logical to assume that an evolutionary world born by accident should end just as haphazardly. In fact, it is illogical to assume otherwise. Ultimate meaning can contain substance only in terms of original design, or purposeful creation, by a Creator.

Frankl's concept of super-meaning may even be self-defeating. An ape used to develop a serum for polio does not understand the meaning of its suffering. The human being may be in the same predicament, not knowing that there may be a world beyond the human world, wherein resides the answer to the question of human suffering (Frankl, 1968a, p. 187).

In carrying this argument to its conclusion, the human, like the animal, will never know the meaning of life, for this exists in a higher sphere. Also, a higher development stage would put the human on relative par with present-day beasts. The human would be reduced to a tool of the next order, an entity destined to serve a higher species. If this is super-meaning, it destroys whatever trust humans have in their own existence.

As in the case of suffering, Frankl, by insisting that logotherapy be available to everyone, detracts from the meaning of death in life. The meaning of death in the form of afterlife is to find itself in another world or another species. This divests death of a this-worldly meaning.

But perhaps we are being unfair, and too analytic in dissecting Frankl's ape analogy. The analogy is merely to suggest that other dimensions of understanding exist, dimensions that are not beyond human comprehension, yet dimensions that are not forthcoming in immediate human experience.

With all that logotherapy seems to point toward a religious, or spiritual ethos, it still tries to maintain an openness to everyone, which is in itself a spiritual and noble desire. But logotherapy is clear and unyielding in enunciating the critical importance of meaning. Frankl long ago accurately pinpointed the lack of meaning as endemic to North America, and warned of the fallout from this meaning crisis. Drugs, delinquency, crime, violence, abuse, are all offshoots of the lack of meaning. And the debate about ending life in itself captures the essence of the problem.

In a world which has no meaning, why suffer? To that question there is no answer. But to the hypothesis that life has no meaning, there is a retort, an eloquent logotherapeutic retort, a retort which precludes the question. And it is unfortunately a retort that escapes the proponents of Kevorkianism.

REFERENCES

Alvarez, A. (1974). *The savage god: A study of suicide.* Middlesex, England: Penguin Books.
Babylonian Talmud (20 vols.). New York: M.P. Press, 1964.
Bulka, R. (1989). *Individual, family, community: Judeo-psychological perspectives.* Oakville, Ontario: Mosaic Press.
Frankl, V. E. (1958). "The will to meaning." *Journal of Pastoral Care,* 12, 82–88.
Frankl, V. E. (1966). "Time and responsibility." *Existential Psychiatry,* 1, 361–366.
Frankl, V. E. (1967). *The Doctor and the soul: From psychotherapy to logotherapy.* New York: Bantam Books.

Frankl, V. E. (1968a). *Man's search for meaning: An introduction to logotherapy*. New York: Washington Square Press.
Frankl, V. E. (1968b). *Psychotherapy and existentialism: Selected papers on logotherapy*. New York: Simon and Schuster.
Frankl, V. E. (1968c). *The will to meaning: Foundations and applications of logotherapy*. New York: The New American Library.
Greenwald, Y. (1965). *Kol bo on mourning*. New York: Feldheim.
The Holy Scriptures (3 vols.). Philadelphia: Jewish Publication Society, 1982.
Judah the Pious (1970). *Sefer Hasidim*. Jerusalem: Mosad HaRav Kuk.
Maimonides, M. *Mishnah Torah* (6 vols.). New York: M.P. Press, 1962.
Stengel, E. (1971). *Suicide and attempted suicide*. Middlesex, England: Penguin Books.
The Talmud (18 vols.). I. Epstein (ed.). London: Soncino Press, 1961.
Tukacinsky, Y. (1960). *Gesher HaHayyim* (Vol. 1). Jerusalem: Private Printing.

10

Dr. Kevorkian and the Rabbis, Detroit, 1996

A Brief Historical Note

MATTHEW B. SCHWARTZ, PH.D.

As Dr. Jack Kevorkian's home town, Detroit has been the scene of many of the doctor's activities and of his court trials as well. The Jewish community of Detroit produced an exchange of opinions in the early months of 1996, prompted by Dr. Kevorkian's trial in Oakland County for two of his assisted suicides. In early February, the local Council of Orthodox Rabbis issued a statement explaining the halachic prohibition on suicide. The statement was reported on local news programs.

Geoffrey Feiger, Dr. Kevorkian's attorney, reacted by calling the rabbis "religious fanatics" and "Nazis." Many people think that Feiger is Jewish. In fact, his father is Jewish, though his mother is not, and Feiger attended afternoon Hebrew school for a time as a child. (Teachers remember him as a difficult student.) However, Feiger does not consider himself Jewish nor does the *halacha*.

The story goes on. Local newspaper editorials criticized Feiger's attack on the rabbis, and a similar attack on several Catholic judges. A local Talmudic scholar, who prefers anonymity, a man of considerable knowledge who is no supporter of Kevorkian, sent a lengthy, scholarly letter to the Council of Orthodox Rabbis citing several obscure sources in rabbinic literature that supported a more lenient stance on suicide than the Council's statement. The letter was private, very respectful, and intended as theoretical scholarship, not as a halachic pronouncement. Rabbi Chaskel Grubner, a senior member of the Council, thanked the letter writer in a personal note, expressing his appreciation of the scholarship involved and reiterating that it did not really change the standard position advocated in the Jewish law codes.

Enter Jack Goldman, a liberal Orthodox rabbi, who operates the local Metropolitan Kashruth Council of Michigan and is a long time critic of the Council. Goldman wrote a letter to the *Detroit News*, February 29, in which he argued that under certain circumstances "suicide would not be reprehensible in the eyes of the Jewish law," and that if a person suffers "excrutiating pain and anguish . . . and takes his life, this is a permissible suicide."

On March 6, the paper carried a response from Rabbi Elimelech Silberberg of the Council. Jewish law, he wrote, forbids hastening a person's death. One's body and life are not his to do with as he wishes but are entrusted to him by his Creator. Goldman's assertion, added Silberberg, that the Bible and Talmud do not specifically prohibit suicide is incorrect. "Instead of supporting medicine, we must expend greater resources to develop new ways to mitigate pain."

Two days earlier, the 9th Circuit Court of Appeals had overruled Washington State's ban on assisted suicide. On March 8, an Oakland County, Michigan, jury acquitted Kevorkian on two charges of assisted suicide. Feiger had argued unsuccessfully that the Court of Appeals decision had effectively nullified all laws in the United States prohibiting assisted suicide for mentally competent adults who were terminally ill. Most of the jurors claimed that the Michigan law was unclear, confusing the issue of intent to cause death versus intent to cause pain.

The foreman of the Michigan jury was Bishop Donald Ott, supervisor of Michigan's United Methodists. When he was selected for the jury, he stated his "belief that there should reside with the individual the right to determine the end of life" but maintained that this belief would not affect his vote in the Kevorkian case. Cardinal Adam Maida of Detroit condemned the verdict, stating that "assisted suicide blurs the fundamental moral distinction between withdrawal of treatment from those who are terminally ill and active intervention to take a human life."

Even as this volume goes to press, new chapters in this story are being written.

REFERENCES

Detroit Free Press, March 9, 1996.
Detroit News, February 29, 1996, and March 6, 1996.

11

Euthanasia and Physician-Assisted Suicide in America Today: Whither Are We Going?

JOSEPH RICHMAN, PH.D.

This paper compares respective position papers on euthanasia and assisted suicide (EAS), from the American Association of Suicidology (AAS) and the New York State Task Force on Life and the Law (NYS). Both papers covered similar issues, but arrived at different conclusions. The AAS took no position, while NYS came out firmly against legalization. Euthanasia and physician assisted suicide is a movement that is gaining momentum. I examined the issues in terms of my own clinical experience, which turned me from a supporter to an opponent of rational suicide and euthanasia.

Euthanasia and physician assisted suicide have been defended as compassionate and rational procedures for those who are suffering, disabled, or dying, while their opponents are heartless and insensitive. In contrast, euthanasia and physician assisted suicide have been opposed as based upon a lack of knowledge and an avoidance of alternative measures, while their supporters are unethical and harbor secret personal motives.

The topic is a controversial and volatile one, as typified by the fate of the Oregon State Physician Assisted Suicide law. Like the suicidal state itself, the Oregon legislation has undergone a symbolic death and rebirth. It was passed following a referendum, declared dead and unconstitutional by one court and recently re-declared alive and constitutional by another.

What would be a rational response to both the opponents and supporters of euthanasia and assisted suicide (EAS)? When intellectuals and politicians are faced with a controversial topic they form a committee. Their discussions are sometimes used to find a resolution and sometimes to prevent a resolution. Recall the riddle, "What is a camel?" the answer is, "A horse made by a committee." I shall compare two committees, one of which made a horse and the other came too close to a camel. The reports are from a New York State group and The American Association of Suicidology.

In 1994 the New York State Task Force on Life and the Law (NYS) published *When death is sought. Assisted suicide and euthanasia in the medical context*. The committee was organized by the then governor Mario Cuomo to study the question of euthanasia and physician assisted suicide (EAS). The members of the committee consisted of eminent authorities who represented a balance of supporters and opponents.

Also in 1994 the American Association of Suicidology (AAS) organized a similar committee composed of members of the Association who represented both sides of the issue and who submitted their report.

I compared the NYS and AAS reports in terms of their implications for medical and psychosocial practice in general and the AAS in particular. The following outline summarizes the issues raised by one or both committee reports:

1. American medicine has failed to treat pain adequately.
2. American medicine has failed to treat depression adequately.
3. The terminally ill is not a high-risk group for suicide compared, say, to major depressive disorders, especially when pain and depression are treated adequately.
4. The forecasting of the time of death for the terminally ill is fraught with uncertainty, and the predictions of the physicians are frequently inaccurate.
5. Social bias against the poor, the elderly, and certain minority groups may make them targets for euthanasia and physician assisted suicide.
6. The American medical system is unsuitable for legalized euthanasia. "Our health care system is fragmented and economically driven." "The relationships between patients and physicians has never been more impersonal." [including] ". . . The absence of a close, long-lasting relationship between the patient and the physician," and the temptation to reduce medical costs through euthanasia and physician assisted suicide (All from the AAS report).

7. There is the danger of the slippery slope, with euthanasia and physician assisted suicide expanded to cover the disabled, the psychiatrically ill, and other groups. (An example is the recently proposed assisted suicide law in Massachusetts that expands the type of patients who would be eligible to include chronic disabilities and other "incurable" conditions. People in the same condition as Christopher Reeve but without his family, social, and medical support would become very vulnerable.) What begins as a voluntary procedure can become obligatory. Both committees noted that thousands of patients in Holland are put to death by doctors without their consent.
8. Instead of legalized suicide, a comprehensive approach is recommended for the terminally ill, which, in addition to pain and depression management and palliative care, includes psychosocial components and help for families who are emotionally burdened and financially drained.
9. Our knowledge is insufficient. For example, some people who want to commit suicide may be depressed and in pain, but the suicidal wish may remain after the pain and depression are treated.
10. There are nonmedical reasons for suicide. (That is presented in the AAS report as a reason for not taking a position.)
11. There are conflicts between society and "issues of individual liberty" (the AAS report).

The AAS committee achieved consensus on two issues:

1. "Involuntary euthanasia can never be condoned," and
2. "Intolerable, prolonged suffering of persons *in extremis* should never be insisted upon against their wishes."

Both reports covered similar issues and background data, but their conclusions differed. Despite the differences in the viewpoints of their members, the New York committee declared, "we unanimously recommend that New York laws prohibiting assisted suicide and euthanasia should not be changed" (p. vii).

The AAS committee recommended "that the American Association of Suicidology take no position on physician assisted suicide or euthanasia. Further, we do not recommend the support of legislation for or against, any of these matters . . . much research is needed to answer many important questions before the Association might properly take positions on these problems" (p. 1).

The committee was inconsistent. For example, to my knowledge, none of the members on the AAS committee ever recommended holding back support for living will legislation or "do not resuscitate" orders until research was conducted.

The AAS committee added that "what you have before you is not a position paper." However, it seems to this reader that not taking a position is a position. Some of the writing was unclear. For example, was the conclusion of the committee not to take a position without more study a unanimous one? Was the consensus against involuntary euthanasia and intolerable suffering unanimous? There is too much use of the editorial we such as, "We do believe that more study is needed," but who are or is "we"?

COMMENTS

Particularly striking was the contrast between the views of the NYS and AAS reports on the value of research to date. For example, the New York report states: "In the course of their research, many Task Force members were particularly struck by the degree to which requests for suicide assistance by terminally ill patients are correlated with clinical depression or unmanaged pain, both of which can ordinarily be treated effectively with current medical techniques. As a society we can do far more to benefit these patients by improving pain relief and palliative care than by changing the law to make it easier to commit suicide or to obtain a lethal injection" (p. ix).

The AAS report agreed that "the assessment and treatment of depression in the seriously physically ill can be taught and the treatment is usually effective" (p. 18). However, the report questioned whether depression always impairs judgment to make a rational choice to end one's life. In addition, depression may sometimes be mistakenly diagnosed, and "On that basis the request for assistance in dying might be denied (p. 19) . . . We need further research, therefore, if we are to understand how depression and its associated affective states (e.g., hopelessness) influence decision making in the face of terminal illness" (p. 21).

Both the NYS and AAS reports agree that pain is associated

with the request for euthanasia and assisted suicide. AAS noted that "physicians in general tend to underestimate the analgesic needs of critically ill patients." NYS concluded that more effective medical teaching and treatment was needed rather than legalized EAS. In contrast the AAS report objects that there was no data on how many patients whose pain was managed better might still choose euthanasia and physician assisted suicide.

The NYS group emphasized the degree to which the request for suicide was precipitated by poorly managed pain as well as depression. The AAS report also noted on p. 20 that when patients requested suicide because of pain, they changed their minds when the pain was treated. The conclusion that additional research was needed must have followed from their own preconceived attitude, not from the data that they themselves reported.

As for depression, the AAS report argued on p. 21 that we cannot exactly determine how much depression enters into the decision for suicide. The authors should have read Kubler Ross's (1969) pioneering work on death and dying, as well as the effective treatment of depression reported in more recent studies. It is not necessary to obsess over whether or not a depressed person's decision to die is related to the depression, but instead to see to it that the depression is treated by a competent therapist.

The committee also argued that "health care providers require more extensive training in the treatment of depression in the terminally ill." I agree with that, as does everyone else I know. However, the committee concludes that "research has yet to be conducted that supplies the knowledge on which that training should be based" (pp. 22–23).

I fear that my friends and colleagues on the AAS committee are not aware of the huge amount of excellent research that has been conducted throughout the country, sponsored by the United States National Institute of Mental Health, comparing the results of cognitive behavior therapy, interpersonal psychotherapy, and drug therapy, and their interactions (National Institute of Mental Health, 1991). The consistent findings were of the positive results of treatment for both older and younger patients with a major depressive disorder.

The connection between the recommendation for more research (which is like being in favor of motherhood and apple pie) and the statement that any position must await more research sounds absurd. The additional recommendations for a continuing committee and educational programs, "to promote the study, development, teaching, and availability of good palliative care," are beyond reproach. The only problem is that they are irrelevant to taking a position.

In some ways, the AAS paper is more optimistic than the NYS report. For example, both groups agree that social bias can make certain groups unfair targets for EAS. The NYS group saw that as one further argument against legalizing euthanasia. The AAS contingent was more hopeful, expressing a great faith in our legal system. Their report said that legislation can correct the bias against the poor, the elderly, and other groups. (They quoted no research in favor of that belief.)

Illustrative examples were vastly more plentiful in the NYS report. The AAS gave seven examples to illustrate euthanasia, suicide, and assisted suicide. Inexplicably, two of the examples were apparently of the same patients, with different endings of how the physician assisted in the death. None of the examples included people who had overcome or found alternate means of dealing with their condition and made the decision to live, often with the intervention of doctors and relatives to make living, genuine living, more possible. NYS also contained many examples of situations in which physician assisted suicide was requested. However, examples of alternatives were also included.

For example, the AAS report described how a 35-year-old musician with ALS was given a lethal injection of barbiturates at her request and with the consent of her family. (In a second version, the physician discontinued the tube feedings.)

The NYS report quoted a journalist, also with ALS, who wanted to end her life when she became unable to speak. However, her husband devised a computer she could operate by using her neck muscles. The patient's emotional state improved dramatically. "Rather than being bound by despair," she wrote, "I look forward to living each day, sharing laughter and joy with my husband, family, friends, and wonderful caretakers." These examples seem to represent two approaches to people while they are alive, one to improve the quality of life; the other to end that life when the quality is unsatisfactory.

The Oregon law legalizing physician assisted suicide has been held up as a model. I greatly fear that it will be used to prevent the proper treatment of the terminally ill, as well as the disabled and despairing, who will probably be included, as the idea of ending lives by physicians becomes accepted. In the Oregon law, alternatives to suicide are disregarded; suicidal people are dichotomized into the mentally ill and incompetent and the mentally well and rational. The rational are allowed to die, with the help of the doctor, while the mentally ill are not—not yet.

Evidently, there are no alternatives in Oregon. The attitude expressed in the Oregon law was reminiscent of the rigid thinking of suicidal people, which has been described at "tunnel vision." A prominent feature of the seriously suicidal state is the belief that there is no alternative, that suicide is the *only* solution.

In the face of tunnel vision, the presentation or discussion of alternatives has been found to be markedly therapeutic, for example by Beck and his colleagues (1979) in their cognitive behavior therapy with depressed and suicidal patients. Considering such findings, the Oregon law might at least have recommended counseling for the suicidal terminally ill and their families.

The Oregon law did legislate "counseling." Counseling to me means a form of psychotherapy, or some kind of advice, guidance, and presentation of information. Unfortunately, in the Oregon law, counseling means only to determine if a person requesting suicide is rational or not, period.

Supporters of euthanasia and assisted suicide often accuse their critics of forcing people to exist in a state of unbearable pain, whereas euthanasia and assisted suicide would allow them a peaceful relief. It is true that suicide is seen as a solution and an escape for people in despair and suffering, especially when they are in a state of tunnel vision, and not able to realize there are alternatives. I do not believe that a defense should be taken away without offering something in return.

The NYS committee recognized that principle. It recommended treatment of pain and depression, but in addition, counseling (real counseling) with patients and relatives, and at least by implication, major changes in our health system. In addition, they agreed that decisions for those who continue to suffer be left between the patient and the doctor. This more comprehensive approach of NYS was a welcome step in the right direction. The AAS, with the Oregon law before the committee as a model, is to be faulted for not including a wider discussion of psychological approaches for pain and depression as well as for despair, hopelessness, interpersonal conflict, and unresolved family matters.

As already noted, research has found cognitive behavior therapy to be a valuable form of therapy with the depressed of all ages. That has also been demonstrated for interpersonal therapy, dynamic therapy, and pharmacotherapy. There is both clinical and research evidence that in addition to reducing pain and depression and providing effective palliative care, a comprehensive biopsychosocial approach is desirable. It brings the individual human organism's ability to cope and adapt, combined with the healing influence of family and social support, acceptance, and integration, into the center of the treatment arena. Psychotherapy for the terminally ill who are suicidal, and counseling and other help for relatives and loved ones should be offered more frequently (see Richman, 1995). It is not that we need more research but that we need more dedication by those who believe that medical and psychological health care can be provided until the very last moment.

Finally, these two reports create a challenge to all the health and service professions. What is our response and responsibility toward terminally ill patients and others who are suffering greatly? Does our responsibility include assisting in their deaths when it is desired by the patient? Does it include devoting our energies toward alleviating pain and suffering and a greater use of psychotherapy for these patients and families? Is it at least as important to study those who do not request assisted suicide and why they do not? These questions cannot be discussed, and certainly not answered, outside of the value systems of the participants.

A PERSONAL TESTAMENT

My professional work with suicidal patients has shaped my personal attitudes toward euthanasia and assisted suicide. The major barrier to the understanding and treatment of suicide has been the mysterious silence that surrounds the topic. As a result, contradictory myths abound. Many people believe that if someone talks about suicide that he or she will not do it. On the other hand, they also believe that to ask a person if he or she is suicidal will precipitate the act.

Both myths are untrue. Open talk could be a major step in reducing the taboo, dispelling false beliefs, and preventing some suicides. I thought that all supporters of euthanasia held the same view, until I learned from an impeccable source, Derek Humphry, that I was mistaken.

I was invited to debate Mr. Humphry, then president of the Hemlock Society, on the topic of euthanasia and rational suicide. In my presentation I thanked the Hemlock Society for helping people to speak more freely about suicide. A dialogue between supporters and opponents of euthanasia would contribute to our understanding. Open discussions would decrease the taboo which has kept many people in despair from obtaining help, and encourage suicidal people to speak more freely about their suicidal state. More people could be relieved of their suicidal despair. After all, suicide was based to a great extent upon problems in living and the false belief that there was no solution.

Mr. Humphry was displeased and revealed that his aim was anything but to *prevent* suicide. He was categorically opposed to the view that people who want or need treatment for their suicidal state are basically like other people. On the contrary, he proposed even more stringent barriers between us and them. *Us* includes rational suicides. *Them* are the disturbed, sick suicidal people who are mentally ill while *us* are the healthy, rational suicidal ones. *Us* are so rational that treatment is anathema. As he expressed it, rational suicidal people "would not go near a psychiatrist." (He meant that as a compliment, illustrating how "normal" they were.) He has been extremely influential with the general public, and his divisive view is one that has found acceptance.

The proponents of euthanasia need to be reminded that dying does not mean being dead, that the quality of life can be improved, and participation in living can take place even in the last days. That point is made in the story of Mr. Jones who was lying in bed, very ill, when he smelled some delicious food his wife was cooking. His mouth watered. He called to his daughter and said, "Could you ask mother if I could have a plate of that delicious meat?" The daughter left and returned shortly. "Mom says you can't have it. We're saving it for the wake."

As a metaphor the joke is an all-too-accurate depiction of how some terminally ill people are treated. The point is that life continues until it is over, but how it is lived depends upon society and other people. There is a tendency, especially among those who are not able to deal with illness and death, to treat a terminally person as if already dead. That particularly includes the supporters of euthanasia and assisted suicide. Therefore their recommended "treatment" for the dying is death.

Mr. Humphry is a polarizing influence, but I subsequently found that the topic of euthanasia generally tends to be polarizing. I have been on both sides of the argument. Euthanasia seemed sensible to me for people in the throes of intractable pain, suffering, and despair. However, the reasons given for euthanasia by its supporters are the same reasons that have made me an opponent. The change occurred because of my experiences with patients in intractable pain, suffering, and despair. These turned out to be meaningful communications, not senseless events.

In 1965 I began working in the psychiatric emergency room of Jacobi Hospital in the Bronx. Most patients were accompanied by a relative or close friend, which, in and of itself, is an important message about the nature of our work. We must pay more attention to the interpersonal and family components of emotional distress. At that time, however, the evaluation was an individual one, where the relatives were advised of the disposition, but took no part.

One of my first patients was a 59-year-old man in a wheelchair with his arms and legs bandaged because of self inflicted wounds. He reported the presence of many distressing ailments, including an inoperable tumor of the spine that kept him in constant pain and a combination of ailments that included but were not limited to diabetes and arthritis. He finally decided that he did not want to continue living this way and would do away with himself.

I sympathized with the patient and agreed with his decision. He was also severely depressed and I arranged for his hospitalization on the psychiatric service. I called in his son, who had been waiting patiently, to inform him of my decision. His son was eager to talk, and presented a very different picture. He described his father as a tyrant who controlled his wife and three children through his symptoms. He refused to allow their friends into the house, and insisted that everyone be at his beck and call. On this particular day, there had been an enormous family quarrel, at the height of which his wife and children all walked out, leaving him in a state of impotent rage. At that point he picked up a knife and slashed his arms and legs.

My experience has subsequently confirmed that pain and suffering were symptoms to be understood and treated. They were rarely sufficient reasons for a poor quality of life and certainly not in and of themselves a basis for ending a life prematurely. I also began my pioneering work on family therapy for suicidal people (Richman, 1986).

My interview with that unfortunate gentleman marked the beginning of 30 years of intensive clinical work with the suicidal. Many patients were rational but both the reason and the emotions are always part of one organism. Of the hundreds of suicidal patients I have seen, the majority were depressed, many were physically ill, and all were involved with problems in living, even those who were terminally ill. Almost all were capable of making rational choices. They were proof of how wrong Derek Humphry was in his statement that the suicidal are different. Suicidal people may not be like Derek Humphry, but they are like me, and I am not suicidal.

A caring attitude combined with a sense of humor can be on the side of life and survival and bring people closer together (Richman, 1995a). An example is found in "A Death of One's Own," by Gerda Lerner (1978), a memoir of the struggles of her husband Carl and the entire family to cope with his brain tumor. When Carl was scheduled to undergo brain surgery, the doctor told him the following story:

A man went to a bar and asked for the usual. The bartender brought him a double martini. The man gulped it down and asked for another. Same routine. After the third round he heaved a deep sigh.
"Feeling better?" the bartender asked. The man nodded. "Had a hard day? How's the brain surgery going, Doc?"
"Not bad," the man said.

Mrs. Lerner was at first upset at the doctor for telling such a joke at such a time. "But Carl was laughing uproariously with real enjoyment," she reported, "and before I knew it I was laughing too . . . In the months to come we would increasingly find sentimentality, pity, or a tragic stance unbearable and ludicrous. We had without knowing, shaped our attitude that day" (1978, p. 28). Can there be a more eloquent statement of the healing power of shared humor and laughter?

The essential factor was the willingness of the doctor through the joke to acknowledge that he was human and that doctors can also be under stress. That brought everyone closer together. How one faces the end of life depends upon many factors, including the presence of a sense of humor that is on the side of life and survival (Richman, 1989).

The education of the public about the availability of alternatives is an area that needs more attention and study. I recently heard a woman on a radio call-in show. She was 89 years old, very depressed, very lonely, and in favor of assisted suicide. The host of the show was very upset and disagreed with the caller. However, all he could tell her was, "You shouldn't think that way."

I have treated many elderly men and women in a suicidal despair, and have written about the successful results achieved by many therapists (Richman, 1993). The response, "Don't think that way," is not a helpful one. Such examples illustrate the need for the public and the news media to understand and be better informed about depression, despair, and hopeless in the elderly. That condition represents what Erik Erikson (1950) called a state of "disgust and despair" in those faced with the end of life.

Loneliness is endemic in the elderly, and it must be addressed. Loneliness is bad enough, but for those who are suicidal, the unconscious meaning is of being rejected and abandoned by the entire universe. My goal is to transform disgust and despair into integrity, acceptance, and cohesion. It can be done, even in the last days of life.

REFERENCES

American Association of Suicidology (no date). Report of the Committee on Physician-assisted Suicide and Euthanasia. Washington, D.C.: American Association of Suicidology.

Beck, A.T., Rush, A.J., Shaw, B.R. & Emery, G. (1979). *Cognitive therapy of depression.* New York: Guilford.

Erikson, E. (1950) *Childhood and society.* New York: Norton.

Kubler-Ross, E. (1969) *On death and dying.* New York: Macmillan.

Lerner, G. (1978). *A death of one's own.* New York: Simon & Schuster.

National Institute of Mental Health (1991). The Consensus Development Conference on the Diagnosis and Treatment of Depression in Late Life. Bethesda, MD, November 4–6, 1991.

The New York State Task Force on Life and the Law (1994). *When death is sought: Assisted suicide and euthanasia in the medical context.* New York: New York State Task Force on Life and the Law.

Richman, J. (1986). *Family therapy with suicidal persons.* New York: Springer.

Richman, J.(1989) "Humor and the fear of death." In Kastenbaum R. and Kastenbaum B., Eds. *Encyclopedia of death*. Phoenix, Arizona: Oryx Press. 153–158.

Richman, J. (1993). *Preventing elderly suicide: Overcoming personal despair, professional neglect, and social bias*. New York: Springer.

Richman, J. (1995a). "The lifesaving function of humor with the depressed and suicidal elderly." *The Gerontologist*, 35 (2), 271–271.

Richman, J. (1995b). "From despair to integrity: An Eriksonian approach to psychotherapy for the terminally ill." *Psychotherapy*, 32 (2), 317–322.

III

Suicide and Suicide-Prevention in Biblical and Graeco-Western Narratives

III

In the first paper of this section, Kalman Kaplan compares biblical and Greek creation stories and draws implications for the modern personality. Kaplan argues that the attempts of secular humanism to liberate and expand the personality by detaching it from its religious underpinnings have often had the opposite effects: they have often constricted and diminished it. This phenomenon is illustrated in three problem areas: (1) suicide and self-mutilation, (2) child-sacrifice and family pathology, and (3) self-esteem.

The next selection in this section deals with the implications of the contrast between Jewish and Western views of life and death in contemporary literature. In this piece, Dr. Joseph Lowin examines the sense of honor in Jewish figures in the literature of Elie Wiesel and contrasts it with the sense of honor emerging in the French romantic writers such as Racine and Corneille. Dr. Lowin examines the question of why the French heroes are often suicidal while the Jewish heroes are not.

The next four papers in this section deal with suicide and suicide-prevention in actual biblical and Graeco-Western narratives. First, Matthew Schwartz and Kalman Kaplan discuss the question of suicide for a biblical figure, Cain, and a Greek figure, Antigone, the daughter of Oedipus. Sophocles' great heroine, Antigone, is often cited as the ideal of the strong, uncompromising, independent, moral woman. Yet, strangely, Antigone's road leads to suicide while

Cain, a selfish murderer, is salvaged by God. Schwartz and Kaplan focus on the motif of a brother's blood to argue that Antigone's whole thought world propels her to self-destruction while Cain's biblical God moves him toward a creative and useful life, even after the murder of Abel. The next paper in this section, "Job: A Biblical Message about Suicide," is by Israel Orbach, a prominent Israeli psychologist and suicidologist. Employing psychological and rabbinic thinking, Orbach focuses on the fact that Job does not commit suicide despite his pain and the breakdown of his human support systems. Instead, Job never ceases to seek meaning and never loses his sense of transcendental values. He is able to attain a clearer understanding of man's relationship with the divine. As the Akedah teaches that God rejects human sacrifice, so the story of Job teaches that God rejects any need for human suicide.

The next paper in this section, "Kill Me I Pray," contains Stanley Selinger's analysis of the despair of Moses in the wilderness. Moses is overwhelmed by his burden and implores God to kill him. Instead, God responds by bringing seventy elders to share Moses' responsibility. Selinger, a psychotherapist, points to the profound implications for Moses of this community reorganization, both in his inner psychology as well as the meaning he attaches to his role. This thoughtful paper draws parallels to the problem of suicide and the role of therapy in modern society. The final paper in this section is by Kalman Kaplan. It compares the narratives of Jonah and Narcissus in a further attempt to pinpoint what is suicide-prevention in the Hebrew Bible as compared with Greek mythology. Narcissism is linked to suicide in the Greek mind and a general biblical approach to suicide-prevention is suggested to the clinician. This approach involves temporary protected regression to allow a suicidal individual time to work out his conflicts, which often involve individuation and attachment.

12

Suicide, Sacrifice, and Self-Esteem in Biblical versus Greek Stories of Creation

KALMAN J. KAPLAN, PH.D.

One of the great paradoxes of Western civilization is that secular humanistic attempts to remove the self from its religious underpinnings and thereby expand and liberate it have often had the effect of constricting and diminishing it. This paper illustrates this phenomenon in three problem areas: (1) suicide and self-mutilation, (2) child-sacrifice and family pathology, and (3) self-esteem. Two underlying principles are stressed: (1) a sense that a concerned God created each human being in God's own image, and (2) an insistence that there is an unbridgeable line of demarcation that separates the creator (God) and the created (human being).

SUICIDE AND SELF-MUTILATION

The belief that life belongs to the self rather than to a divine creator has had the effect of legitimizing self-mutilation and suicide. In Athens, for example, as well as in Massilia and Ceos, the suicide was actually supplied with hemlock (*Valerius Maximus*, 2, 6:7–8). According to Libanius (quoted by Durkheim, p. 330), the law of Athens read as follows: "Whosoever no longer wishes to live shall state his reasons to the Senate, and after having received permission shall abandon life."

The Greek and Roman Stoics seemed to feel overwhelmed by necessity or fate in all things except the time and manner of their death. For example, Seneca, an actual suicide, along with his wife Paulina, gave an impassioned plea that life belongs to the self and he advocated suicide as a means of control over the kind of life one should accept. "For mere living is not a good but living well." He also stresses the quality and not the quantity of his life. Dying well means escape from the danger of living ill (Seneca, *Epistle*, LXX). Seneca went on to equate suicide with liberty. "You see that yawning precipice? It leads to liberty. You see that flood, that river, that well? Liberty houses within them . . . Do you inquire the road to freedom? You shall find it in every vein of your body" (Seneca, *De Ira* III, 15:3–4). The attitude in the biblical world is totally different. Freedom is seen in vastly different terms. God controls matters of life and death. "Against your will you are born, against your will you live, against your will you die. Against your will you shall in the future give account before the King of Kings" (*Avot*, 4.29). Paradoxically, this frees the individual to devote his attention wholly to those tasks that are peculiarly his, that is, loving God and man and studying and fulfilling God's commandments. The Mishna (the oral tradition in normative Judaism) goes on to offer its own statement on freedom. The Ten Commandments were carved (*harut*) on stone: Read not *harut* but *herut* (freedom). One is not free unless he devotes himself to the study of the Torah (Hebrew Scriptures) (*Avot*, 6.2).

God gives and takes life and humans must not intervene in this process under ordinary circumstances. God clearly instructs humans to choose life rather than death "so that you and your children may live" (Deuteronomy 30:19). The first rule of criminal law, which God gave Noah and his sons, i.e., all humankind, after the Flood, namely, "whoever sheds the blood of man, by man shall his blood be shed" (Genesis 9:6) was preceded by this solemn warning: "For your lifeblood too I will require a reckoning" (Genesis 9:5).

The contrast in these views can be seen in the comparative incidence of suicide in Greek tragedy versus the Hebrew Bible. In the surviving plays of Sophocles and Euripides alone, there are seventeen suicides and self-mutilations (see Kaplan and Schwartz, 1993, p. 71). In the entire Hebrew Bible, in contrast, there are only six deaths that can even begin to be classified as suicides (Kaplan and Schwartz, 1993, p. 95). Furthermore, several other narratives illustrate suicide-prevention (Kaplan and Schwartz, 1993, p. 99).

CHILD-SACRIFICE AND FAMILY PATHOLOGY

A second example of protection provided by the sense of a divine creator may be found in the problem of child-sacrifice. It is true that the Christological interpretation of the Hebrew Scriptures seems to

Suicide, Sacrifice, and Self-Esteem

equate God's love with child sacrifice; "For God so loved the world that he gave His only begotten son, that whoever believes in Him should not perish but have eternal life" (John 3:16). Nevertheless, such an emphasis on child-sacrifice does not emanate from the Hebrew Bible, which regards human sacrifice as murder and is particularly repulsed by the implications of child sacrifice in the cult of Moloch (Leviticus 18:21, 20:2–5). Rather, it seems to derive from the Greek culture, which lacked the biblical sense of a divine creator and often carried out child exposure.

Compare the creation stories in the Hebrew Bible and Greek mythology. The Hebrew God exists before nature and creates both heaven and earth. "In the beginning, God created the heaven and the earth" (Genesis 1:1). Although divided, the two elements are harmonious. Adam himself is made of the ground and is given a soul: "Then the Lord God formed man of the dust of the ground, and breathed into his nostrils the breath of life, and man became a living soul" (Genesis 2:7). The Greek theogony is very different. Nature, which itself is polarized by gender, precedes the gods and child-sacrifice and family pathology abound.

Grieved at the loss of the children who were thrown [by Sky] into Tartarus, Earth [their mother] persuaded the Titans to attack their father [Sky] and gave Cronus a sickle. Cronus cut off his father's genitals and threw them into the sea. Having thus eliminated their father, the Titans brought back their brothers who had been hurled to Tartarus and gave the rule to Cronus (*Apollodorus*, 1.1.4).

This vicious family pattern continues as Cronus swallows his own newborn children to avoid being supplanted by them. Zeus, his youngest son, survives and overpowers Cronus with the collusion of Rhea, his mother, and becomes king. Zeus, in turn, devours Metis with an embryo still in her womb (*Apollodorus* 1.1).

The most dramatic comparison can be seen in the narratives of Isaac and Oedipus. The story of Oedipus begins with a warning to King Laius that there is danger to his throne at Thebes if his newborn son should reach man's estate. This warning leads Laius to give his son to a herdsman to be destroyed. The herdsman, after piercing the infant's feet, gives him to a fellow shepherd, who carries him to King Polybus of Corinth and his queen, by whom the infant is adopted and called *Oedipus* (meaning swollen feet). Many years afterward, Oedipus received a riddle from an oracle telling him he was destined to kill his father. Thinking that referred to Polybus, his stepfather, and trying to avoid this fate, Oedipus left Corinth and returned to Thebes. On a narrow mountain road, Oedipus met his biological father Laius, whom he had not seen since birth and presumably did not recognize. A quarrel broke out and Oedipus slew his father. Subsequently, Oedipus saved Thebes from the Sphinx and was given in marriage Queen Jocasta, his biological mother (*Apollodorus* 3.5.7–8).

The story of the Akedah (the binding of Isaac) is quite different. As described in the first nineteen verses of the twenty-second chapter of Genesis, God commands Abraham to make of his son Isaac a sacrifice.

> "And he said, Take now thy son, thine only son Isaac, whom thou lovest, and get thee into the land of Moriah: and offer him there for a burnt offering upon one of the mountains which I will tell thee of." (Genesis 22:2).

Abraham follows God's commandment and Isaac himself seems to acquiesce to the plan.

> And Abraham stretched forth his hand, and took the knife to slay his son. (Genesis 22:10).

At the last moment, however, an angel of the Lord stays Abraham's hand.

> And he said, Lay not thine hand upon the lad, neither do thou anything unto him, for now I know that thou fearest God, seeing thou has not withheld thy son, thine only son, from Me. (Genesis 22:12).

Abraham is provided with a ram, which he substitutes for Isaac.[1]

> And Abraham went and took the ram and offered him up for a burnt offering in the stead of his son. (Genesis 22:13)

The difference in the narratives of Oedipus and Isaac seems to

---

1. While most traditional accounts hold that Isaac is not sacrificed, a tradition does exist in Judaism that holds that Isaac was indeed sacrificed and that the ram was a second offering (Genesis Rabbah 22:13). Shoham's (1979, p. 300) analysis of child-sacrifice rests on this dissenting interpretation.

Suicide, Sacrifice, and Self-Esteem

illustrate our theme dramatically. There is no divine creator in the Oedipus legend to keep Laius from attempting to kill his son. The biblical God, in contrast, ultimately prevents Abraham from sacrificing Isaac after putting him through a test of faith.

SELF-ESTEEM

Our final example of the lack of a sense of a divine creator constricting the human personality lies in the area of self-esteem. Here the contrast is between the biblical sense of being loved and accepted unconditionally and the Greek obsession with competition (either in its heroic or self-sacrificing forms).

The stance of the Hebrew Bible is quite clear on this issue. God is a concerned and loving Creator who has created each person in His own image.

> And God created man in His own image, in the image of God created He him; male and female created He them. (Genesis 1:27)

Several consequences flow from this approach. First, and we cannot emphasize this enough, *each* person is created in God's image. Secondly, each person's worth is unconditional, guaranteed by the experience of the secure love of a heavenly parent. A person may succeed or fail at various tasks in life. But his sense of worth is more intrinsic than this. The Divine source frees the individual from the vagaries of achievement, social approval and even interpersonal love as the basis for his self-worth. Inclusion of a sense of the divine in one's sense of self actually gives the individual room to develop. It makes it easier for an individual to experience the various aspects of love and work, without placing onerous burdens of self-confirmation on either work achievement or love relations. This allows the healthy balance of self-love and other-love displayed in Hillel's famous dictum:

> If I am not for myself, who will be for me? If I am only for myself what am I? If not now, when? (*Avot* 1:14)

The Greek world, without the biblical sense of a loving divine creator, lacks this basis for self-esteem. Everything in the Greek world seems to be turned into a competition (Finley, 1959, pp. 128–129; Huizinga, 1955, p. 73; Slater, 1968, p. 36). One person wins at the expense of another losing. The desperate and futile attempt to gain self-acceptance leads to Karen Horney's (1950) neurotic polarities of heroism (self-aggrandizement) and martyrdom (self-effacement). Carried to the ultimate, these solutions become suicidal. The heroic solution, as we have discussed previously, manifests itself as Durkheim's egoistic suicide, and martyrdom as Durkheim's altruistic suicide.

THE CREATOR AND THE CREATED: PROTECTION AND DEMARCATION

We have presented three examples of how introducing the sense of a divine creator into modern psychology seems to liberate and protect the human personality rather than to restrict it. These examples lie respectively in the areas of (1) suicide and self-mutilation, (2) child-sacrifice and family pathology, and (3) self-esteem. Left unexamined heretofore is the question of how the idea of a divine creator generally works to strengthen the individual personality.[2]

Here we focus on two lines of thinking regarding the relationship between the creator and the created: (1) a sense that a concerned God created *each* human being in His own image, and (2) an insistence that there is an unbridgeable demarcation line between the creator (God) and the created (man); in other words, that God is God and man is man. Both of these positions are stressed in the Hebrew Bible, central to Judaism and Christianity alike. We offer the hypothesis that both of these conditions, either in theological, informal or secular form, are essential to the full preservation and flowering of the personality.

We have emphasized the importance of the first point: the insistence that each individual personality is anchored in the unconditional love and acceptance of God frees it to develop in its

---

2. Ross and Kaplan (1993–1994) have recently developed a questionnaire designed to measure an individual's life-ownership orientation. The Life-Ownership Orientation Questionnaire (LOOQ) assesses whether an individual feels his life belongs to himself, to the state, or to a divine being. Ross and Kaplan have begun to investigate the influence of this orientation on attitudes toward abortion, suicide, and capital punishment.

own unique manner. Such a foundation frees the individual from the pressures of social conformity in a futile attempt to gain social approval, either in a direct or a counter-dependent manner. Such conformity can manifest itself either in the areas of love or of work.

In love, an individual may be afraid to express unique, even idiosyncratic, aspects of his own personality for fear of being rejected by the other. Instead, he will disguise more personal expression of his own self under the mask of social convention. The result, unfortunately, is a limitation imposed on the resultant intimacy, both in depth and in breadth.

The situation in work is analogous and equally constricting. The individual may be afraid to express his own ideas and thus his own creativity because of his fear of social criticism and his need for social approval. He will literally be afraid to be different and therefore inhibit what might be his most valuable contributions.

In both cases, paradoxically, the dependence of an individual's self-esteem on the social milieu prevents the individual from truly expressing his personality and letting it develop. The sense of a loving concerned creator frees the individual from this social milieu, whether it be love or work, and allows him to express his own personality more fully in relation to it.

The second point, a line of demarcation between the Creator and the created may even be more important. This view is stressed by the Hebrew Bible and in later Jewish philosophy through the ages. But it is not self-evident and is a position clearly not shared by many religions and philosophies, both Eastern and Greek, which seem to yearn for an apotheotic experience merging man and God.

The Hebrew Bible, in contrast, is insistent that the human being should not attempt to cross over the line separating him from God. Adam is expelled from the Garden of Eden before he can eat of the tree of life and live forever (Genesis 3:22). This punishment comes not because of man's obtaining technology, as in the Greek account (Prometheus punished by Zeus after stealing fire for man; Hesiod, *Works and Days*, 60–86) but because he tried to be like God, foolishly arrogating to himself the authority to reject God's plan for him.

Later, man is punished again for trying to usurp God by building the Tower of Babel into the heavens. God scatters him over the face of the earth and confounds his language (Genesis 11). This does not mean that man should not pray to God, only that the human personality needs to be separate from God to relate truly to him.

How different this view is from the Greek myths that continually portray an intermingling, often sexual, of the worlds of gods and humans. A striking parallel may be seen between the respect for the line of demarcation between creator and created and between parent and child. The Greek world blurs both distinctions, yearning for apotheosis between God and man and symbiosis between parent and child. Incest and abuse (see Bakan, 1971; Orbach, 1988) occurs frequently at both levels! This is despite, and perhaps because, of the lack of a sense of a nurturant and protective creator in the Greek mind and certainly the absence of any sense of secure parenting (Ainsworth, 1972).

The Hebrew vision, in contrast, because of its sense of a concerned creator and the experience of secure parenting, is able to maintain a firm line[3] separating God from man and parent from child. It is prayer that is pursued, not apotheosis. It is communication that is desired, not symbiosis. Incest is forbidden at both levels and the unique human personality is protected in its development (Kaplan and O'Connor, 1993; Kaplan and Worth, 1992–1993).[4]

REFERENCES

Ainsworth, M. D. S. (1972) Attachment and dependency: A comparison. In Ed: J. Gerwitz. *Attachment and dependency* (pp. 97–137). Washington, DC: V. H. Winston and Sons.

Apollodorus (1976) *The library*. Trans: M. Simpson. Amherst: University of Massachusetts Press.

Avot d' R. Nathan (1887) Ed: S. Schechter. Vienna: n.p.

Babylonian Talmud (1975) New York: Rom Edition.

Bakan, D. (1971) *Slaughter of the innocents*. San Francisco: Jossey-Bass.

---

3. Minuchin (1974) has emphasized the importance of a "line of demarcation" in his analysis of boundaries in family structure.

4. A recent study by Kaplan and Maldaver (1993) has found that three times as many completed adolescent suicides seem to come from pathological parents incapable of giving secure parenting (i.e. either enmeshed or disengaged) as compared to healthy parents capable of giving secure parenting. This relationship is reversed for a matched control group of nonsuicidal adolescents. Here healthy parents outnumber pathological parents in the ratio of three to one.

Durkheim, E. (1897/1951) *Suicide.* Trans: J. A. Spaulding & G. Simpson. Glencoe, Illinois: Free Press.
Faber, M. D. (1970) *Suicide and Greek Tragedy.* New York: Sphinx.
Finley, M. I. (1959) *The World of Odysseus* New York: Meridian.
Genesis Rabbah (1961) Jerusalem: Vilna Edition.
Hesiod & Theogonis (1973) *Theogony and works and days (Hesiod) and elegies (Theogonis)* Trans: D. Wender. Middlesex, England: Penguin Classics.
The Holy Scriptures (1955) Philadelphia: The Jewish Publication Society of America.
Horney, K. (1950) *Neurosis and human growth: The struggle toward self-realization.* New York: W. W. Norton.
Huizinga, J. (1955) *Homo ludens.* Boston: Beacon Press.
Jerusalem Talmud (1866) New York: Krotoschin Edition.
Kaplan, K. J. (1987) Jonah and Narcissus: Self-integration versus self-destruction in human development. *Studies in Formative Spirituality,* 8, 33–54.
Kaplan, K. J. (1990) Isaac and Oedipus: A reexamination of the father-son relationship. *Judaism.* 39, 73–81.
Kaplan, K. J. (1991–1992) "Suicide and suicide-prevention: Greek versus Biblical perspectives." *Omega,* 24, 227–239.
Kaplan, K. J. & Maldaver, M. (1993) "Parental marital style and completed and adolescent suicide." *Omega,* 27, 131–154.
Kaplan, K. J. & O'Connor, N. (1993) "From mistrust to trust: Through a stage vertically." In Eds: S. I. Greenspan & G. H. Pollock. *The Course of Life,* Vol. 6. (pp. 153–198). New York: International Universities Press.
Kaplan, K. J. & Schwartz, M. B. (1993) *A Psychology of Hope: An Antidote to the Suicidal Pathology of Western Civilization.* New York: Praeger.
Kaplan, K. J., Schwartz, M. B. & Markus-Kaplan, M. (1984) *The Family: Biblical and Psychological Foundations.* New York: Human Sciences Press.
Kaplan, K. J. & Worth, S. (1992–1993) "Individuation-attachment and suicide trajectory: A developmental guide for the clinician." *Omega,* 27, 207–237.
Kazantzakis, N. (1960) *The Last Temptation of Christ.* Trans: P. A. Bien. New York: Simon and Schuster.
Kohut, H. (1971) *The Analysis of the Self: The Psychoanalytic Study of the Child.* Monograph no. 4. New York: International Universities Press.
Minuchin, S. (1974) *Families and Family Therapy.* Cambridge, Massachusetts: Harvard University Press.

Mishna (1969) New York: M. P. Press.
NASB Interlinear Greek-English New Testament (1984) Grand Rapids, Michigan: Zondervan.
Oates, W. J. & O'Neill, E., Jr. (Eds.) (1938) *The Complete Greek Drama* (2 Vols.) New York: Random House.
Orbach, I. (1988) *Children Who Don't Want to Live.* San Francisco: Josey-Bass.
Plato (1955) *Phaedo.* Trans: R. Hackforth. Cambridge: Cambridge University Press.
Ross, L. T. & Kaplan, K. J. (1993–1994) "Life-ownership orientation and attitudes toward abortion, suicide, doctor-assisted suicide and capital punishment." *Omega,* 28, 17–30.
Seneca, L. A. (1620) *Works.* London: Willi, Stansby.
Shoham, S. G. (1979) *The Myth of Tantalus.* Australia: University of Queensland Press.
Slater, P. (1968) *The Glory of Hera: Greek Mythology and the Greek Family.* Boston: Beacon Press.
Valerius Maximus (1823) *Valeri Maximi Factorum Dictorumque Memorabilium Liborinovem.* London: A. J. Valpy.
Wellisch, E. (1954) *Isaac and Oedipus: Study in Biblical Psychology of the Sacrifice of Isaac.* London: Routledge and Kegan Paul.

13

A Dialectic on Life and Death: Elie Wiesel, from the Tragic to the Midrashic Mode

Joseph Lowin, Ph.D.

Focusing on Elie Wiesel's 1985 novel, The Fifth Son, *and comparing it to Pierre Corneille's seventeenth-century French play,* Le Cid, *this essay draws a distinction between the ways Western and Jewish civilizations look at life and death. The essay attempts to demonstrate that crucial to the Jewish insistence on the value of life is a turning away from the basic Western concepts of honor and heroism. These concepts often seem to lead to the acceptance of death as a solution to life's tragic dilemmas. In his novel, Wiesel, recognizing the beauty of the tragic mode, nevertheless swerves away from the tragic into a more Jewish literary mode, the midrashic, which constantly emphasizes, through study and commentary, and an ongoing engagement with the Jewish textual tradition, the primacy of life over virtually all other values.*

> Passover eve we are recounting, chanting, the ancient tale of our ancestors' departure, a wild exhilarating race, I am looking for Moses and Moses is looking for us and the Egyptian soldiers are hounding us, driving us into the sea and they are following us into the sea and it is victory and like the angels I love to sing and like the angels I am reprimanded by God one does not sing in the presence of death and I say to God thank you thank you Lord for having killed our enemies thank you for having killed them yourself thank you for having spared us that task and God answers one does not say thank you in the presence of death one does not say thank you to death.
> —Elie Wiesel (1985), *The Fifth Son*, p. 34[1]

---

1. It is important to recognize that the English version of this novel, originally published in French as *Le Cinquième Fils* (1983), has been recast in

Virtually at the center of Elie Wiesel's 1985 novel, *The Fifth Son*, one of the novel's four narrators describes a defining moment, a "tragic" moment, one that places the reader at the ethical center of Wiesel's fictional—and therefore philosophical—universe. By posing a series of questions about tragedy, honor, and heroism, Wiesel emphasizes the distinctions to be made between the ways Western and Jewish civilization look at life and death:

- Is there a place for tragedy—both the literary genre and the outlook on life—in the Jewish value system?
- How is the Jewish idea of honor different from that of Western civilization?
- How is the Jewish hero different from the Western hero?

THE JEW AS HERO

In the city of Davarowsk, somewhere in Eastern Europe during the darkest years of this century, three Jewish men, Reuven Tamiroff, Simha Zeligson, and Bontchek, are called upon to encounter and do battle with a personification of Evil, Richard Lander, the Nazi commandant of the Ghetto that has been created in the city. One of these men, Reuven Tamiroff, has, in his past, displayed a tendency to adopt the behavioral standards of the surrounding culture. In an earlier, more benign, war, for example, he had tried to emulate the values of Western society, his efforts only grudgingly rewarded. "Reuven Tamiroff is drafted and leaves to join the army. There he volunteers for the front lines, determined to be a hero. Rarely tired, never at rest. At first, his fellow officers make fun of him: 'Really this son of rabbis is trying to give us lessons in patriotism!' Then, their mockery turns to grudging acceptance: 'Never mind his motives, fact is: he's not a coward, not like the rest of them.' In the end, one or two of them offer him their friendship" (p. 69).

---

several ways, including the transposition of several chapters and the deletion of some philosophical passages. In a letter to me about this, Wiesel writes, "*All* the changes have to do with the need to speak to the *American* reader whose sensitivities must be taken into consideration" (Letter from Wiesel to Lowin, 8/12/90). Nevertheless, both versions lead equally to the conclusions I will draw from the novel, including the positing by Wiesel of a philosophical viewpoint.

As a young man, Reuven recounts further, he was like the first son of the Passover Haggadah, faithful to Jewish tradition. It did not take long, however, for him to be seduced into becoming a "second son," one who cuts himself off from the Jewish community, one who says to his community, "Your history does not concern me." He learns the perverse lesson that it is "not only the right but the duty of Jews to repudiate their ancestral bonds, to assimilate, to forget their heritage" (p. 36). He devotes his life, not to immersion in the Jewish textual tradition, but rather to the study of Western philosophy. He does manage, barely, to resist baptism.

Ironically, years later, this is the man Commandant Richard Lander chooses to appoint, on the establishment of the Davarowsk Ghetto, President of the Jewish Council. It goes without saying that although he accepts the appointment reluctantly, Reuven acquits himself dutifully in the position. He even shows some good old-fashioned Jewish righteousness, playing no favorites with members of his own family in the allocation of apartments and other physical comforts. It is in the central episode, however, that his behavior is defined by his education in the larger culture.

The Jewish men in Workshop #4 have been sent out of the Ghetto to carry out a task of forced labor; they do not return. With great difficulty, because Lander is talented at dissimulating, Tamiroff learns that the men have been summarily killed by their Nazi guards. In a gesture of defiance, Tamiroff leads the men of the Council to resign in protest. Lander arrives to conciliate, by lying about the fate of the men. He offers to Reuven the opportunity to rescind his resignation. For Reuven it is a dilemma. Here is how the state of mind of the members of the Council is described years later to Tamiroff's American son by Bontchek, a narrator who is capable of making the people of the Ghetto come to life again by the power of his words:

> Everybody held his breath. I half-hoped your father would answer that he agreed to close the parentheses, and yet I would be lying if I denied having another reaction: the hope that your father would not allow himself to be duped by this wretched would-be actor. If he did, I would be ashamed of him; if he did, I myself would be ashamed in front of all my friends still staring at me out of that ditch, staring at me as if to tell me the story of their end, a story nobody will ever know. But, of course, my thoughts and my wishes were of little

importance; the decision was your father's and it was sublime: he did not answer, I mean: he did not speak; he simply shook his head from left to right, from right to left, his jaw set, his eyes unblinking. He is strong, your father, and I admired him, we all admired him. Even those among us who would die and knew it, admired him. (pp. 120–121)

The center of this episode is a verbal outburst by the Nazi commandant to the would-be "hero," Reuven Tamiroff. "Abruptly, the German officer drew himself up, stood at attention and declared dryly: 'You meant to give us a lesson in dignity—well, you didn't succeed. You see, Mr. President of the Jewish Council, we are German officers and our concept of honor differs from yours. Also be assured that we shall never agree to take lessons from you Jews, in this or any other matter.'" (p. 121). And so, the commandant forces Reuven Tamiroff to draw from among twelve lots the names of six members of the Council who shall die for this insurrection, for this sublime and therefore tragic gesture of heroism on the part of their leader. The question remains: however admirable the gesture performed by Reuven Tamiroff, did he perform a Jewish act? And if he did not, did he not commit a cardinal sin against Judaism and against the Jewish meaning of human existence? An older, wiser Tamiroff seems to think so. Years later, Reuven, who is in the habit of unburdening himself psychologically by composing letters to his dead son, Ariel, writes, ". . . Daring? Honor? Dignity? What foolishness! . . . I should not have defied our Angel [so called by the inmates, by antiphrasis] . . . Why did we insist on playing heroes? . . . I should have thrown myself on the ground, crawled at his feet, and begged him to spare us . . . I feel responsible for the deaths of my comrades. Had I overcome my pride, they might have lived another year, another month, another day. For someone about to die even a single day is a long time. I could not resist the temptation of courage . . . I was destined to lose either way" (pp. 123–24).

A CLASSIC DILEMMA OF TRAGIC HEROISM

"I was destined to lose either way." Let us turn for a moment to *Le Cid*, a play by seventeenth-century French dramatist Pierre Corneille. It is fair to speculate that Elie Wiesel, who became a student in Paris after the war, was exposed to the theatrical writings of both Pierre

Corneille and Jean Racine, the great writers of tragedy of the French neo-classical moment. Wiesel's prose, spare and intense, can with justice be called Racinian. Nevertheless, it is Corneille's *Le Cid* (1637)—a tragedy which sidesteps the tragic at the last moment to become a tragi-comedy—which offers the most clear exposition of the tragic dilemma presented in this novel and analyzed in this essay. There are, moreover, at least fifteen allusions to theatricality in the novel, including, e.g., "a tragedy in the making" (p. 112); "like a martyred king in one of those plays from antiquity" (p. 120); "I remember it as though I had seen it on the stage" (p. 140); more than enough to license an initial consideration of the novel in theatrical and even tragic terms. Wiesel will, as we shall see, swerve, like Corneille, from the tragic mode. Unlike Corneille, Wiesel will turn his text toward a Jewish literary genre. The exposition of the tragic dilemma encountered by the play's hero, and his resolution of the dilemma, will provide a case study of the strict code of honor found in certain texts of the tragic tradition of Western civilization. It will also provide a basis for comparison with the Jewish idea of honor as expressed by Elie Wiesel in the novel.

The play, although it takes place at the court of the King of Spain, begins like a domestic French comedy. Rodrigue is in love with Chimène; Chimène is in love with Rodrigue. For the fathers, it is a perfect match. Rodrigue's father, Don Diègue, is the former national hero, now in retirement. Chimène's father, Don Gomès, is Diègue's worthy successor. It is even understood that Rodrigue will be trained to succeed his future father-in-law as hero of the realm when the time comes. There is, therefore, a perfect meshing of family rank, accomplishment, and expectations.

A complication arises, however; the King announces that it is time to choose a tutor for his son and that he is hesitating between the hoary wisdom of Rodrigue's father and the passionate activity of Chimène's. The King chooses experience over vitality and in the debate that ensues between the two gentlemen over the King's choice, Count Gomès insults the honor of Diègue. Having unfortunately passed his physical prime, the elderly hero no longer has the strength to defend his honor: his sword, symbol of his masculine vigor, has become too heavy for him to lift out of its scabbard. Diègue's only recourse is to turn to his son—full of youthful vim and eager to prove his manliness—to avenge his honor.

For Rodrigue, it is a dilemma. If he takes up his father's

challenge and kills the Count, Chimène will no longer be able to marry him. Indeed, she will have to avenge *her* honor and somehow pursue the killer of her father. If, on the other hand, Rodrigue, in the name of love, were to refuse his father's assignment, Chimène, in obedience to the code of honor she follows, would find him unworthy of her and therefore unsuitable for marriage. In a dramatic monologue (Act I, scene 6)—the French equivalent of Hamlet's "To be or not to be"—Rodrigue accepts his tragic situation. Since in either case he must lose Chimène, "Let us at least preserve our honor." When choice is no choice, death is the only possible resolution. The resolution of the tragic dilemma is not merely to kill the Count, however; it is to resign oneself to a life circumscribed by death.

It would seem that such is the case in the novel for Reuven Tamiroff and Simha Zeligson. After the war, because Richard Lander had murdered Reuven's son, Ariel, and Simha's wife, Hannah (in an episode which will be analyzed below), the two survivors vow to take revenge on the murderer. They even carry out their plot. Unknown to them, however, it fails and Lander goes on to become a wealthy industrialist in the German city of Reshastadt (a bilingual pun meaning "city of evil"). A by now familiar pattern reproduces itself. The father having proven weak and incapable of defending his own honor, the son will passionately take up his cause. In fact, the main plot of the novel describes the efforts of the American-born son of Reuven Tamiroff, thoroughly acculturated into Western modes of thinking, to become the hero that his father no longer can be. He will hunt down the criminal and assassinate Lander in his father's place.

THE WIESELIAN DIALECTIC: THE TRAGIC MODE AND THE MIDRASHIC MODE

Wiesel, however, will provide another conclusion. He will do so by recasting his novel from the tragic mode into the midrashic mode. "Ariel" will not be a hero but a *tsaddik*, a righteous man.

Just as the tragic mode has its own poetics, so too does the midrashic mode. Midrash, the quintessential Jewish literary genre, is a term that describes the rabbinical method of adding an interpretive texture to a narrative text by filling in some of the blanks in a biblical story or by smoothing out what James Kugel calls surface irregularities in the text. Kugel provides quite a picturesque—if unkosher—description of the work of the midrashist: "The text's irregularity is the grain of sand which so irritates the midrashic oyster that he constructs a pearl around it. Soon enough—pearls being prized—midrashists begin looking for irritations and irregularities . . . whose connection with 'problems' [in the text commented on] is remote indeed" (p. 93). Kugel also reminds us that in its classical form "midrash is an exegesis of biblical verses, not of books" (p. 93). Modern writers, "in the midrashic mode," will not hesitate to make their books out of previous books as well as verses. Sometimes a midrashist will simply create a narrative out of disparate fragments of text. The rabbinical story never violates the "intactness" of the biblical story. The rabbinic method recognizes, however, that once a biblical story is seen to have other stories latent within it, the original can no longer be divorced from the new story, which, in effect, is henceforth one of its implied, inherent interpretations. The text quoted at the beginning of this essay is a story in the midrashic mode, a commentary on the biblical story of the Exodus.

The new story is a commentary not only on the previous text or texts, it is also a commentary on the universe, a lesson to be learned about living in the universe. Midrash, a narrative art, is unabashedly a didactic genre, one that, in commenting on the words and the world, is aimed at teaching a lesson about the writer's value system.

Such is the case with Elie Wiesel's novel, written in the midrashic mode. The very title of the novel, *The Fifth Son*, is an allusion to the rabbinical story in the Passover Haggadah of the four sons. It is no accident that there are four storytellers in the novel—Reuven Tamiroff (whose first name means "behold a son" and whose last name might mean "son of simplicity"), Bontchek (whose name mimics the Yiddish *boytchik*, little boy), Simha Zeligson (the word "son" evident in his last name), and the nameless narrator of the novel, Reuven Tamiroff's American son, who will "become" a fifth son, his brother Ariel, who was murdered as a child by the commandant Richard Lander.

Wiesel's midrashic intention is further emphasized by his placement of the rabbinic story of the four sons—itself a midrash on several biblical verses in which the word son appears—as the epigraph to the novel, thus indicating to the reader that it is to be read in a midrashic key.

To demonstrate how complex and non-linear the midrashic

mode means to be, we need only recognize that *The Fifth Son* is a continuation and a rewriting of Wiesel's 1961 novella, *Dawn*. That book is essentially the interior monologue of eighteen-year-old Elisha, a spiritual older brother to fifteen-year-old Eliezer of *Night*, who is chosen as an instrumentality of the policy of the Jewish underground in post-World War II Palestine.

This policy is designed to demonstrate that despite their atavistic aversion to killing, Jews do fight back. "We shall kill in order that once more we may be men" (Wiesel, 1982, p. 26). A Jewish state must be born and Elisha will be instrumental in the dawning of this new era in Jewish history. But Elisha will face a dilemma, one that is presented in tragic terms. What is one to do if tragic circumstances call on the Jew to play a role that goes against the grain of 2,000 years of his history? Elisha hallucinates. In a vatic vision, he calls together "all those who had contributed to [the] formation of my permanent identity" (Wiesel, 1982, p. 54). Not only his Master, not only his father and mother, but also the little boy he had been are recalled into existence. It is this little boy who reminds Elisha that he is not only himself but also "the sum total of all that we have been" (Wiesel, 1982, p. 57). If Elisha executes John Dawson, all Jews do. And yet, it is not that Elisha has to decide whether to kill an innocent hostage—that has been decided by the first page. It is that he has to come to terms with the ways in which his existential act will affect not only his own soul but the soul of the entire Jewish people. One act can change an entire essence. By bringing us into Elisha's deliberations, Wiesel makes us feel that we are all implicated in his act.

In spite of his night-long deliberations about accepting the responsibility for the morality of taking another's life—"When is a man most truly a man? When he submits or when he refuses? Where does suffering lead him? To purification or to bestiality?" (Wiesel, 1982, p. 12)—Elisha is nevertheless capable of pulling the trigger on an *innocent* British hostage. One might say that *Dawn* is a commentary on the Sixth Commandment, a midrash on it.

In the 1985 novel, neither the father, Reuven Tamiroff, nor his young adult son, "Ariel," even after *years* of deliberation, will be able to execute the murderously *guilty* commandant of the Davarowsk ghetto. They have immersed themselves in the Jewish textual tradition and can find neither in it nor in their *midrashim* on it justification for death.

THE LEARNING OF REUVEN TAMIROFF

The Fifth Son is a didactic novel not only because it is a teaching text; it is also a learning text, presenting fascinating variations on traditional modes of Jewish study. In effect, the episodes which describe these learning situations become a new type of midrashic writing, a recasting of the novel into a *beit midrash*, the traditional Jewish House of Study.

"Ariel" recounts how on the last Thursday of every month his father and Simha meet for textual study. A witness to these evenings of study, he is able to report how they all seem to revolve around capital punishment; the two men are in search of proof texts to justify the act of vengeance they believe that they have committed but which they sense is a betrayal of their Jewish ethical system.

One of these evenings revolves around the study of the biblical text which narrates the killing by Moses of the Egyptian overseer whom Moses had observed beating an Israelite slave. The study session begins with an invitation to the midrashic mode, "Let us reread the text." Rereading in their system means commentary and it does not take long for rereading to become rewriting, an updating of the story into modern terms. "You see in him [i.e., Moses] only the prophet impassioned with legislation, poetry, teaching, but in fact, he was also a warrior, strategist and military leader. A hero of the resistance. A commander of a national liberation army" (57). By using this anachronism, Simha seeks to turn the story into a parable, a story from which one can learn that what is justifiable for Moses is also justifiable for modern man. Tamiroff concludes the session however with a fine distinction between what is justified and what is just. "The Talmud claims that Moses could not enter the Promised Land precisely *because* he had shed blood. Even Moses had no right to kill. In other words, God did not forgive, not completely. And yet, at the moment it took place, the murder seemed necessary if not indispensable, thus justified." And then he adds to this "political" discussion an ethical dimension, one laden with Jewish values, "Justified perhaps, *just* never" (p. 57). In this way Wiesel's "hero" paves the way for the distinction between the man of honor and man of justice.

THE TEACHINGS OF RABBI AHARON-ASHER OF DAVAROWSK

The Jewish meaning of justice is presented in the novel in yet another setting in which Jewish study takes place, the streets of the ghetto. Reuven Tamiroff and Rabbi Aharon-Asher of Davarowsk are walking and talking. Not unnaturally, in that setting, where "death [is] everywhere," the subject of suicide will arise, even without being brought up. Although the conversation may be peripatetic, only its form and not its content is Socratic. For the Jews, according to Rabbi Aharon-Asher, there is no escape from life through Hemlock. "'Our Law, since Moses is opposed to human sacrifice and suicide is just that,' said the Rabbi. 'Our Law, centered on life, is opposed to death, even when it is summoned for so-called lofty motives. To die in another man's place is forbidden'" (p. 100). The rabbi goes on to elucidate the conflict between the Jewish and the Western value systems by teaching a Talmudic story whose appositeness to their situation, where people are dying of starvation, is poignant. The narrator presents both the story and its commentary:

> The Rabbi was telling my father a controversial story about Rabbi Akiva and Ben P'tura. The two Talmudic sages had quarreled over the following problem: two men are walking in the desert; they are thirsty but all they have is one jug of water, enough for one man, not for two. What to do? Said Ben P'tura: let them share it; friendship is worth more than water, more than life. But Rabbi Akiba decreed: let the jug's owner drink the water and cross the desert and let him defeat death. Because, according to Rabbi Akiba, that is the Law: *Khayekha kodmin*, your life comes before any other life; though you may be able to save a life in the desert you may not do so by sacrificing your own. (p. 100)

This recounting of the law jars the sensibilities of a man raised in the modern Western tradition of honor and its cognates. Reuven Tamiroff protests that he finds such a law shocking. "It lacks generosity, compassion, brotherliness." The Rabbi, in the true dialectical spirit, goes on to explain. "*Khayekha kodmin* simply means that your life is not your own. In other words, friend, you are not free to dispose of it. That is the basis of our tradition; one may not play with another's life nor with one's own; one may not play with death."

THE JEWISH HEROISM OF HANNAH ZELIGSON

The Rabbi, for the sake of completeness, concludes his lesson with a statement of the exception to the rule. "And yet . . . there are times when we must choose death over shame. Over abdication" (p. 101).[2] Tamiroff, eager to understand his tradition's value system, responds with a modest but earnest "Teach me." In the novel, the lesson will be taught not by the Rabbi in conversation, but by the one defiant act of authentic Jewish heroism in the novel, that of the wife of Simha Zeligson, Hannah.

It is Yom Kippur, the most holy day in the Jewish calendar. The SS Officer, Lander, has gathered a group of people in an outdoor plaza to taunt them for hours on end about their traditional religious practices. He wants to hear them chant the High Holy Day service. But he asks them to change the liturgy and to pray to him, to imagine that *he* is God. The Jews recognize that this would be an act of idolatry and that moreover it would be like praying to death itself. After a standoff of several hours' duration, Hannah Zeligson, we are told, "straightens up, stands there erect and dignified, dusting an imaginary speck off her dress" and begins to speak. Hannah is educated, she knows both the liturgy and the law. She tries to explain to the commandant that, "For a Jew to pray is an affirmation of faith only when it is freely made. It is up to us to choose the object—or subject—of our faith. Faith in God, yes; faith in our ancestors, yes again. Faith in Death, never" (p. 154). In response to this heroic proclamation, Richard Lander orders his men to shoot the two hundred people standing in the plaza, thus proving to his own satisfaction, "I am Death and I am your God."

Like Reuven Tamiroff in a previous episode, Hannah here demonstrates a sense of honor. But, unlike in the Tamiroff episode, her heroism does not stem form the Western tradition but comes straight from the Jewish textual tradition itself.

Indeed, this scene is a commentary on the passage in Sanhedrin referred to by Rabbi Aharon-Asher which states that one must "suffer death and not transgress" (*ye-hareg ve-al ya'avor*) in cases of idolatry, incest, and murder. This episode thus asks to be read in the

---

2. The source of this law is in the Babylonian Talmud, Tractate Sanhedrin, Folio 75a.

midrashic mode. It is clear from the passage that Wiesel believes that idolatry and murder are organically related, that idolatry is an unfailing premonition of murder.

THE NEWSPAPER AS JEWISH TEXT

In the Yom Kippur episode, ancient law and liturgy are made to coalesce into modern life and literature. When Wiesel brings the drama of Hannah Zeligson to a conclusion, he avoids the tragic mode. He does so by rewriting the liturgy of the Holy Day and making it a part of the drama. "Who shall live, who shall die? The two hundred shall die. Before the day is over, before the *Neila* service is ended, all will have perished" (p. 154).

For an extreme case of midrash and modernity, it is necessary to return to the Thursday evening study sessions of Reuven Tamiroff and Simha Zeligson. They do not limit their texts to the ancient books, but find that there is Torah and a Jewish ethical lesson to be learned even from a newspaper account of the interrogation of a captured Arab terrorist in Israel. Clipped from an Israeli newspaper, the article is far from being straight-forward eyewitness reportage. Rather, it tells of a metaphysical confrontation between Ilan, an Israeli intelligence officer, and Tallal, the captured Palestinian terrorist.

The interrogation is going nowhere and Ilan has to decide whether it is necessary to use torture to gain what might be crucial information about other planned terrorist activities. Ilan is aware that if he uses torture, he dehumanizes not only Tallal but himself as well. He finds it hard to understand why Tallal would not understand this. "Then, he sees a shudder quick as lightning go through the prisoner. It lasts only a fraction of a second but Ilan notices. What is he so afraid of if it is not suffering? And suddenly, the answer is obvious: he wants to suffer. He has prepared himself for suffering, for torture, probably for death. The reason? Perhaps to set an example. To lengthen the list of Palestinian martyrs. To feed anti-Israeli propaganda. And also to force the Jewish adversary to practice torture, therefore, to betray himself, therefore to choose inhumanity. For Ilan it is a dilemma . . ." (p. 142).

The newspaper account is interrupted at this point by the irruption of Reuven Tamiroff and Simha Zeligson into the story. It is crucial to realize that what Reuven and Simha seize on is the statement "For Ilan it is a dilemma." They have taken hold of the tragic nature of Ilan's predicament. Like all tragic heroes when confronted with a dilemma—like Rodrigue and like the Reuven of the Davarowsk Ghetto—Ilan is aware that, no matter what decision he makes, he will lose. But we will never learn the outcome of this interrogation, because it is what goes on outside the story—its commentary—that is important to Wiesel.

The narrative frame has been broken to let two new authors inside so that they can create by the use of their imagination a new story, one from which an ethical lesson can be learned. Says Reuven, "Let us imagine that Tallal knows that a bomb will explode the next day and cause the death of many human beings; let us imagine that Ilan knows that Tallal knows. A Tallal of superior intelligence determined to turn Ilan into a torturer could definitely force him into that position. What would Ilan do? If Tallal is permitted to remain silent, it spells disaster. How can one make him talk?" (p. 144).

Reuven's answer, that he is against torture and death in all cases, is much more complicated than it appears at first. It is not that death must be avoided at all costs—this cannot be overly emphasized—but that the tragic must be overcome. He states that the responsibility for solving the dilemma resides with the person facing the dilemma. It is almost as if Wiesel were positing an eleventh commandment. Faced with a tragic dilemma, "Thou shalt be creative and find a solution that leads to life." Reuven realizes that he is demanding of the Ilans of the world perhaps more than they are able to deliver. Simha accuses Reuven of judging Ilan too harshly. Reuven knows that the responsibility for his position that "Nothing justifies torture" and "Nothing justifies death" remains with himself and himself alone. He concludes, "I let him act and I judge myself."

THE MAKING OF A WISE SON

Reuven's son, the central narrator of the novel, has learned the lesson of these study sessions well. He is in complete agreement with his father's conclusions, however complicated and demanding. Nevertheless, a fully assimilated American young man, he undertakes to go to Europe to accomplish his existential heroic act, the act that his father had proved incapable of accomplishing.

His adventure will, in admittedly different circumstances,

recapitulate his father's ordeal. Just as his father had sought to learn the *halakha*, the Jewish legal tradition, from Rabbi Aharon Asher of Davarowsk, so, too, "Ariel" will seek a *pesak halakha*, a religious legal decision, from a local hasidic rebbe, Rebbe Zvi Hirsch of Brooklyn. He wants to get religious sanction for the Rodrigue-like vengeance he is about to seek. The Rebbe responds that vengeance belongs only to God. He goes further: "Jewish tradition is opposed to capital punishment . . . The Law permits it, but it behooves us not to implement it. A court that issues such a verdict is considered murderous. Think: if a tribunal is encouraged not to enlarge the kingdom of death, what about an individual? To punish a guilty man, to punish him with death, means linking yourself to him forever" (p. 190). The Rebbe is careful to add that this does not mean that a Jew may not defend himself. "Scripture teaches us that it is our duty to kill whoever is preparing to kill us. But does this mean that we are to throw ourselves on just anyone who looks to us like a killer? On the contrary, Torah enjoins us to contemplate this defensive action only if we are certain that the assailant has come with the purpose of killing us. But how can one acquire such certainty? Supposing that he even states his purpose, how can one be sure that his threats are not meant merely as a deterrent? In other words, the Biblical verse prohibits assassination. It can never be justified" (p. 191). Curiously, because his adventure is just beginning, "Ariel" does not respond to the Rebbe's lesson by asking to be taught further, as his father had done. He does not say "Teach me"; he says "Listen to me." He does not want a ruling about the legitimacy of his planned act; he wants it to be blessed.

And so he sets out for Germany, to the city of Reshastadt and to his confrontation with Richard Lander, whom he is determined to assassinate. On the train, feeling a knot in his stomach from his very presence on German soil, he meets a German woman, Theresa. Her reaction to his announcement that he is Jewish is to demand a parity with the descendant of the victim of German murderousness. "Why do you refuse to understand *our* tragedy?" It is by now obvious that the word "tragedy" as used here has metaphysical resonances. Will "Ariel" find the creativity in his own soul to overcome his own tragic dilemma?

On its way to Reshastadt, the train makes a stop in Graustadt, the grey city, a city propitious for the fantasy world of dreams. Indeed, "Ariel" is never sure that he has left the train for the adventures he encounters wandering about Graustadt, or that he has merely dreamt them while the train was in the station. Wiesel's version of Kafka's fantasy is not a trial however but a funeral, in which "Ariel" is invited to deliver the eulogy. Curiously, in his fantasy, the narrator winds up by delivering a eulogy not only of Ludwig Semmel, the deceased, but also of the English poet John Donne (1572–1631), the author of the sonnet "Death Be Not Proud," a poem that proclaims the death of Death. A eulogy is, if it is truthful, a verbal settling of accounts with both the living and the dead, and perhaps that is the lesson that "Ariel" learns in the fantasy world of Graustadt.

For, when he finally arrives in Reshastadt, he no longer feels the need to settle accounts by using violence. He will sidestep the tragic choice, refuse it. He will use words, instead. He has come to Germany, he now realizes, to testify, not in his own name, but in the name of the Jewish people. "My name is Ariel and I am a Jew, I come from Brooklyn and Davarowsk, from Wizhnitz and Lodz, from Debrecen and from Bendzin . . ." (p. 204).

He recounts to Richard Lander the story of his father's ordeal, of the humiliations suffered at his hands, and of his identification with his little brother and with all his brothers. In the course of telling this story, he realizes that by telling and retelling—however futile it might seem at times—he will be fulfilling the ethical wishes of his father, of Rabbi Aharon-Asher of Davarowsk and of Rebbe Zvi Hirsch of Brooklyn.

He vows to become the type of storyteller who bears witness. "I shall speak. I shall tell the tale. The *Angel* must be, will be, unmasked. I shall describe the solitude of the survivors, the anguish of their children. I shall relate the death of my little brother. I shall set forth, I shall recall the wounds, the moanings, the tears. I shall speak of the voices of dusk, the mute violence of night. I shall recite the *Kaddish* of dawn. The rest is no longer within my scope" (p. 214).

In essence this is the vow of Elie Weisel, the author of *Night* and *Dawn*. Like Wiesel, Ariel[3] has learned that Jewish heroism

---

3. The quotation marks around the name Ariel are no longer necessary, for the Wieselian fusion of two characters representing past and present has mystically taken place. The narrator has, as is constant in Wiesel's writing, blended with his older/younger brother. Creating unity out of duality seems to be a major preoccupation of the novelist.

consists in bearing witness, in dealing with the first question asked by the Wise Son in the Passover Haggadah, *"Ma ha-eidot?"* "What are these witnessings?" For Elie Wiesel, as demonstrated in his novel *The Fifth Son*, this is the essence of the Jewish hero, one who is immersed in the Jewish literary genre par excellence, the literature of the midrashic mode.

Let us return to the epigraph of this essay, the breathless, unpunctuated dialogue with God about the place of death in His creation. It appears that in Elie Wiesel's thought, the dialectic on death can and must become a dialogue with God. Since it is of necessity a dialogue between a living human being and a living God, the subject of the conversation, and its conclusion, can only be the primacy of life.

REFERENCES

Kugel, James L. (1986). "Two Introductions to Midrash," in Geoffrey Hartman and Sanford Budick, *Midrash and Literature*. New Haven, Connecticut: Yale University Press, pp. 77–103.

Wiesel, Elie. (1982). *Dawn*. New York: Bantam. Originally published at *L'Aube*. Paris: Éditions du Seuil, 1960. First edition in English, translated from the French by Frances Frenaye, dates from 1961.

Wiesel, Elie. (1985). *The Fifth Son*. New York: Summit Books. Translated from the French by Marion Wiesel. Originally published as *Le Cinquième Fils*. Paris: Bernard Grasset, 1983.

14

The Blood of Thy Brother

Antigone Suicides, Cain Doesn't

MATTHEW B. SCHWARTZ, PH.D.
KALMAN J. KAPLAN, PH.D.

The striking two-part image of the earth calling out over the blood of a slain brother is a central feature both in the biblical story of Cain and in the ancient Greek literature as well, particularly Sophocles' Antigone. The images are remarkable both for their seeming similarity at the surface level, and at the same time for certain subtle and profound differences which they indicate between Hebraic and Greek thinking. Implications are drawn from the contrasting views toward suicide shown by the two cultures.

In a number of papers during the last few years, we have attempted to compare the way in which suicide was viewed in the biblical and classical Greek worlds. As our modern society draws heavily upon the traditions of both Hebraism and Hellenism, it seemed reasonable that an understanding of the differing places of suicide within these two cultures would be instructive for our current concerns.

A considerable variation appears in Graeco-Roman attitudes on the question of suicide. Socrates, on the one hand, condemns suicide on the grounds that human beings are the property of the gods and have no right to do away with that which does not belong to them (Plato, *Phaedo* 62 b–c). At the same time, however, he describes philosophy as a preparation for death (*Phaedo* 64a) and goes on to argue that death frees the soul from the prison of the body and allows it then to achieve pure knowledge impossible in life (*Phaedo* 66e). Aristotle opposes suicide, but not for any valuation of human life *per se*. Rather, he opposes it on the grounds that it treats the state unjustly (Aristotle, *Ethica Nichomachea*, 1138a:11–13). The Roman

Stoic Seneca, an actual suicide, eloquently defends suicide as a means of control over the kind of life one should accept. "For mere living is not a good, but living well. . . . He also reflects concerning the quality, and not the quantity of his life. . . . Dying well means escape from the danger of living ill." (Seneca, *Epistle* LXX). Further, suicide is equated with liberty (*De Ira* III, 15:3–4).

The attitude toward suicide in the biblical world is far more uniform. The deliberate taking of one's own life is strongly condemned by traditional Judaism, and it is generally agreed that the biblical basis for the condemnation of suicide can be found in the Noahide laws. Cohen (1976) argues as follows: "The first rule of criminal law which God gave Noah and his sons, i.e., all mankind, after the Flood, namely, whoever sheds the blood of man, by man shall his blood be shed." (Gen. 9:6) was preceded by this solemn warning: "For your lifeblood, too, I will require a reckoning." (Gen. 9:5) This warning of a divine reckoning for shedding one's own life blood has typically been interpreted as the prohibition of suicide (Rashi). The Hebrew Bible generally seems to contain a prohibition against self-injurious behaviors per se. In Deuteronomy, a man is forbidden to mutilate himself. "Ye are the children of the Lord your God: ye shall not cut yourselves, nor make any baldness between your eyes for the dead" (Deut. 14:1). Much the same prohibition is given specifically to the priests (the sons of Aaron) in Leviticus. "They shall not make baldness upon their head, neither shall they shave off the corners of their beard, nor make any cuttings in their flesh" (Lev. 21:5).

This attitude is expressed quite concretely. For example, Judaism does not award a suicide full burial honors. The Talmud and Code of Jewish Law decree that rending one's garments, delivering memorial addresses and other rites of mourning which are an honor for the dead are not to be performed for a suicide victim. In practice, however, Judaism takes a far more complicated position. For example, one is obliged to allow oneself to be martyred when the alternative is idolatry, incest or murder (Talmud, Sanhedrin 74a). Further, the definition of who is truly a suicide has become progressively narrower to require announced willful intent (Talmud, Semahoth 2:2, 2:3), full wits, nondeficiency in behavior (i.e., not a *shoteh*) and noninebriation.

Far more striking than this attitudinal difference is the comparative incidence of suicide in the Hebrew Bible and in Greek

Tragedy. We have compiled a list of sixteen suicides occurring in the twenty-four surviving plays of Sophocles and Euripides. In addition, there is one case of self-mutilation (the blinding of Oedipus) and only one case of aborted suicide (Hermione). In the Hebrew Bible there are only six suicides. Furthermore, a number of characters express suicidal ideation, but overcome their despair (e.g., Jonah, Job, Elijah).

We go on with this work in a comparison of the biblical story of Cain and the Sophoclean treatment of Antigone. A striking theme common to both stories is the image of the earth calling out over the blood of a slain brother. The images are remarkable both for their seeming similarity, at the surface level, and at the same time for certain subtle and profound differences which they indicate between Hebraic and Greek thinking.

Greek thought is generally termed fatalistic and, in truth, it is. However, the problem goes beyond the level of the theoretical and abstract. Impelled by terrifying fears, the Greek moved toward a very real and horrible outcome—suicide. Many famous Greeks and Romans (Socrates, Zeno, the younger Cato, Mark Antony and others) did take their own lives, pushed at least partly by the feeling that only by giving away their entire existence could they satisfy the terrible demands which they anthropomorphized in the motif of the earth demanding human blood. Greek literature and history indeed seem obsessed with the problem of suicide.

The Cain story contains a motif which at a quick glance looks very similar. Yet, Cain does not destroy himself. A nurturant God bears with Cain, even though he hardly seems to deserve it. There is no fatalistic mood: there is no suicide. Man can still look forward to a better world.

ANTIGONE SUICIDES

Let us briefly recount the main parts of the story of Antigone. After the death of Oedipus, one of his sons, Eteocles, becomes king of Thebes, and the other, Polyneices, leaves the city only to return with an army to dispute his brother's throne. It is arranged that the two brothers shall meet in mortal combat at one of the gates of Thebes. They duel there, and both are killed. Creon, the new king, orders an honorable burial for Eteocles, who fell defending his homeland. However, the body of Polyneices, the invader, is to be dishonored by being left unburied. Their sister, Antigone, is deeply disturbed by this sacrilegious decree. The thirsty earth, she says, demands the blood of the slain (1.246–47, 429), and she is determined to bury Polyneices, even though for breaking Creon's law she will be put to death.

Why does Polyneices' situation so strike Antigone, and why is she impelled to duty by this strange and ghastly image of the earth demanding her brother's blood? To understand more precisely the use of this image, we must view the character of Antigone as Sophocles presents it. This, of course, is a central focus of the play.

Antigone, as daughter of Oedipus and Jocasta and as descendant of Laius and before him Labdacus, bore the burden of a wretched family background of violence, especially to one's own offspring. Antigone speaks of what seemed to be almost a primal curse, "the ancient sorrows of the house of Labdacus . . . no generation can free the next." (1.592). Antigone feels overwhelmed with living out and repaying to her ancestors a terrible debt, which can be paid in full only by her total self-sacrifice and her joining them in Hades without producing any offspring of her own. (e.g. 1.2, 75–76, 90, 859–869, 898–900).[1] The demand of the insatiable earth for the blood of her brother is only part of the demand which she feels that her ancestors make of her for the supreme sacrifice—her own self. Antigone shows suicidal inclinations from early in the play, "If I die before my time, I say it is a gain. Who lives in sorrows as many as mine, how shall he not be glad to gain his death" (1.461f.).

The immense dilemma of the original Oedipal family is not merely academic. It is a serious and persisting trauma, proceeding in an intensifying crescendo from one generation to the next until it succeeds in bringing about the total destruction of the line of Oedipus. Antigone, condemned to death by King Creon, takes her own life leaving no children to carry on the line of Labdacus. Before

---

1. This motif, the demand of the earth for the blood of the slain, occurs several times in the Athenian dramas, and it apparently touched an important chord in the mind of the Athenian theater goer. The *Odyssey*, Chapter 11, contains a memorable description of the shades in Hades lapping up an offering of blood.

the play is over, her fiance Haemon, son of Creon, and Eurydice, Creon's wife, have also killed themselves.

As Sophocles in his drama fleshed out the ancient Greek myths, the rabbinic scholars fleshed out the very brief treatment of the Cain-Abel story in Genesis (only 17 verses). Again a man (Cain) slays his brother (Abel), but now the continuation of not only one family but of the entire human race is in dire jeopardy.

Cain is guilty of deliberate fratricide and is not largely a victim of outside forces, like Antigone, whose only visible offense was to bury her slain brother. Yet, while Antigone hurtles straight to suicide, Cain is not only salvaged but goes on to lead a productive life and to produce very creative descendants, who build cities, invent machinery and produce the first musical instruments (Gen. 4:20–23).

The key to the pleasanter result of Cain's story is that in the Genesis narrative there is a stopper, an active and benevolent Deity Who, rather than hound Cain like a fury or thirst after his blood like a devouring god or a shade in Hades, instead intervenes to offer Cain care, protection, a realistic outlook, and a new way to live more productively.

CAIN DOESN'T

The biblical saga of Cain describes, like *Antigone*, a challenge of earth and of blood and of the continuation of family. However, point by point its aims and its conclusions are quite at variance with the Greek. We shall deal with the story of Cain, in terms of its interpretations in the rabbinic literature.

Cain's first mistake was becoming a farmer and then bringing a sacrifice of his farm produce. *Meshekh Hochma*[2] points out that the later biblical laws of the sacred service exclude the use of unrefined produce as a sacrifice in the Temple cultus (likewise, honey is forbidden). However, something made from the produce of the soil, like flour or baked goods, is suitable. In contrast, Abel's offering of sheep was very acceptable, and in later times animal sacrifices are, in fact, brought in the Temple in Jerusalem. *Meshekh Hochma*'s explanation is very original but very significant. Cain's farm work is

---

2. Written by Rabbi Meir Simcha HaCohen of Dvinsk.

uncreative and drudging, and it contains little of man's singular creative effort. It is therefore unsuitable as a gift to God. The raising of animals requires creative nurturance from man, and animals are an acceptable gift as Abel's was. Man must give of his own creativity to God.[3]

Still, God does not punish Cain for his misguided sacrifice but instead tries to clarify Cain's dilemma for him. What Cain must do is try better next time. God understands that Cain, something like Antigone, suffers from an irrational fear of and connection to the earth with its supposed punitive powers, and that his life as a farmer is bound up in those fears.

> If you do well you shall be raised up,
> and if you do not do well,
> then sin couches at the door (Gen. 4:7).

This imagery recognizes that Cain has forebodings about the earth not unlike those in Sophocles' play. The rabbis offer two main opinions to explain the image of "sin couching at the door": (1) The door to the netherworld. (2) The maternal womb.[4] For one who does not live as God commands, (1) the door to the netherworld is beckoning and (2) insatiable parents and ancestors *seem* to be

---

3. In taking a crop from the earth and giving it back unimproved as a sacrifice to God, Cain is reversing the order of life and of development (almost as Oedipus did by returning to live with his own mother). God cannot accept Cain's offering or his view of life without accepting this reversal in the order of Creation. Let it be noted that the Bible makes a point of saying that the twelve sons of Jacob, plus Moses, David and Amos were all shepherds.

4. See commentaries on Genesis 4:7—Rashi, Onkelos, Mizrachi, Kli Yakar Sifte Hachamim. Also references in M. Kasher, *Torah Shelemah* on Genesis 4:7. BT sabh 139a. Significantly, the second explanation is cited in the Talmud. Sanhedrin 91b has an opinion offered by "Antoninus," a Roman emperor, to Rabbi Judah Hanasi. Modern historians have debated widely but inconclusively as to whether Antoninus might have been Emperor Marcus Aurelius or one of the rulers of the Severn family. For purposes of our passage, it is important that the Talmud felt that "Antoninus," learned in the Classics and in contact with rabbinic scholars as well, was something of a scholar of comparative literatures, understanding better than most the variant views of the two cultures.

demanding total submission even to the death. However, the biblical God does not at this point abandon Cain to be overwhelmed by his fears and problems. Instead, God offers Cain hope for better things. If he only tries his best, then he can be free of these terrors.

Cain does not follow God's good advice. Driven by depression, by an unreasonable need for security, or by a sense that man's actions are predetermined beyond his ability to control them,[5] Cain murders his brother. God now confronts the murderer, "Where is Abel, your brother?" Cain will not admit to any responsibility in the matter, "Am I my brother's keeper?" (Gen. 4:9) i.e. surely the Creator, and not I, is my brother's keeper. God cuts quickly to the core of the issue, pointing out how drastic Cain's act was, "The voice of your brother's bloods (sic) cry out to me from the soil." Here the story of Cain comes closest in its imagery to Sophocles' *Antigone*. However, significantly, in Genesis it is not morbid subterranean powers who hunger after human life and blood. It is the blood itself crying out from the earth to God.

The Mishna (Sanhedrin 4:end) wonders why the blood is crying and why the word blood is in the plural form (Heb. *demei* instead of *dam*)? The Mishna explains that the *bloods* bewail the many descendants who might have come forth from Abel and now will not. The continued existence of mankind is so highly important. The opposite was true of Antigone, who felt that she owed more to her netherworld dwelling ancestors than to any continuation of mankind and specifically her family, and Antigone makes the horrifying choice of giving up offspring to please forbears. In Genesis, Abel's bloods bewail instead his descendants who will never be.

SUMMARY

Antigone is courageous and intelligent, and she has a strong sense of higher law. Yet, her loyalties, overzealous and misplaced, lead only to her suicide despite or indeed because of her heroism. Her mother had also killed herself, and her father had put out his own eyes. Suicide seemed the natural way out of her problems, as it so often

---

5. See Joseph Dov Soloveitchik, *Bet Halevi. Meshekh Hochma op. cit* and M. L. Malbim on Genesis 4.

was in the Greek world. There was no supportive, benevolent god to offer hope to Antigone.

Cain, although likewise in a very serious situation, does not destroy himself, for there *is* a supportive and benevolent God Who helps him, although Cain seems hardly willing to repent or even to acknowledge his crime. God removes Cain from tilling the soil and gives him a sign of Divine protection. Cain goes on to build cities and to produce new generations of talented and creative descendants (Gen. 4:20–22). For the biblical God, it is more important to make things right than to destroy Cain. The creativity of Cain's descendants (and their ultimate union, in one midrashic opinion, with the progeny of Seth through Noah and Naamah, Genesis Rabbah 23:3) helps to make up in some measure for what Cain destroyed when he murdered Abel. The supra-human powers in the Greek world are seen as promoting the misery and destruction of even the most heroic and best intentioned of people. In Genesis, God intervenes personally almost in the role of a Divine counselor to give Cain a better grip on reality and a new lifestyle and to set him into a process of healing.

Why, in fact, is Cain not immediately put to death as a fratricide would seem to deserve? It is because the situation requires not only revenge but an acceptance by Cain of responsibility and liability and a turning from bad to good. Cain must now carry through in matters that Abel would have had to accomplish. The call of what Abel and his descendants would have accomplished cries out from the earth for fulfillment. Zeus and his earth call back Antigone to surrender to their dominion. The God of Genesis tells Cain that he and his own children must not be swallowed up in the earth, must not regress.

The contrast between Greek and biblical conceptions of God and earth are very telling. To the Greeks, Zeus himself is a child of earth and unable to free himself from it. To the Hebrew, God is neither earth nor sky but is the Creator and Lord of both. The idea of a dominating and devouring earth mother is also very Greek, Zeus himself being the son of an earth goddess. In the Hebrew Bible, significantly, Eve is not an earth mother but is the "mother of all the living" (Gen. 3:20). It is the man who is created by God partly of earth and named Adam (ground), and partly of the "breath of life" (Gen. 2:7). But Adam too is entirely a creation of God, and he carries no burden of debt to a devouring earth mother. Indeed, there is no devouring earth mother in the Hebrew Bible.

REFERENCES

Aristotle (1939). *The Nichomachean Ethics*. H. Rackham (trans.), Cambridge, Mass: Harvard University Press.
Babylonian Talmud (1973). Vilna Edition.
Cohen, H. 1976. "Suicide in Jewish legal and religious tradition." *Mental Health and Society*, 3, 129–136.
HaCohen, M. S. (1972). *Mesheleh Hochma*. Jerusalem.
Pentateuch: Mikraot Gedolot (1978). New York.
Plato (1955). *Phaedo*. R. S. Bluck (trans.), London: Routledge and Paul.
Seneca, L. A. (1979). Cambridge, Mass.: Harvard University Press (The Loeb Classical Library).
Soloveitchik, J. (1973). *Bet Halevi*. New York.
Soloveitchik, J. (1983). *Halakhic Man*. Philadelphia: Jewish Publication Society.
Sophocles (1954). *Antigone*. E. Wyckoff (trans.), Chicago: University of Chicago Press.

15

Job—A Biblical Message About Suicide

ISRAEL ORBACH, PH.D.

The book of Job deals with the existential paradigm of meaning in life and man's stand before God. Job is overwhelmed by endless suffering through which his unshakable faith in God is being tested. However, this story has more than one message. It is suggested that the story carries a clear message against suicide. From an anachronistic perspective it would be assumed that Job had every reason to commit suicide, but he did not. This paper elaborates the above assumption from psychological and literary perspectives.

The biblical story of Job is a story of man's quest for meaning of the relationship between man and God in face of unbearable and unjust human suffering. However, as other biblical stories, it is a complex one and has many faces and messages. The hypothesis which I will elaborate in this paper is that Job also has a clear message about opposing suicide. The incomprehensible, drastic, traumatic, and painful events occurring to Job may lead us, the modern researchers of suicidal behavior, to expect Job to put an end to the unjust suffering by suicide, just as his wife suggests to him. Nevertheless, for Job this is out of the question. On the contrary, in spite of his suffering from a certain moment, Job seems to gain unexplained strength and emerges as a powerful personality with inner mental resources which enable him to sustain his tragic existential situation.

Why didn't Job commit suicide? The biblical story unfolds two types of answers: one pertains to the mental processes which determine Job's behavior and resiliency which are described in the text, and the other pertains to a message with regard to norms of behavior as reflected from the general structure of the story. This paper attempts to deal with the question of suicide through the two avenues described in the Book of Job.

Job—A Biblical Message About Suicide

Job begins as a legendary story: "There was a man in the land of Uz, whose name was Iyyov, and that man was perfect and upright, and one who feared God" (Job 1:1). Uz is an unknown place and Job is depicted as a perfect human being—an unrealistic quality attributed to no other human being in the Bible.

The idealistic life of Job described in the following verses shows him to be a man not only with moral perfection, but one who enjoys an idealistic family life, economic wealth, and the highest social status and happiness. "And there were born to him seven sons and three daughters. His possessions also were seven thousand sheep, and three thousand camels and five hundred yoke of oxen and five hundred she asses and very many servants; so that this man was the greatest of all the men on earth. And his sons used to go and feast in the house of each one on his day; and they used to send and call for their three sisters to eat and drink with them. And when the days of their feasting were gone about, Iyyov sent and sanctified them, and rose up early in the morning, and offered burnt offerings according to the number of them all: for Iyyov said, it may be that my sons have sinned and despised God in their hearts. Thus Iyyov did continually" (Job 1:2–5). The idealism is curtly interrupted by a series of abrupt calamities designed by the adversary and the permission of God. First, there is a collapse of the economic empire. "The oxen were ploughing, and the asses were feeding . . . and men of Sheva fell upon them, and took them away . . ." (Job 1:15). "The fire of God has fallen from heaven, and has burned up the sheep, and the servants, and consumed them" (Job 1:16). "The Kasdim formed three bands, and fell upon the camels, and have carried them away, and have slain the servants . . ." (Job 1:17). The calamities happen one after another, one worse than the other, leaving Job no time to get reorganized. The tragedies culminate with the death of his children, ten of them in one breadth of time. "While he was yet speaking, there also came another, and said, Thy sons and thy daughters were eating and drinking wine in their eldest brother's house: and, behold, there came a great wind from across the wilderness, and smote the four corners of the house, and it fell upon the young men, and they are dead" (Job 1:18, 19).

In the first round of disasters, Job suffered a total economic loss and the most unbearable pain of all—the death of all his children. However, Job is strong; he mourns his losses, but accepts his destiny and says: "Naked I came out of my mother's womb, and naked I shall return there: The Lord gave, and the Lord has taken away; blessed be the name of the Lord" (Job 1:21).

The second series of disasters added more suffering. This time the adversary is determined to physically hurt Job himself. "So the adversary went forth from the presence of the Lord, and smote Iyyov with vile sores from the sole of his foot to his crown" (Job 2:7). Not only physical illness and suffering resulted from the infliction of the vile sores, but also deep humiliation: "And he took him a potsherd with which to scrape himself; and he sat down among the ashes" (Job 2:8).

The next blow to Job comes not from heaven, but from his wife, the only survivor of his close family. Job hears no comforting words from his wife, no encouragement, no support, and no hope. On the contrary, his wife gives him a clear message to commit suicide: "Then his wife said to him, Dost thou still retain thy integrity? curse God, and die" (Job 2:9). The wife projects her own anger with God onto Job and encourages him to commit suicide as a protest against God. But Iyyov "did not sin with his lips" (Job 2:10).

The social support system breaks down completely with the visit of his good friends Elifaz the Temanite, Bildad the Shuhite, and Zofar the Na'amatite. First, they comfort him and empathize with his sufferings. This allows Job for the first time to open up and in an emotional outburst to cry out. But soon his friends turn against him and the empathy turns into a serious accusation of Job's moral and ethical behavior: "Is not thy wickedness great? and thy iniquities infinite? For thou has taken pledges from thy brother for nought, and stripped the naked of their clothing. Thou has not given water to the weary to drink, and thou has withheld bread from the hungry . . . thou hast sent widows away empty, and the arms of the fatherless have been broken" (Job 22:5–9). The support system has been broken down. His friends do not understand him, accusing him of wrongdoings which he never committed, thus increasing his loneliness and suffering.

The phenomenological experiences of Job are unfolded throughout the story. While his religious integrity remains unshaken, he experiences unbearable mental pain. Using modern psychological jargon, he experiences some symptoms of depression in the form of restlessness and insomnia: "When I lie down, I say, When shall I arise, and the night be gone?" (Job 7:4). He is pent up with unexpressed anger: "I had no repose, nor had I rest, nor was I quiet;

yet trouble came" (Job 3:26—the word "trouble" is actually a translation of the Hebrew word "rogez" which means anger). Job finds no outlet for his anger, but directs it towards himself and internalizes it as he declares: ". . . Oh that the day had perished wherein I was born, and the night which said, There is a man child conceived" (Job 3:2-3). Moreover, the psychological and physical pain culminate to a deep repulsion for life on one hand: "Though I were innocent, yet would I not know myself: I would despise my life" (Job 9:21) and a deep attraction to death on the other hand: "Why did I not die from the womb?" (Job 3:11) and "For now should I have lain still and been quiet, I should have slept: then had I been at rest, with kings and counsellors of the earth, who built desolate places for themselves, or with princes that had gold, who filled their houses with silver . . . There the wicked cease from troubling; and there the weary are at rest" (Job 3:13-17). All these culminate in the most painful emotion of all, the feeling of total hopelessness. In one short verse he says it all: "My days are swifter than a weaver's shuttle, and are spent without hope" (Job 7:5). He feels useless, worthless, and an existential being of "nothingness."

Job is not suffering only from the sudden collapse of his secure environment, reduced status and health, loss of his beloved children, and the love of his friends. The crisis in his belief in God and his struggle to gain meaning from a religious standpoint comes across as the most important paradigm that Job faces. Leibovitch (1991) interprets the Book of Job as a confrontation with an existential religious dilemma. It represents a search for meaning in an existence in which God is not revealing the laws of reward and punishment and the principles of control over human life in a clear-cut way. Job discovers that he does not understand God's laws of individual supervisions of the righteous or the wicked. In other words, Job has lost the meaning of the relation of God to men. According to Leibovitch, Job starts his arguments with subjective complaints about his personal injustice, namely, searching for his wrongdoing for which he is punished so cruelly. Little by little, his arguments turn from the private and subjective cry to a statement of a more general and objective problem of God's leadership of the world. The largest part of the book is devoted to this question which is reflected in arguments between Job's friends and Job himself. His friends hold the position that God's control of the world is firm and that it is expressed through reward and punishment and, therefore, accuse

Job of wrongdoing. Job finds it impossible to accept this accusation and the meaning of his punishment.

Job's lack of comprehension of God's leadership of the world constitutes a loss of meaning in life. This has a tremendous emotional impact. He is shaken by fear, anxiety, and loss of direction: "Why is light given to a man whose way is hidden, and from whom God has screened himself? For my sighing comes before I eat, and my roarings are poured out like the waters. For the thing which I had feared is come upon me, and that which I was afraid of is come to me. I had no repose, nor had I rest, nor was I quiet; yet trouble came" (Job 3:23–26). "Fear came upon me, and trembling, which made all my bones to shake" (Job 4:14). "Shall mortal man be more just than God? shall a man be more pure than his maker?" (Job 4:17).

Summarizing all these processes, Job emerges as a person under severe suicidal risk. He suffered multiple losses—his children, his status, his wealth, and his support systems, and feels rejected. His wife gave him a direct message to commit suicide. He feels lonely, full of anger, and experiences anxiety. He feels humiliated, suffers physical pain, and is depressed. He is repulsed by life, feels attracted to death, and has lost any hope for change in the future. Most lethal of all, phenomenologically he lives a life without meaning. All the above have been pointed out as most potent risk factors in suicide and suicidal behavior (Frankl, 1962; Freud, 1917; Crook and Raskin, 1975; Roy, 1982; Motto, Heilbron and Juster, 1985; Whitlock, 1986; Curren, 1987; Orbach, 1989; Beck, Brown, Berchick, Stewart and Steer, 1990; Kuda, 1990; Platt and Kleiton, 1990; Maris, 1991).

What prevented Job from killing himself? Why didn't he listen to his wife's advice to curse God and die? The Scripture lends itself to two types of possible explanations—a psychological and a theological.

The most potent motivational force against suicide in Job can be attributed to his unwillingness to give up the search for meaning in life, namely, in the relation of man to God. Search for meaning in life in spite of an unfortunate destiny is a most powerful life-enhancement motivation. Frankl has described the search for meaning as a life-sustaining force in the most traumatic personal and historical tragedies. Meaning in life has nothing to do with personal gains or with a cure for pain and sufferings. Rather, the power of meaning lies in the ability to see oneself as a part of a transcendental existence or when one's behavior is related to a set of transcendental values. Job's quest for meaning has never been given up. Job says indeed: "My soul is weary of my life" (Job 9:35), but he continues to be determined: "I will give free utterance to my complaint; I will speak in the bitterness of my soul. I will say to God, Do not condemn me; inform why thou dost contend with me" (Job 10:1–2). He continues to search for meaning and for understanding God: "Why dost thou hide thy face, and hold me for thy enemy?" (Job 13:24). His friends urge him to give up his search for meaning just accepting his destiny: "What is man, that he should be clean? and one born of a woman, that he should be righteous?" (Job 15:14). But Job does not give up. He knows that giving up the search for meaning can be detrimental: "Far be it from me that I should justify you [the friends]: till I did I will not put away my integrity from me" (Job 27:5).

The arguments with his friends have a paradoxical effect on Job; instead of weakening his position, his belief and convictions get stronger. Job changes in front of our eyes, from the humiliated and suffering person into a powerful and confident figure. The sense of hopelessness turns without apparent reason into a new hope: "For there is hope of a tree, if it be cut down, that it will sprout again, and that its tender branch will not cease" (Job 14:7–8).

The escalation of the argument with his friends (Job 21:34 and 22:5) only increases Job's sense of righteousness and gives him new hope—two powerful life-sustaining forces. Job comes out from this struggle victorious. But what meaning did he gain in this struggle? In what way was his theological stand different from that of his friends? Leibovitch (1991), interpreting the approach of Maimonides to the issue at hand, provides an enlightening insight. What Job learned is that the essence of God's supervision and control of the world is not in the simple reward and punishment relationship between God and man. The essence of belief in God is the acceptance of his existence and man's obligation to him, regardless of reward and punishment. In other words, the worship of God should be independent of reward and punishment. Man's belief in God and his following of God's commands do not guarantee satisfaction of man's needs. The natural order of the world is independent of man's behavior. This is the highest form of worshipping God.

Attitudes of self-righteousness, the stubborn search for meaning, holding onto hope for finding meaning can constitute the psychological aspects of inhibition and create a psychological hardiness against mental breakdown and suicide. However, the Book of Job uses a special literary device to convey the theological message about suicide. The theological stand is one that suicide, as an option for solving problems and escaping pain, is forbidden. The author of Job portrays a protagonist struggling with extreme circumstances which may lead to suicide, but he stops short of committing this act, as though telling the reader that from a religious point of view suicide is unacceptable. Although there are several cases of suicide throughout the Bible, the Book of Job opposes suicide due to personal and psychological causes. Judaism does permit certain forms of self-destruction, from a normative perspective, under conditions of coercion to idolatry, to incest, and to the murder of others.[1] But the Book of Job takes the clear approach against suicide for personal psychological reasons.

A similar technique to convey an important message prohibiting certain behaviors is, I believe, presented in the story of the Akeda (the binding of Itzhak). Human sacrifice was a common way of worshipping God at the time of Abraham. Possibly it was one of the highest forms of worship. In this story the reader is taken through the preparations for the human sacrifice, making him believe that this is yet another example for an acceptable way to worship God. But at the last minute, when Abraham is ready to slaughter his son demonstrating his unshakable belief in God, he is stopped. Aside from the other morals of this story, it teaches us that human sacrifice is not an acceptable way to worship God.

Leibovitch (1991) points out some links between the story of the Akeda and Job, not only in the theological morals, but also in some verbal associations. The story of Job took place in the legendary place of Uz and one of the friends who came to comfort him was Elihu the son of Barakh'el the Buzite. Both names of the places Uz and Buz appear also in the Book of Genesis immediately following the story of the Akeda: "And it came to pass after these things, that it was told Avraham, saying, Behold Milka, she also has born children to thy brother Naḥor; Uz his firstborn, and Buz his brother . . ." (Genesis 22:20–21). These verbal associations give

---

1. The "Iggeret Ha-Schmad" by Maimonides presents a more flexible approach with respect to at least the first of these three conditions.

validity not only to the similarities in the theological issues presented in the two stories, but also the special literary techniques to convey the prohibition of certain unacceptable behaviors: human sacrifice and suicide.

REFERENCES

Beck, A. T., Brown, G., Berchick, R. J., Stewart, B. L., & Steer, R. A. (1990). "Relationship between hopelessness and ultimate suicide: A replication with a psychiatric outpatient." *American Journal of Psychiatry,* 147, 190-195.
Crook, T., & Raskin, A. (1975). "Association of childhood parental loss with attempted suicide," 43, 272-278.
Curren, D. K. (1987). *Adolescent Suicide Behavior.* Washington, DC: Hemisphere.
Frankl, V. E. (1962). *Man's Search for Meaning.* Boston: Beacon Press.
Freud, S. (1917). "Mourning and melancholia." In J. Strachey (Ed. and trans.), *The Standard Edition of the Complete Psychological Works of Sigmund Freud.* (Vol. 14, pp. 243-258). London: Hogarth Press.
Kuda, M. (1990). "Values, economic estimation, and suicidal intent." *Crisis,* 11, 20-31.
Leibowitch, Y. (1982). *Faith, History and Values.* Jerusalem: Academon Press.
Maris, R. W. (1991). "Introduction to assessment and prediction of suicide." *Suicide and Life-Threatening Behavior,* 21, 1-17.
Motto, J. A., Heilbron, D. C., & Juster, R. P. (1985). "Development of a clinical instrument to estimate suicide risk." *American Journal of Psychiatry,* 142, 680-687.
Orbach, I. (1989). "Familial and intrapsychic splits in suicidal adolescents." *American Journal of Psychotherapy,* 43, 356-367.
Platts, A., & Kreitman, P. S. (1990). "Long-term trends in parasuicide and unemployment in Edinburg, 1986-87." *Social Psychiatry and Psychiatric Epidemiology,* 25, 56-61.
Roy, A. (1982). "Risk factors for suicide in psychiatric patients." *Archives of General Psychiatry,* 39, 1089-1095.
Whitelock, F. A. (1986). "Suicide and physical illness." In A. Roy (Ed.), *Suicide* (pp. 151-170). Baltimore: Williams & Wilkins.

16

Moses: "Kill Me I Pray"

Stanley S. Selinger, Ph.D.

In the wilderness the people complain bitterly and discover the insecurity of freedom. Moses questions his role and responsibilities. He struggles with his own limitations. Exasperated and feeling burdened and alone, Moses asks to be killed. This paper analyzes the psychology behind such self destructive thinking and what resolves it.

> I am not able to bear all this people myself alone, because it is too heavy for me. And if You deal thus with me, kill me, I pray thee out of hand, if I have found favour in they sight; and let me not look upon my wretchedness! (Numbers 11:12–15)

These words were spoken by Moses as he led the Hebrews through the wilderness. The purpose of this paper is to analyze what leads to such self-destructive thinking and what resolves it?

The pain of the people and his wish to respond is so great that Moses cannot tolerate the situation. He believes that he cannot feed them, i.e. "give to all this people." These thoughts and feelings reflect a fear of pending failure. For if the people die, he cannot take them to the promised land. Here we sense the initial purpose of self-destructive thought. It seems to offer a way out of feeling trapped in a hopeless situation.

Psychologically, there is a possibility of repressed anger. We find, *"the anger of the Lord was kindled greatly, and Moses was displeased"* (Numbers 11:10). Why isn't Moses angry at them too, like God is? After all, Moses went through many trials to lead them out of slavery to freedom. Is his anger not accessible to him, or is he more than angry? In the unconscious, rage, disappointment and love co-exist side by side. It is not uncommon to be dominated by one emotion in order to mask another emotion that is psychologically unacceptable. To think that a feeling is unacceptable ("my wretchedness") leads to guilt for having that unacceptable feeling. For someone, even Moses, to cleanse himself from such guilt or psychologically to punish himself, for such unacceptable feelings, he could transform the guilt, turning the aggression on himself and into the wish for his own destruction (i.e., "kill me").

The tendency of traditional Jewish comment is to vindicate Moses. Some (Ginsburg, 1966; Plaut, 1981) have suggested that the scribes changed the text to avoid disrespect. They claim that Moses had really said either *their* wretchedness (that is, he did not want to see the misfortunes which would befall the people) or *Your* wretchedness (ascribing evil to God).

Psychologically, more than one possibility, even opposing thoughts can co-exist in the unconscious. Certainly all those thoughts are feasible. A straight reading of the text (*my* wretchedness) emphasizes the expressions of Moses' own internal feelings. The attempts to exculpate Moses miss the significant aspects of his development. In order for him to mature psychologically and overcome his death wish, Moses must face his own limitations or failures ("my wretchedness") and accept his own inner feelings.

A NURSING-FATHER

Moses, in frustration, tries to reject the notion that he is responsible for the people as both a mother and father. He asks:

> Have I conceived all this people? have I brought them forth, that Thou shouldest say unto me: Carry them in thy bosom, as a nursing-father carrieth the sucking child, unto the land which thou did swear unto their father? (Numbers 11:12)

Our attention is focused on a unique struggle for Moses. And it highlights a time when the Children of Israel are likewise struggling with their development. Moses essentially is saying, "I did not give birth to these people, why should I be responsible for them like a mother is responsible for her young child?" He is feeling tremendous demands from the people and especially from God to "bear," "carry" and feed the people. Essentially, he equates the demands with filling the role that a nursing mother does for its baby ("carrying them in thy bosom as a nursing father carrieth the sucking child"). This example, while symbolic, represents a demand which he cannot fulfill, yet he feels that he must meet the needs of the people. That self-imposed demand evokes psychological conflict and emotions that drive him to suicidal thought.

He hears his people *"weeping, family by family, every man at the door of his tent"* (Numbers 11:10). A quick reading of these lines might lead one to suggest that the people were crying in public, because they were without food. But there is more interaction between the people and Moses, and Moses and God that suggests that these lines reflect significant aspects of development and needs. The people have just left Egypt where as slaves they were essentially told how to run their lives. Having walked through the threshold of emancipation, they are faced with the responsibilities of making their own decisions about how their lives and families are to be. Now every man and every family struggles to be a family without the slave masters ordering them and structuring their lives. This is the birth that Moses also refers to, the birth of the family constituted in freedom. We find "every man at the door of his tent" weeping. Why at the door and not inside their home? The context and subtlety suggests more psychological possibilities. For instance, does family conflict occur and lead to or result from the men not knowing how to be *in* their families, where freedom had changed and made new demands and responsibilities. These family demands and the anguish parallel the tremendous expectations and distress that Moses felt.

Moses questions his role and responsibility. He questions whether God has acted like an active and supportive parent. Moses has led the people and clearly is deeply concerned for them. In the past, he has argued to save them from destruction, from Pharaoh, and from God's anger after the golden calf. He has been a strong masculine model, but currently, he is rejecting a role, "nursing father," that he feels is beyond him. A crucial distinction is necessary here. Moses is *not* simply rejecting the role of symbolic mother or father. He is saying that he can't be *both* a nursing mother and a father. In other words, "I have limits!" We are faced with the implications of what roles men and women play in the development of their children. Some have tried to differentiate the role of "mothering" from the role of "teacher" (Besdin, 1981). Moses seems to be struggling with whatever special experience a mother may offer, that he as a male cannot. Neither the mother nor the father can be all things for the child, and Moses is not omnipotent.

Moses' leadership helped free these people and created a community. The "whining" and complaints against him and God reflect nostalgic looks back to a past that had become in fantasy satisfying and nurturing rather than dangerous in comparison to the present. This look to the past is their defense, to avoid looking at the difficulties of the present, that they do not yet know how to resolve. They say:

> we remember the fish which we used to eat in Egypt for nought, the cucumbers, and the melons, and the leeks, and the onions, and the garlic, but now our soul is dried away; there is nothing at all; we have nought save this manna to look to. (Numbers 11:5)

Why after all that has happened, e.g., the ten plagues, freedom from slavery, the passage through the sea, and the destruction of the Egyptian army, do the people complain so bitterly? Do they need to be given hope and nurturance even beyond the food that they cry for?

Soloveitchik (Besdin, 1981) insightfully suggests that the people's cry for "flesh" is a euphemism for that which is sensual. From a psychological perspective, these cries are regressive. The references for "flesh" and melons, etc. to feed their "soul," coupled with the associations that Moses makes of the demands, i.e., "carry them in your bosom, as a nursing-father carries the sucking child," reflects very early longings (pre-Oedipal) for the feelings and sensations of a young child being taken care of. This was also the role that Moses, in exasperation, cried that he could not fulfill.

There are numerous lessons from this scenario. Initially, Moses speaks as though he should have been able to meet the demands except that there has been a change in plans, saying to God, "Wherefore hast though dealt ill with thy servant?" (Numbers 11:11) Then he doubts that he can provide for them, "Whence should I have flesh to give unto all this people." And finally he cries for assistance in this task. "I cannot carry all this people by myself." If he cannot be relieved of this demand he cries for the mercy of death.

To fully understand Moses' death wish, we must also consider the experience of the whole group consciousness. Moses is in some ways articulating the unconscious issues of the people he is identified with. When Moses feels overwhelmed by demands, he also reflects the people feeling overwhelmed by demands on them, e.g., to flee their homes, to survive suddenly in the desert, constantly moving, changing family demands and the responsibilities of their own decisions. These changes leave the people filled with doubts and uncertainties. They struggle with the ambiguities of this life, and perhaps are unsure of what is expected of them. They do what members of groups often do when the rules are ambiguous and they haven't yet accepted responsibility for their own lives. They criticize their leader.

At the same time, we find an attitude in Moses that is similar to the danger that can be found when professionals take on too much responsibility in helping others. In spite of requests for help, resistance emerges, personality factors interfere, defenses against change are mobilized and the professional is defeated or "burns out."

A different type of similarity also may exist to the parents of suicide victims. This occurs when parents view their adolescent's attempts at individuation or separation as a sign of family "disloyalty" and rejection instead of an attempt (albeit sometimes misguided) to grow up. An example of such biblical similarity is, "For you have rejected the Lord who is among you by whining before Him and saying Oh why did we ever leave Egypt!" (Numbers 11:20). Jung held the idea that the Israelites' experience represented a constant individuation process (Edinger, 1986).

THE INSECURITY OF FREEDOM

Where am I? Where am I going? What am I doing? These are questions that strike terror in people as they begin to face the difficulty of taking responsibility for themselves.

Moses and the people struggled to overcome and be free from the harsh superego, represented by the Egyptian Pharaoh and his task masters. We all face the slavery of this way of thinking. Submission is a way to avoid aloneness and anxiety. And freedom leads to an awareness of limitations (Fromm, 1969). Being free leaves people in a position where they must struggle with new feelings. How do we make the decisions that represent and maintain our freedom? How do we nurture each other or even ourselves, once we find ourselves free? There is no one easy solution. For in freedom, one faces the consequences of their decisions and actions. So Moses turns in anguish as he faces the people's struggle with their new found needs and questions, who will nurture us?

LIMITATIONS

By facing the fears that the people held, Moses stirred up very powerful feelings in himself. He questions and doubts:

> The people among whom I am are six hundred thousand men on foot; and yet thou hast said: I will give them flesh that they may eat a whole month! (Numbers 11:21)

Moses doubted that enough could be provided to meet the needs of the people, even after he was told it would be provided. He faced the possibility that the people he had freed could die in the wilderness he led them into. Even if he knew that their children would go on to the "promised land," his strong reaction and emotions suggest it would have been an agonizing realization. This means that Moses had to recognize what he could and could not do. And that he could not completely help them in the way they expected.

This is the challenge that we sometimes face with patients. We can't always expect to completely help everyone. We are limited, even when they ask, can't you do more?

When the people weep and say, "what have you saved us for?" (Numbers 11:20), this is a crucial question for Moses. It forces him to face some bitter truths, some that have been repressed. It is not simply to take them into the promised land that they have left Egypt. It is for them to become a strong group or nation that will survive attacks and the struggles of life. To become that, they cannot whine for their "need" of nurturance like infants, they have to find it in other ways. They cannot stand at the door weeping and not knowing whether to be in or out of the family. They have to make certain decisions and accept certain obligations. They must develop so that their slave mentalities and yearnings for the harsh superego of Egypt will be shed, even if it means that their generation will die in the process. Moses is limited, he despairs and feels helpless in the face of such forces. This is an emotional turning point in the development of Moses and the community.

THE SPIRIT FOR CHANGE

On the surface it appears that the solution to Moses' despair and repeated crises, "I am not able to bear all this people myself alone, because it is too heavy for me" (Numbers 11:14 and 11) is the reorganization that shares his spirit and burden with seventy elders of the people.

> Gather unto me seventy men of the elders of Israel, whom thou knowest to be the elders of the people, and officers over them; and bring them unto the tabernacle of the congregation, that they may stand there with thee. And I will come down and talk with thee there; and I will take of the spirit which is upon thee, and will put it upon them; and they shall bear the burden of the people with thee, that thou bear it not thyself alone. (Numbers 11:16-17)

Moses transforms the frustration and anger that both he and the people feel into an experience of community. He achieves this after facing the agonizing aspects of his limits. He asks for help, gathers together with the seventy elders, talks and shares his special spirit.

Picking a specific number suggests that a certain structure is being built into the system. However, the number chosen, seventy, is very unusual. Since there are 12 tribes, six from each of the 12 tribes would equal 72. Seventy cannot be picked without the potential of offending someone or some tribe(s).

So the next step was the task of picking seventy with minimal offense to the people and the tribes. The Babylonian Talmud (Sanhedrin 17a) suggests that 72 were actually picked, but two either did not partake or were not chosen to be among this group. The experience of these two further elaborates the resolution of conflicts for Moses:

> and the spirit rested upon them: and they were of them that were recorded, but had not gone out unto the tent; and they prophesied in the camp. And there ran a young man, and told Moses and said: 'Eldad and Medad are prophesying in the camp.' And Joshua the son of Nun, the minister of Moses from his youth up, answered and said: 'My lord Moses, shut them in.' And Moses said unto him: 'Art thou jealous for my sake? would that all the Lord's people were prophets, and that the Lord would put his spirit upon them.' (Numbers 11:26-29)

The two continued to prophesy, much to the chagrin of Joshua who came to Moses asking that he stop them. This continues the theme of jealously and offending others that Moses must have considered when he picked only seventy. Moses is not threatened, to the contrary, he suggests the hope of a new goal, that all God's people should be prophets. Would contemporary political scientists interpret grass roots democracy being suggested here?

To better understand the solution that involved the picking of seventy elders who prophesied, we must ask another question. What is a prophet? Note that Moses referred to the people all becoming prophets and not just prophesying. One of the controversies in a democracy is whether the role of a leader is to protect and safeguard the people, or to advance the moral development of the people. This latter role is what prophets do. They raise the moral issues and sincerely question values. They urge the people to take responsibility for their own lives. They ask the crucial questions.

We find Joshua being told that he is envious. Moses is encouraging Joshua to accept responsibility for his *own* feelings ("jealous for my sake?"). The model reflected here is one of self exploration, as Moses did, struggling with his feelings, limitations and "wretchedness."

The lesson that Moses teaches Joshua is the lesson that has helped Moses transcend his own despair and his fears. His mission is no longer to just lead the people through the desert to a land promised to their fathers. His calling is refined. Seventy can share the task and overcome the isolation, and the possibility exists for all the people to follow. The promised land he is leading them to is a land where they can discover themselves, the problems of living, and how to deal with others and their needs.

To live in the present, Moses has found a purpose that gives his life meaning. This is part of his solution to the trap of self-destructive thought. He has revised his goal. He continues the process of raising the level of self understanding by sharing not only his spirit with seventy, but his insight with one (Joshua). He is gratified that others continue this process and pick up the spirit to teach the people.

The people will be in a better position, both individually and as a group, to answer the questions "who am I" and "where are we going," by their struggles to master their feelings and gain the insights of self awareness. Awareness, rather than their old memories, becomes the basis for their new identities.

The community will find itself in a new emotional place, where the people can survive their most horrendous thoughts and fears, e.g., annihilation, failure, self destruction, jealousy, etc. New to freedom, they are learning the boundaries of their emotions and how to cope with fears and wants. They need these changes and the experiences of their powers and vulnerabilities as much as they need bread.

PRESENT—FUTURE—PAST

At the burning bush Moses asked God what his name was. He was told:

> I am what I am, I will be what I will be. And when you tell your people of this experience tell them it is the same YHVH they know about. (Exodus 3:14).

This response has great significance. It is the meaning of this name that sends Moses on the quest to free the Hebrews. It suggests an internal focus not an external one. It suggests a merging of the present with both the future and the past. What can be more powerful than having access to those three dimensions. Finding the answer to who we are, what we have been and what we can be is a challenge that we all face at many times in our lives.

Moses is told that he will be like a god to Aaron (Exodus 4:16) and will also be placed in the role of God to Pharaoh (Exodus 7:1). Will Moses, in these relationships and in his relationship with the people he sets out to free, discover what he is and what he can and cannot be? This is an appellation and a task "for all eternity" (Exodus 3:15).

For Moses, confidence re-emerges after experiencing his own emotional struggle. He expresses his deepest feelings ("I cannot bear this alone"), and struggles to define his responsibility. He stands with others, talking and sharing his spirit.

Moses recovered from intense exasperation, feeling overwhelmed, despairing and hopeless with no view of a viable future. By accepting his limitations, he could ask the questions that allowed him to define his responsibility in context with God's responsibility.

After doubting the possibility of surviving, he integrates his past (hidden feelings) with a refined future (the promised land of prophets). Picking the seventy elders was a masculine alternative to nurture the people. It offered structure, transformed their emotions and gave them a system and a model beyond the present. He values the changes, advocates accepting help and is hopeful that all the people can be involved and join in this growth. He now sees his calling as sharing his spirit and raising the people's awareness of themselves. This will develop a nation that can not only possess a land, but fulfill their promise.

REFERENCES

Babylonian Talmud. 1975. Jerusalem: Vilna Edition.
Becker, E. 1971. *The Birth and Death of Meaning*, 2nd Edition. New York: The Free Press.
Besdin, A. R. 1981. *Reflections of the Rav.* Israel: World Zionist Organization.
Edinger, E. 1986. *The Bible and the Psyche: Individuation Symbolism in the Old Testament.* Toronto: Inner City Books.
Fromm, E. 1969. *Escape From Freedom.* New York: Avon Books.
Ginsburg, C. D. 1966. *Introduction to the Massoretico-Critical Edition of the Hebrew Bible.* New York: Ktav.
Ginzberg, L. 1956. *Legends of the Bible.* Philadelphia: The Jewish Publication Society.
Greenstone, J. 1948. *The Holy Scriptures: Numbers with Commentary.* Philadelphia: The Jewish Publication Society of America.
Hertz, J. H. (Ed.). 1981. *Pentateuch and Haftorahs*, 2nd Edition. London: The Soncino Press.
Heschel, A. J. 1975. *The Insecurity of Freedom: Essays on Human Existence.* New York: Shocken Books.
Leibowitz, N. 1980. *Studies in Bamidbar* (Numbers). Jerusalem: The World Zionist Organization.
Noth, M. 1968. *Numbers: A Commentary.* Philadelphia: Westminster Press.
Plaut, W. G. 1981. *The Torah.* New York: Union of American Hebrew Congregations.
Wildavsky, A. 1984. *The Nursing Father: Moses as a Political Leader.* The University of Alabama Press.

17

Jonah versus Narcissus

A Biblical Approach to Suicide Prevention

KALMAN J. KAPLAN, PH.D.

Examination of suicide narratives in Greek tragedy and the Hebrew Bible reveals the following pattern; some sixteen suicides occur in the writings of Sophocles and Euripides alone while only six suicides occur in the Hebrew Bible. Further, the Hebrew Bible contains a number of suicide-prevention narratives. The present paper compares two classic narratives, those of Narcissus and Jonah, in an attempt to understand what, if anything, is *suicide-promoting* in the Greek world and what is *suicide-preventing* in the biblical world. The theoretical point of departure follows from Durkheim's (1897/1951) distinction between egoistic, altruistic, and anomic suicides. Egoistic suicide is seen as resulting from an isolation of self from society. Altruistic suicide is seen as resulting from a lack of differentiation between self and society. Anomic suicide, finally, refers to a confusion in boundaries between self and society.

NARCISSUS AND GREEK SUICIDE

The Durkheim typology can be directly applied to the sixteen suicides in the writings of Sophocles and Euripides (see Table 1). Consider, for example, the *egoistic* suicide of Ajax in Sophocles' great play of the same name. What is learned in the play is essentially this: "Ajax has run amok because Achilles' armor has been given to Odysseus. In a 'frenzied' state and filled with 'grievous wrath' he attempts to murder Odysseus. He is prevented by the goddess Athena, who guides him in his 'ecstasy' to a herd of sheep upon

Table 1. Suicides in Greek Tragedy

Character	Gender	Source	Method	Type
Ajex	M	Ajax (Sophocles)	Sword	Egoistic
Oedipus	M	Oedipus Rex (Sophocles)	Self-blinding	Egoistic
Jocasta	F	Oedipus Rex (Sophocles)	Hanging	Egoistic
Haemon	M	Antigone (Sophocles)	Sword	Egoistic
Eurydice	F	Antigone (Sophocles)	Knife	Egoistic
Deianeira	F	The Trachinae (Sophocles)	Sword	Egoistic
Heracles	M	The Trachinae (Sophocles)	Burning	Anomic
Antigone	F	Antigone (Sophocles)	Hanging	Anomic
Hermione	F	Andromache (Euripides)	Suicidal threats	Anomic
Phaedra	F	Hippolytus (Euripides)	Hanging	Anomic
Evadne	F	The Suppliants (Euripides)	Burning	Altruistic
Iphigenia	F	Iphigenia in Aulis (Euripides)	Axe	Altruistic
Memoeceus	M	The Phoenissae (Euripides)	Jumped	Altruistic
Macaria	F	The Heracleidae (Euripides)	Knife	Altruistic
Polyxena	F	Hecuba (Euripides)	Sword	Altruistic
Alcestis	F	Alcestis (Euripides)	Poisoned	Altruistic

Note: M=Male, F=Female.

which he wreaks great slaughter, believing it to contain both Odysseus and those who were responsible for his getting the armor . . . Before long, the 'ecstasy' passes and Ajax discovers himself amidst the animals he has killed. The realization of what has happened has a devastating effect on him . . . He winces at the thought of Odysseus laughing over his plight. He will kill himself, he announces, 'because his former glory is gone'" [pp. 463–467].[1] Many of the suicides in Sophocles, mostly male, are of exactly this type (see Table 1).

Suicides in Euripides are portrayed with a marked difference. The majority can be thought of as falling into Durkheim's *altruistic* type. Macaria, the daughter of Heracles in The *Heracleidae* provides an excellent example. Demophon, King of Athens, announces that a royal maiden must be sacrificed if the Athenians are to succeed in repelling the attacks of Heracles' old enemy when Eurystheus "ventures forth" to inquire into the trouble. She encounters Iolaus,

---

[1] This quotation and all subsequent quotations from Greek Tragedies come from W. J. Oates and E. O'Neill, Jr.: *The Complete Greek Drama*, 1938.

her father's old friend and companion who puts pressure on her, saying to her [pp. 482–491]:

> My daughter, tis nothing new that I should praise thee, as I justly may, above all the children of Heracles. Our house seemed to be prospering, when back it fell again into a hopeless state; for the King declares the prophets signify that he must order the sacrifice of some tender maid of noble lineage, if we and this city are to exist. Herein is our perplexity; the King refuses either to sacrifice his own or any other's child. Therefore, though he use not terms express, yet doth he hint, that, unless we find some way out of this perplexity, for he this country fair would save.

The embedded quality of Macaria's internalization of the group superego classifies her suicide as altruistic. It is typical of many suicides in Euripides, many of whom are female.

Some of the most lethal suicides in Greek Tragedy may actually classify as Durkheim's *anomic* type. Consider the examples of Sophocles' (*Antigone*) and of Euripides' Phaedra (*Hippolytus*). Antigone defies Creon's edict that no one, on pain of death, bury Polyneices, son of Oedipus and Jocasta and brother of both Antigone and Ismene. Antigone decides to go ahead and give her brother the burial rites she feels are due him. Although Antigone is typically singled out in this regard as the most individualistic of Greek heroines, she may be also one of the least individualistic, over integrated with her idealized sense of family and community to such an extent that her desire to bury her brother cannot be separated from her desire to die. Consider Phaedra as a second example of anomic suicide. *Hippolytus* opens with Phaedra being consumed by her passion for the title character who is the illegitimate son of her husband Theseus. At the same time, Phaedra shows an intense preoccupation with her honor throughout the drama—with her self as it exists in the eyes of other people.

Although the term "narcissistic" is an extremely popular term in modern psychology and psychiatry, we may be less aware that the myth of Narcissus in fact is a suicide story. We turn to it for a direct and simple Greek understanding of the psychodynamics of suicide. Earliest sources of the myth of Narcissus are long since lost. The most complete account from antiquity is to be found in the first-century Roman poet Ovid's *Metamorphoses* [1955, iii, 11.339–510]. Yet it is Conon's version [1798] that specifically articulates the death of Narcissus as a suicide. The following events are highlights in the life and death of Narcissus (Ovid, 1955).

1. A seer prophesied that Narcissus would live to a ripe old age provided that he never knew himself [iii, 11.347–349].
2. Although anyone would have fallen in love with him, he heartlessly rejected lovers of both genders, because he had a stubborn pride (hubris) in his own beauty. Among those lovers was Echo, who had no voice of her own and could only reflect back what Narcissus said. Narcissus rejected Echo roughly, saying, "I will die before I would have you touch me" [iii, 11.359–400].
3. One of those Narcissus scorned raised his hands to heaven and prayed: "May he, himself, fall in love with another, as we have done with him; May he, too, be unable to gain his loved one!" [11.402–407].
4. Nemesis, hearing this righteous prayer, caused Narcissus to seek shelter from the sun near a pool and to fall in love with his own reflection. At first, Narcissus tried to embrace and kiss the beautiful boy who confronted him [iii, 11.408–433].
5. Subsequently, he recognized himself and lay gazing at his image for hours. "How I wish I could separate myself from my body" [iii, 1.463].
6. Grief was destroying him, yet he rejoiced in the knowledge that his other self would remain true to him. Saying "alas" (which Echo repeated), Narcissus plunged a dagger into his breast (Conon, 1798). [Ovid here describes Narcissus as pining away unto death; iii, 11.480–495].

What is suicide-promoting in this myth? In the first part of the narrative, Narcissus tends to be self-absorbed, treating his lovers as mere extensions or mirrors of himself. This trend becomes accentuated in his relationship with Echo who becomes a perfect mirror for Narcissus, reflecting back everything Narcissus says (see Kohut's, 1971, distinction between mirroring and idealizing narcissism). Narcissus is thus egoistic in Durkheim's terms, insufficiently connected with his environment; yet, he is not suicidal at this time. The events in the story proceed. A rejected suitor prays that Narcissus himself will experience unrequited love. Nemesis answers this prayer, causing Narcissus, for the first time, to fall hopelessly in love. He now idealizes the face in the brook (not realizing that it represents his own reflection). Narcissus is now altruistic in Durkheim's terms, insufficiently differentiated from his environment; yet, he is still not suicidal. Ultimately, however, Narcissus recognizes that the face in the brook is his. The reflection becomes simultaneously an ideal and a mirror. He is not self-invested, but self-empty, driven to grasp his self, which has now been projected onto the outside world. Such a psychotic juxtaposition rips Narcissus apart. As Ovid expressed it, "How I wish I could separate myself from my body." This represents an extreme statement of an anomic confusion in the boundaries between self and the outside world and is suicide-promoting.

JONAH AND BIBLICAL SUICIDE PREVENTION

The Durkheim typology can also be applied to suicidal behavior in the Hebrew Bible. Of the six suicides listed in Table 2, three (Ahitophel, Zimri, and Abimelech) can be classified as egoistic, and three (Samson, Saul, and Saul's armor bearer) can be classified as altruistic. None fall into Durkheim's lethal anomic category.

The story of Ahitophel represents a prime example of egoistic suicide in the Hebrew Bible (2 Samuel 17:23). One of several reasons all egoistic, probably prompted Ahitophel's suicide. First, he knew that Absalom's attempt to overthrow David was doomed, and he would die a traitor's death. Secondly, and less likely, is the disgust of Ahitophel at Absalom's conduct in setting aside his counsel, thus wounding Ahitophel's pride and disappointing his ambition. Finally, David's curse [Makkot, 4a] may have prompted Ahitophel to hang himself. Ahitophel, significantly, is listed in the Mishna [Sanhedrin X, 2] as among those who have forfeited their share in the world to come.

A good example of altruistic suicide may be Samson's final effort in bringing down the Philistine temple upon himself as well as his enemies. It is vividly described in the Book of Judges: "And he bent with all his might; and the house fell upon the Lords, and upon all the people that were therein, so the dead that he slew at his death were more than that he slew in life" (Judges 16:23–30).

What may be of greater significance here is the number of suicide preventions in the Hebrew Bible of characters in seemingly hopeless and perhaps anomic positions (see Table 3). Job, for example, expresses a clearly suicidal wish out of the depths of his affliction (Job 7:15). Yet Job does not commit suicide, and, indeed, seems to recover his faith: "Though he slay me, yet I will trust in Him" (Job 13:15). The prophet Elijah represents another example of suicide prevention. He, too, clearly expresses a renewed strength and faith (I Kings 19:8). Finally, Moses himself expresses suicidal wishes to God while he is in the desert. He is overwhelmed by his burdens, which he must shoulder alone (Numbers 11:14–15). Once again, God successfully intervenes by offering to share Moses' burden (Numbers 11:16–17).

The Book of Jonah provides an understanding of what is suicide-preventing in the biblical narratives. The following events are highlighted from the Book of Jonah:

Table 2. Suicides in the Hebrew Bible

Character	Gender	Source	Method	Type
Ahitophel	M	2 Sam. 17:23	Strangling	Egoistic
Zimri	M	1 Kings 16:18	Burning	Egoistic
Abimelech	M	Judg. 9:54	Sword	Egoistic
Samson	M	Judg. 16:30	Crushing	Altruistic
Saul	M	Sam. 31:4 2 Sam. 1:6 1 Chron. 10:4	Sword	Altruistic
Saul's Armor bearer	M	1 Sam. 31:5 1 Chron. 10:5	Sword	Altruistic

Table 3. Suicide Preventions in the Hebrew Bible

Character	Gender	Source	Method
Elijah	M	1 Kings 18–19	Protected withdrawal and nurturance
Moses	M	Numbers 11	Support and practical advice
David	M	Psalms 22	Renewal of faith in God
Job	M	Job	Renewal of relationship
Rebecca	F	Genesis 27–28	Appropriate matchmaking
Jonah	M	Jonah	Protected withdrawal and guidance

1. Jonah was ordered by God to go to Nineveh to warn it of its wickedness. Jonah attempted to escape God by running away to Tarshish (Jon. 1:1–1:3).
2. God sent a great wind after him, endangering his ship. When asked his identity by his shipmaster, Jonah admitted to being the cause of the storm. Jonah asked his shipmates to throw him into the sea to spare them. "Take me up and cast me forth into the seas, so shall the sea be calm unto you; for I know that for my sake this great tempest is upon you" (Jon. 1:4–1:16).
3. They did so and Jonah was saved by a great fish prepared by God: "And the Lord prepared a great fish to swallow up Jonah; and Jonah was in the belly of the fish for three days and three nights, Jonah prayed to God and the fish vomited Jonah out into dry bones" (Jon. 2:1–2:11).
4. God sent Jonah to Nineveh a second time. This time Jonah went and gave the people of Nineveh God's message. They repented and were saved, but Jonah expresses his anger that they were saved and expresses a strong desire to die: "Therefore, now, O Lord, take, I beseech Thee, my life from me; for it is better for me to die than to live" (Jon. 3:1–4:4).
5. Jonah left the city to sit on its outskirts. There he was shielded from the sun by a gourd prepared by God: "And the Lord prepared a gourd and made it come up over Jonah, that it might be a shadow over his head, to deliver him from his evil" (Jon. 4:5–4:6).
6. God then destroys the gourd with a worm. Jonah again expresses the wish to die: "And it came to pass, when the sun arose, that God prepared a vehement east wind; and the sun beat upon the head of Jonah, that he fainted, and requested for himself that he might die, and said: "It is better for me to die than to live" (Jon. 4:7–4:8).
7. God again intervenes, asking Jonah, "Art though greatly angry for the gourd?" When Jonah admits that he is, God tries to implant his lesson of divine mercy: "Thou hast pity on the gourd, for which thou has not labored, neither madest it to grow, which came up in a night and perished in a day; and should not I have pity on Nineveh, that great city, wherein are more than six score thousand persons that

cannot discern between their right hand and their left hand, and also much cattle?" (Jon. 4:9–4:11).

What is suicide-preventing in this narrative? Jonah is presented with a terrible dilemma in the beginning of the story. As can be seen in Jonah's later words, Nineveh represents a symbol of evil to him, and he thinks that it should not be spared through God's mercy. At the same time, Jonah does not want to deny God. In Lewis's (1961) terms, "He is too God-fearing to defy and too opinionated to submit." In Durkheim's terms, he avoids both altruistic and egoistic solutions. He runs in anomic confusion and tells his shipmates to throw him overboard. The story could thus end in anomic suicide, *but it doesn't*—God intervenes as a protective parent, swallowing Jonah in the protective stomach of a great fish until he overcomes his confusion. This same pattern occurs later in the story as well. Jonah again becomes suicidally torn between egoistic individuation and altruistic attachment. Again God provides protection (this time a gourd) until Jonah can end his anomic confusion with regard to self and others. After the protective gourd is destroyed by a worm, Jonah once again expresses suicidal thoughts. God once again intervenes, this time engaging Jonah in a mature dialogue in a successful attempt to end his anomic confusion with regard to individuation and attachment.

NARCISSUS AND JONAH: A COMPARISON

Table 4 compares the life narratives of Narcissus and Jonah with regard to suicide and suicide-prevention. The suicidogenic element in the myth of Narcissus is the inability of Narcissus to successfully integrate his individuation and attachment behaviors. First he is individuated at the expense of attachment (i.e. egoistic); then he is attached at the expense of individuation (i.e., altruistic). Finally, he is overwhelmed by the irreconcilable confusion between his individuation and attachment issues (i.e., anomic) and resolves the conflict through self-murder.

The suicide-preventing element in the story of Jonah, in comparison, is God's covenantal intervention providing a protective shield to allow Jonah to harmoniously reconcile his individuation-attachment dilemma.

Table 4. Suicide, Suicide Threats, and Suicide Prevention, for Narcissus and Jonah

Act	Outcome
Narcissus	
1. Narcissus mirrors and abandons Echo.	Egoistic position
2. Narcissus idealizes face in brook.	Altruistic position
3. Narcissus recognizes face in brook as his own and stabs himself with a dagger.	Anomic suicide
Jonah	
1a. Jonah runs away in confusion from God's command to go to Nineveth. Asks to be thrown overboard.	Anomic confusion and suicidal intent
1. God protects Jonah with big fish.	Covenantal suicide prevention
2a. Jonah leaves Nineveh, again expressing suicidal desires.	Anomic confusion and suicidal intent
2b. God protects Jonah with gourd.	Covenantal suicide prevention
3a. Jonah again expresses suicidal desire when gourd is destroyed.	Anomic confusion and suicidal intent
3b. God engages Jonah in dialogue regarding divine mercy.	Covenantal suicide prevention

Jonah's rejection of egoistic and altruistic resolutions need not lead to suicidal oscillation or to anomic suicide. A covenantal *wall* can be seen to allow the individual time to work out his *boundary* confusion at his own pace. He may need to regress to an earlier stage to do so, and he will need protection to do so. In the biblical world, God provided this shield with a fish and a gourd (Jonah), with special support (Moses), with trustworthiness (Job), and with food and drink (Elijah). In the modern world, parental understanding, therapeutic protectiveness and hospitals may provide some of this same protective function. Covenantal walls may be suicide-preventive, shielding the anomically confused individual from external pressures until he can straighten out his individuation-attachment dilemma.

Interestingly, Table 1 shows only one Greek story that did not end in suicide or self-destructive mutilation. This one exception is Hermione in Euripides; *Andromache* who is rescued from her suicidal dilemma through the protective walls provided by her father, Menelaus. Faber (1970) looks upon such escape as regressive and no solution whatsoever. "Instead of coming to understand the reasons for her disappointing marriage, for her aggressive and self-aggressive behavior. Hermione "goes back" to the old dependent union, to the very bond which provoked her "woe" in the first place, and which is now preventing the emergence of her adult personality" [pp. 203–204]. Faber may be correct if Hermione's move is permanent. From a biblical perspective, such protected regression, if temporary, may be exactly the intervention required to prevent suicidal confusion from becoming action, whether such intervention is performed by God, parents, or therapists. Hopefully, we will know when the time is right to lift the protective wall.

REFERENCES

The Babylonian Talmud 18 vol. (1961). I. Epstein (ed.), Soncino Press: London.

Conon. *Narrations Qvingvaginta et Parathenii Narrationes Amatoriae* (1798). J. C. Dietrich, Gottingae.

Durkheim, E. (1897/1951) *Suicide.* A. J. Spaulding and G. Simpson (trans.), The Free Press: New York.

Faber, M. D. (1970). *Suicide and Greek Tragedy.* Sphinx Press Inc.: New York.

Kaplan, K. J. & Schwartz, M. B. (1993). *A Psychology of Hope: An Antidote to the Suicidal Pathology of Western Civilization.* Praeger: Westport, Conn.

Kohut, H. (1971). *The Analysis of the Self.* International Universities Press: New York.

Lewis, C. (1961). Jonah—A Parable for Our Time. *Judaism.* 21. pp. 159–163.

The Midrash 10 vol. (1972). H. Friedman and M. Simons (ed.), Soncino Press: London.

Oates, W. J. & E. O'Neill Jr., (1938). *The Complete Greek Drama.* Random House. New York.

Ovid (1955). *The Metamorphoses.* M. Innes (trans.), Penguin Classics: London.

The Holy Scriptures (1955). The Jewish Publication Society of America: Philadelphia.

Epilogue

This volume has explored the issues of suicide, martyrdom and euthanasia in Jewish civilization ranging from philosophy to law to traditional narratives to specific life stories. Judaism emphasizes life in a number of central areas. First, unlike Greek mythology, the Hebrew Bible describes God as a concerned and all-powerful Creator. To destroy any life defaces the divine image and does damage to the divine plan of love in which the world was brought into being. Second, Judaism sees life belonging to God rather than to man. The Mishna, unlike the Greek and Roman stoics, does not posit illusory freedom or choice in matters beyond human control. "Against your will you are born, against your will you live, against your will, you die. Against your will you shall in the future give account before the King of Kings." (*Avot* 4, 29). Third, the rabbinic view emphasizes that the body and soul should function together harmoniously. Though the body supports the soul in their joint service of God, there is none of the Platonic sense that the body must die to liberate the soul. Finally, Judaism does not glorify martyrdom nor does it idealize death or sacrifice. Clearly, suicides do sometimes occur among Jews. However, they are not encouraged nor do Jewish martyrs actively court death as do martyrs in other religious cultures.

A case in point is the tragic mass suicide of David Koresh and the Branch Davidians in their compound in Waco, Texas in 1993. A number of articles and editorials have rushed to compare Waco with Masada as mass suicides. Hopefully, this collection will alert the reader to be more critical about such comparisons. We can think of three major differences between Waco and Masada.

First, it must be remembered that the only contemporary account of the Masada incident comes from Josephus, who was not an eyewitness and who hated the defenders of Masada (i.e., the

Sicarii). We cannot be sure that *any* point of his account is accurate, for example, he implausibly puts Graeco-Roman Platonic and Stoic arguments which praise death as "liberating the soul from the body" into the mouth of Eliezer Ben Yair, the leader of the Sicarii (Josephus, *The Wars of the Jews*, VII, p. 601). Judaism had and has little or none of this body-soul dualism and indeed Josephus gives himself a traditional rabbinic anti-suicide speech at another mass suicide at Jotapata in Galilee several years earlier (Ibid, III, p. 515).

This brings us to our second point. Whatever Eliezer Ben Yair may personally have felt about suicide, it is probable that his followers were largely not suicidal cultists. They fought off their human attackers for a long time. Even when their final defense structures were destroyed and defeat was imminent, Eliezer could not persuade the defenders to join a suicide pact through the Stoic and Brahmin arguments mentioned above. Only after he portrayed the cruel tortures and enslavement of their wives and children by the Romans did the Jewish defenders agree to mass suicide (Ibid, VII, p. 602). Nor was this an empty threat, for previous Jewish captives by the thousands had been sent to the galleys or fed to wild beasts in the arenas. Indeed mass suicide unfortunately was a common response for peoples in Asia Minor besieged by Greeks and Romans (Cohen, 1982). Men first slaughtered their families to save them from Roman torture and then themselves. The point is that the ancient Roman army was not governed by the same restraints as modern American law enforcement agents, however imperfect, and that the fear of being tortured and killed was quite *realistic* for the defenders of Masada. For the Branch Davidian group at Waco, in contrast, it is clear that there was a considerable amount of *paranoia and delusional thinking* as to what would happen to them if they turned themselves in. Despite this, it is important to stress that traditional Judaism did not glorify the "suicide" at Masada. First, it is not mentioned in the Talmud. Second, Josippon, a medieval Jewish historian who drew on Josephus, tells a story different than Josephus' account of Masada. Instead of a mass suicide, the men first kill their wives and children, to save them from prostitution and slavery, and then fight to the death against the Romans (Yosippon, 2, Ch. 87). Although modern Israel does induct elite trainees into its army at Masada, the message is not to suicide but to be strong so that Masada does not fall again.

This brings us to a third difference between Waco and Masada.

And this involves a subtle but important distinction between Jewish and Christian conceptions of martyrdom. According to the Babylonian Talmud (*Sanhedrin*, 74a), one is obliged to accept death when the alternative is being forced to commit idolatry, incest or murder. However, this means allowing oneself to be killed under certain prescribed circumstances, not actively killing oneself, which is no better than murdering someone else. Further, a Jew does not actively court death nor is martyrdom sought for its own sake. *It gains the Jew nothing theologically.* The paradigmatic Jewish martyr is Rabbi Akiba who was tortured cruelly by the Romans for teaching the Torah. As the story is told in the Babylonian Talmud (*Berachot*, 61b), a Roman officer saw Akiba smiling and asked him why. Akiba responded that he was in great agony and that he knew he would soon die. He was glad only that in his last moment, he could still sanctify God's name through prayer (the Shema). It is clear, however, that Akiba did not seek martyrdom for its own sake nor did his death have any sacrificial meaning. It would have been far better had Akiba not died. However, he could not avoid teaching the Torah and thus died. Historically, rabbinic advice often counselled prudence in matters such as this for the death of a martyr was not desired in Judaism.

The case is very different for Christianity and Christian martyrs, especially those before St. Augustine (354–438). The problem emerges from some interpretations put on the death of Jesus himself. Tertullian, for example, held that "Jesus Christ on the cross gave up the ghost freely and of His own volition before death by crucifixion overtook him." (*To the Martyrs*, 4) St. Augustine agreed on the voluntary aspects of the death of Jesus. "His soul did not leave His body constrained, but because He would and where He would and how He would." (*The Trinity*, 4) Centuries later, St. Thomas Aquinas argues very much the same position. (*Summa* 3.47.1) Indeed, the New Testament itself focuses on the mystery and passion of the sacrificial death of Jesus as part of a divine plan to save mankind. (*John* 3:16).

It is little wonder that Augustine was faced with a host of martyr-suicides in the early Church who seemed to actively court death in an imitation of Christ (*Imitatio Christi*). Ignatius and Cyprian represent two examples as do the heretical Circumcelliones and Donatists who often seemed to provoke their death. Ignatius, for example seems to feel an urgent need to prove his nothingness: "Pray leave me to be a meal for the beasts, for it is they who can provide my way to God . . . ground fine by lion's teeth to make pure bread for Christ." (*Epistles*, 4) Cyprian is even clearer, stressing that Jesus' crucifixion brought salvation to the world. His act of self-sacrifice and suffering was so immense, however, that it must now be "a great matter to imitate Him who in dying convicted the world." (*On the Glory of Martyrdom*, 29)

Augustine responded firmly to this challenge, strongly condemning many of these martyr-deaths as "veiled suicides." He strongly condemns suicide as a "detestable crime and a damnable sin." (*The City of God*, 1.27) He portrayed Jesus as urging flight from persecution rather than self-murder (Ibid, 1.22). Official Church decrees followed Augustine's lead and became increasingly more disapproving of suicide (The Council of Orleans, 533, The Council of Braga, 563, and the Council of Antisidor, 590). Nevertheless, a sense of the voluntary sacrificial aspect of the death of Jesus (albeit an altruistic suicide in Durkheim's terms) lingered on. In his famous work, *Biathanatos*, John Donne (1573–1631) stresses the implications of Jesus' death for a Christian tolerance and almost idealization of suicide. "It is a heroic act of fortitude, if a man when an urgent occasion is presented, exposes himself to a certain and assured death as He did." (*Biathanatos*, 3:45). Further, "And that Apollonia and others, who prevented the fury of the executioners, and cast themselves into the fires did therein imitate this act of our savior, of giving up his soul before he was constrained to do it."

And this takes us back to our basic point. We do not feel all mass suicides are alike and we most certainly do not feel that Waco and Masada are alike! If Masada in fact involved a mass suicide (and this is no historical certainty), it finds no justification in normative Judaism, past or present. The threat from the Romans was real, not imagined. Further, there is absolutely no theological reason within Judaism for Eliezer and the Sicarii to kill themselves. For misguided and shadowy fanatics such as Jim Jones (Jonestown) and David Koresh (Waco), the case is very different. They may well have seen themselves as "good Christians," and in fact, as Messianic figures in the process of dying, despite formal Church opposition to suicide. Their very fringe and cut-like status may have released Jones and Koresh from the inhibitions toward suicide provided by the contemporary organized church and left them prey to the wild and delusional strains so prevalent in pre-Augustinian Christianity. Koresh's identification with the New Testament Book of Revelations provides evidence of this. There was no comparable book in normative Judaism to haunt Eliezer at Masada or a Jew of today. The link between distorted conceptions of Christian (and Moslem, for that matter) martyrdom and suicide is a major problem for contemporary society and one with which religious leaders and mental health professionals must become more acquainted.

For example, Raphael Israeli, an internationally recognized expert in Islamic fundamentalism, points out that "when the PLO calls its casualties *shuhada* (martyrs) and its guerrillas *fidaiin*, it is clear that they imply the redemption inherent in dying for one's homeland, in the Muslim sense of the concept, since *fida'i* equals a *mujahid* (fighter for the cause of *jihad*, the Holy War)," (1993, p. 127).

The term "fida'i", roughly translated as "devotee," was used by the Ismaili Shi'ite sect of Islam in the eleventh and twelfth centuries to describe their offshoot, the Assassins, from the Arabic *hashish*. The Assassins were groups religious in inspiration, who used planned systematic murder as a political weapon, being willing to die themselves in the process. Established in Iran in the eleventh century, they spread to Syria in the twelfth century and operated from castles in remote mountain areas under a mysterious and shadowy leader known as "The Old Man of the Mountain" (*aloadin*) (See Bernard Lewis' *The Assassins: A Radical Sect in Islam*, 1987).

Israeli warns us that the emergence of fundamentalist Islam may have staggering consequences for Israel, the Middle East and the world, "A religiously-motivated Islam is likely to act far more boldly and with far more sense of self-sacrifice than a politically-oriented guerrilla/terrorist. *The fida'i tradition in Islam can make death a desirable end unto itself*" (1993, p. 199, italics ours). This tendency has been tragically evidenced by the terrorist "suicide" bombings carried out by Hamas in Tel Aviv, Jerusalem and throughout Israel, even while "peace talks" were being carried out between Israel and the PLO. We have attempted to address many of these issues in our book: *A Psychology of Hope: An Antidote to the Suicidal Pathology of Western Civilization* (Kaplan and Schwartz, 1993).

REFERENCES

Aquinas, Thomas. (1981). *Summa Theologica*. 5 vols. Trans. Fathers of the English Dominican Province. Westminster, MD: Christian Classics.

Augustinus, Aurelius. (1957–1972). *The City of God Against the Pagans*, 7 vols. Trans. William M. Green. Cambridge, MA: Harvard University Press.

Augustinus, Aurelius. (1963). *The Trinity*. Trans. D. McKenna. Washington, DC: The Catholic University of America Press.

Babylonian Talmud. (1975). Vilna Edition. Jerusalem, Israel.

Ben Gurion, Joseph. (1956). *Sefer Yosippon*. Jerusalem: Hotstaat Hominer.

Cohen, S. J. D. (1982). "Masada, literature, tradition, archaeological remains and the credibility of Josephus." *Journal of Jewish Studies*, 33, 385–405.

Cyprian. (1951). In *The Ante-Nicene Fathers*, 5. Ed. A. Roberts & J. Donaldson. Grand Rapids, MI: Wm. B. Eerdmans.

Donne, J. (1984). *Biathanatos*. Ed. Ernest W. Sullivan II. Cranbury, NJ: Associated University Press.

Durkheim, E. (1897/1951). *Suicide*. Trans. J. A. Spading & G. Simpson. Glencoe, IL: Free Press.

The Holy Scriptures. (1955). Philadelphia: The Jewish Publication Society of America.

Ignatius. (1968). *Epistles. Early Christian Writings*. Ed. B. Radice. Baltimore: Penguin Books.

Israeli, R. (1993). *Fundamentalist Islam and Israel: Essays in Interpretation*. University Press of America, Lanham, MD.

Josephus, Flavius (1985). *Completed Works*. Trans. W. Whiten. Grand Rapids, MI: Kernel.

Kaplan, K. J. & Schwartz, M. B. (1993). *A Psychology of Hope: An Antidote to the Suicidal Pathology of Western Civilization*. Westport, CT: Praeger.

Lewis, B. (1987). *The Assassins: A Radical Sect in Islam*. Oxford University Press, New York.

NASB Interlinear Greek-English New Testament. (1984). Grand Rapids, MI: Zondervan.

Index

Acceptance, unconditional, 137
Afterlife, 107–112
Akiba, Rabbi, 41, 70, 152, 199
Altruistic suicide, 138, 187
American Association of Suicidology (AAS), report of, compared to NY State Task Force's, 117–123
Anger, 26, 176
Anomic suicide, 188
Antiquities of the Jews (Josephus), 66
Anti-Semitism, 37–56
Aristotle, 9–10, 159
Asher, Rabbi Jacob ben (Tur), 71
Assassins, 201
Assisted suicide. *See* doctor assisted suicide
Athens and Jerusalem (Shestov), 33
Atonement, suicide as, 107
Avuyah, Elisha ben, 35

Balance suicide, 107
Beck, A. T., 122
Bible, suicide in
  incidence of, 62–65, 134
  preventions of, 190–193, 191
  prohibition against, 61–62, 75
Blood libel, 47–52
Boaz, Rabbi Joshua, 87–88
Body and soul, relationship between, 13–14
Book of the Pious (Wistinetzki), 87

Childhood suicide, 70, 72
Child-sacrifice, 134–137
Christianity, message of, 37–41
Christians as survivors of suicide, 41–53, 42
Le Cid (Corneille) compared to *The Fifth Son*, 143–158
Cognitive behavior therapy, 122–123
Competition, 137
Cowardice, 19
Creation stories
  Biblical vs. Greek, 133–142
  Greek, 28–29
  Hebrew version of, 32–33
Creator and created, relationship between, 138–140

Death
  choosing, 75

Death (*continued*)
  control over, 14–16
  dimensions of, 103
  Frankel's concept of, 109
  hastening, 88
  incomprehensibility of, 110
  logotherapy on, 102–103
  meaning of in life, 103–105
  and philosophy, link between, 8
  praying for, of another, 93
  problem of, 107–108
A Death of One's Own (Lerner), 126
Definition of Suicide (Shneidman), 78
Depression, 119, 120
Destiny, 31
Doctor assisted suicide, 98–112, 116–129. *See also* euthanasia
Doctor's mandate, 100–101
Droge, A. J., 75
Durkheim, E.
  suicide, definitions of, 38–39
  typology of, 186, 190

Easter persecutions, 48–52
Egoistic suicide, 138, 186
The Eight Chapters (Maimonides), 23
Elderly, loneliness in, 127
Emotional distress, components of, 125
Euthanasia. *See also* doctor assisted suicide; Kevorkianism
  active, 84–86, 89–96
  in America, 116–129
  forms of, 81–82
  Jewish position on, 89
  King Saul's death as, 64
  passive, 81, 86–89
  precedent for, 82–83, 91
  problem of, 80–84
Execution of criminals, 95
Existence, meaningful, 106–107
Existence after life, 7–8
Existential analysis, 104
Experimental therapy, 95

Failure, 105–107, 110
Family components, 125
Family pathology, 134–137
Fatalism
  Aher and, 35–36
  and suicide, interrelationship of, 27–34
Fate, 31
  and self-destruction, 32
  Stoics' view of, 14
The Fifth Son (Wiesel) compared to *Le Cid*, 143–158
Finiteness, human, 105–107, 109
Frankel, Viktor, logotherapy of, 101–112
Freedom, 134
  Greek vs. Hebrew thinking on, 5–6
  insecurity of, 180–181
  Stoics on, 15
  and suicide, relationship between, 13–14
Freud, Sigmund, 24–25, 27

God
  personification of, 26
  as psychological projection, 33

Graeco-Roman attitudes on suicide, 159
Greek thinking
  on acceptance, 28
  on suicide, 6–13, 159–167
  vs. Hebrew, on freedom, 5–6
Greek tragedy
  incidence of suicide in, 134, 160–161
  suicide in, 187
Greenwald, Rabbi Jekuthiel Judah, 73
Greenwald, Y., 99
Group consciousness, Moses' death wish and, 179–180
Guilt, 105–106, 110

Halakhic option, suicide as, 80–96
Halakhic prohibition on suicide, 114
Hebrew thinking
  on freedom and suicide, relationship between, 13–16
  vs. Greek, 5–6, 159–167
Heiman, Aaron, 35
Heracleidae, 41
Heroism, 138, 146–148, 153
Homicide. *See* murder
Hope, 173, 174
Hopelessness, 17, 95
Horney, Karen, 138
Host desecration slander, 47–48
Human responsibility. *See* responsibleness
Humor, healing power of, 126

Humphrey, Derek, 124
Hysteria, as result of wrongdoing, 24

Ideal Truth, 7
Imperfection, 106
Instinct, 19
Intellection, and misconduct, 23
Intellectual apprehension, 24–25
Intentional suicide, 70, 71, 79
Interpersonal components, 125
Iphigenia in Aulis, 41
Irretrievability, 105
Irreversibility, 104
Isaac
  compared to Job, 174
  compared to Oedipus, 135–136
Isaac and Oedipus (Wellisch), 27–28
Israeli, Raphael, 201
Isserles, Rabbi Moses, 87

Jakobovits, Rabbi Immanuel, euthanasia, Jewish position on, 89
Jesus, death of
  and anti-semitism, 37–56
  blame of Jews for, 46–47
  Christian as suicide survivor of, 43
  as martyr/suicide, 38–39
  potential responses to, 43–46
  ritual murder charges in, 47–48
  voluntary aspects of, 37–38
Jew as hero, 144–146

Jewish Law, Code of, on burial honors, 160
Jewish laws
    criteria for suicidal act, 79
    on Kevorkianism, 101
    on mourning, 72
    on murder, 95–96
    suicide in, 61–76, 71–72
Jewish views
    on euthanasia, 85–86, 89
    on life and death, 143–158
    on martyrdom, 73–74
    on Masada, 66
    misinterpretation of, 75
    on suicide, 22, 61–62, 73, 99–100
Job, 168–175, 190–191
Jonah, compared to Narcissus, 186–195
Josephus
    account of Masada, 16–17
    near suicide of, 66
Josippon, 20
Justice, Jewish meaning of, 152
Justifiable suicide, 107
Justified homicide. *See* murder

Kaplan, Kalman J., 28
Karo, Rabbi Joseph, regulations regarding suicide, 72
Kerygma of Christianity, 37–41
Kevorkian, Jack, 98, 114–115
Kevorkianism. *See also* doctor assisted suicide
    reactions to, 98–112
Kimchi, Rabbi David (Radak), 63, 65, 91
Koresh, David, 197–199. *See also* mass suicide

Kugel, James, on Midrash, 148–149

Lack of meaning, 112
Laughter, healing power of, 126
Leaders, role of, 183
Leah, King, 64–65
Legislation, church, against suicide, 40
Leibovitch, Y.
    interpretation of Book of Job, 171
    on stories of Akeda and Job, 174–175
Lerner, Gerda, 126
Le Suicide (Durkheim), 38–39
Liberty, 134. *See also* freedom
Life
    after death, 7–8
    goal of, 10
    Jewish and Western views on, 143–158
    meaning of, 172
    meaning of death in, 103–105
    quality of, 126
    value of, 62, 90
"Little St. Hugh," 48–49
Logotherapy
    on afterlife, 107–112
    on death, 102–103
    on meaning of death in life, 103–105
Loneliness, 127

Maimonides
    on Garden of Eden story, 24
    intentional suicide, definition of, 71

mental functioning, views on, 22
on murder and suicide, 99
on physicians' obligations, 101
on self-destructiveness, 22–26
Malice, 95
Martyr death, vs. suicide, church on, 44
Martyrdom
as exception to rule on suicide, 82
Horney on, 138
Jewish and Christian conceptions of, 199–201
in Judaism, 73–74
Masada as model of, 16–20
in Talmud, 83, 91
Martyrs, Christian vs. Jewish, 40–41
Martyr-suicide, 39
among early Christians, 39
Masada
Josephus's account of, 20
as mass suicide, 16
as model of Jewish martyrdom, 16–20
and Waco compared, 197–199
Mass Suicide, 200
in Talmud, 68–69
Meaning, lack of, 112
Meaningful existence, 106–107
Mental illness, suicide as sign of, 74
Midrash, suicide in, 70–71, 99
Midrashic mode, 148–150
Misconduct, and intellection, 23

Mishna(h), on freedom, 14–15
Mita yafa, 95
Moses
analysis of self destructive thinking, 176–185
character of, 25–26
Mourning
laws of, 72
prohibition of, 71
rites of, 76, 160
Murder
compared to suicide, 99–100
exceptions to rules on, 82
justifiable, 82, 151, 156

Narcissism, 188
Narcissus, compared to Jonah, 186–195
Near suicide, 66
Necessity, 32
Nefesh. *See* soul
Neurosis, and religion, Freud on connections between, 25
New York State Task Force, report of, compared to AAS's, 117–123
Noahide laws, 160

Oblivion, 108–109
Oedipal conflict, birth of, 29
Oedipus
compared to Isaac, 135–137
compared to the Akedah, 27–28
Oedipus complex, 27
Oregon State Physician Assisted Suicide law, 116. *See also* doctor assisted suicide; euthanasia

Pain, 119–120
Palaggi, Rabbi Hayyim, 94
"Parasuicides," 78
Parental approval, 28
Paris, Matthew, case of "Little St. Hugh," 48–49
Passion plays, ritual murder in, 52–53
Passive suicide, 100
Perfection, 106
  intellectual and moral, 24
Personification of God, Maimonides on, 26
Pessimism, 35–36
Philosophy, and death, link between, 8
Physician assisted suicide. *See* doctor assisted suicide
Plato's *Republic*, 7–9
Praying for death of another, 93, 94
Premeditation, 95
Prometheus Bound (Aeschylus), 29–32
Prophecy
  conditions for, 24
  psychological conditions and, 22
Prophets, 183
Psychiatry, suicide and, 74–75
Psychotherapy, biblical approach to, 27–28
Ptolemy, 65
Punishment, 24
Pythagoras, on suicide, 6–7

Quality of life, 126
"Quasi-suicidal attempts," 78

Rabbinic attitudes, toward suicide, 72–73, 100

Reality, 7
Regulations, governing suicide, 69–70, 72
Religion, and neurosis, Freud on connections between, 25
Republic, Plato's, 7–9
Responsa literature on suicide, 72–73
Responsibleness, 104–105, 106, 110–11
Right to commit suicide, 74–75
Ritual murder
  charges of in death of Jesus, 47–48
  in contemporary passion plays, 52–53
Rules
  exceptions to on murder/suicide, 82
  governing suicide, 69–70

Sacrifice
  child-, 134–137
  in creation stories, 133–142
  human, opposition to, 152
  suicide as, 107
Samson, 62–63
Saul, King, 63–64, 90–91
Second Book of Maccabees, suicides recorded in, 65
Self-defense, 156. *See also* murder, justifiable
Self-destructiveness
  explanation of, Freud's, 26
  and fate, 32
Self-destructive thinking, 183
Self-esteem, 137–138
Self-murder. *See* suicide

Self-mutilation, 133–134, 160
Self-righteousness, 173
Seneca, Lucius Anneaus, 11, 36, 133–134, 160
Shestov, Lev, 33
Shneidman, Edwin, definition of suicide, 79–80
Singularity, 104–105, 106
Socrates, 7–9, 159
Soul, and body, relationship between, 13–14
Stern, Rabbi Yehiel Mikhel, murder vs. suicide, graveness of, 73
Stoics, views of, 10–13, 14, 15, 133
Subintentional death, 79
Suicide
  an act of martyrdom, 73–74
  in America, 116–128
  in ancient Jewish writings, 66
  Antigone and Cain stories compared, 159–167
  in the apochrypha, 65
  arguments for, 18, 40
  barriers to understanding, 123
  in Bible, 62–65
  church legislation against, 40
  Cicero on, 10–11
  compared to homicide, 99–100
  as cowardice, 19
  in creation stories, 133–142
  defense of, Donne's, 40
  doctor assisted (*See* doctor assisted suicide)
  Easter as anniversary of a, 47–53
  as escape, 9
  exceptions to rules on, 82
  and fatalism, interrelationship of, 27–34
  fear of, 10
  as form of creativity, 6
  and freedom, relationship between, 13–14
  halakhic prohibition on, 114
  legitimizing, 133–134
  mass. *See* mass suicide
  and modern psychiatry, 74–75
  parents of victims of, 180
  permission for, 91, 174
  preventions of in Bible, 190–193
  prohibitions against, 40
  psychodynamics of, 188
  rates of, 61
  right to commit, 74–75
  risk factors for, 172
  rules and regulations governing, 69
  vs. martyr death, church on, 44
Suicide, definitions of
  altruistic, 186
  anomic, 186
  attempted, 78
  Durkheim's, 38–39
  intentional, 70, 71, 79
  "redefinition," 92
  Shneidman's, 79–80
  Stengel's, 100
  willful, 72, 73
Suicide notes, Gospel of John, 42
Suicide-prevention narratives, 186, 193

Super-meaning, 109, 111–112
Szasz, Thomas, 74–75

Tabor, J. D., 75
Talmud
  burial honors for suicides, 160
  case of Haninah ben Teradion, 86
  intentional suicide, definition of in, 79
  precedent for euthanasia in, 82–83
  suicide in, 67–70, 71–72, 99
Tam, Rabbenu Jacob, 91
Temporality, 104–105
Terminal illness, 93–96
Toledot Tanaim Veamorain (Heiman), 35
Torah, study of, 23–24
Tragic mode, 148–150

Treatment, withdrawal of, 115
Tukazinsky, Rabbi Yehiel Mikhel, on suicide, 72–73
Tusculan Disputations (Cicero), 11

Urbach, Ephraim, 14

The Wars of the Jews (Josephus), 16–19, 66
Wellisch, Erich, on Oedipus complex, 27–28
Wiesel, Elie, *The Fifth Son* compared to *Le Cid*, 143–158
Willful suicide, 72, 73
Withdrawal of treatment, 115
Wrong-doing, hysteria as result of, 24

Yaacov, R., 35
Yair, Eleazar ben, speech of, at Masada, 16–19

About the Editors

Kalman J. Kaplan, Ph.D., is a licensed clinical psychologist and the Director of the Suicide Research Center at Columbia-Michael Reese Hospital and Medical Center and Professor of Psychology at Wayne State University. He is also Adjunct Professor of Psychology at the University of Illinois at Chicago and at Spertus College of Judaica, and has recently served as guest lecturer at Bar-Ilan University. He is also associate editor of the *Journal of Psychology and Judaism* and is on the editorial board of *Omega, The Journal of Death and Dying*. He is author of *TILT: Teaching Individuals to Live Together* (1997), coauthor of *Family: Biblical and Psychological Foundations* (1984), the *Psychology of Hope* (1993), *Living with Schizophrenia* (1997) and a contributor to *Metapsychology: Missing Links in Mind, Body, and Behavior* (1991). He has also written numerous articles about biblical psychology, interpersonal relations, human development, and suicide. Kalman Kaplan is currently conducting a study of Dr. Kevorkian's patients.

Matthew B. Schwartz, Ph.D., teaches history and Near East studies at Wayne State University and is co-author, with Kalman Kaplan, of the *Family: Biblical and Psychological Foundations* (1984), and the *Psychology of Hope* (1993). He serves on the editorial boards of the *Journal of Psychology and Judaism* and *Menorah Review*. He is also coauthor of *Roman Letters* (1991), and a contributor to *History of the Jews of Detroit II* (1992). His scholarly interests include the Bible, Rabbinics, and Classical literature.